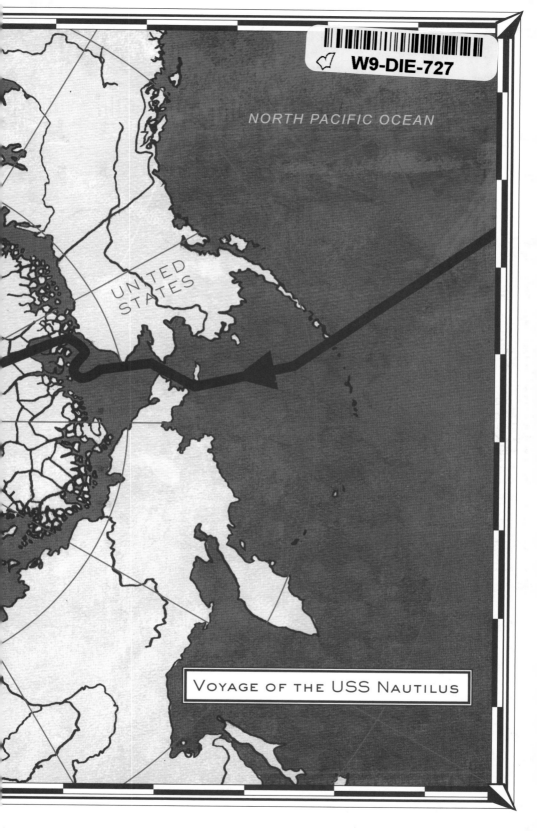

NORTH PACIFIC OCEAN

UNITED STATES

Voyage of the USS Nautilus

THE ICE DIARIES

ALSO BY WILLIAM R. ANDERSON:

Nautilus 90 North (with Clay Blair Jr.)

The Useful Atom (with Vernon Pizer)

First Under the North Pole

ALSO BY DON KEITH:

The Forever Season

Wizard of the Wind

The Rolling Thunder Stockcar Racing Series
(with Kent Wright)

Final Bearing (with Cdr. George Wallace)

Gallant Lady: The Biography of USS Archerfish
(with Ken Henry)

In the Course of Duty

Final Patrol

The Bear: The Life and Times of
Coach Paul "Bear" Bryant

THE ICE DIARIES

THE UNTOLD STORY OF THE COLD WAR'S MOST DARING MISSION

CAPTAIN WILLIAM R. ANDERSON
WITH DON KEITH

THOMAS NELSON
Since 1798

NASHVILLE   DALLAS   MEXICO CITY   RIO DE JANEIRO   BEIJING

Published in Nashville, Tennessee. Thomas Nelson is a registered trademark of Thomas Nelson, Inc.

Published in association with the literary agency of Bob Robison and Associates, 2977 Nautilus Drive, Nashville, TN 37217.

For movie rights contact Bob Robison and Associates, 2977 Nautilus Drive, Nashville, TN 37217, 615-366-6386.

Thomas Nelson, Inc., titles may be purchased in bulk for educational, business, fund-raising, or sales promotional use. For information, please e-mail SpecialMarkets@ThomasNelson.com.

Page Design by Casey Hooper

Library of Congress Cataloging-in-Publication Data
Anderson, William R., 1921–2007.
  The ice diaries : the untold story of the Cold War's most daring mission / by Captain William R. Anderson (with Don Keith).
    p. cm.
  Includes bibliographical references and index.
  ISBN 978-0-7852-2759-5
  1. Nautilus (Submarine : SSN-571) 2. Arctic regions—Discovery and exploration—American.
3. Northwest Passage—Discovery and exploration—American. 4. Underwater exploration—Arctic Ocean.
5. United States. Navy—Officers—Biography. 6. Submarine captains—United States—Biography. 7.
Cold War. I. Keith, Don, 1947– II. Title.
  VA65.N3A49 2008
  359.933—dc22

                                                                              2007038817

Printed in the United States of America
08 09 10 11 QW 6 5 4 3 2 1

CONTENTS

Preface ix

Introduction xiii

PART I: A TRUE SUBMARINE

Chapter 1   The Journey Begins 3

Chapter 2   An Audience with the Admiral 16

Chapter 3   Giving Myself a Job 27

Chapter 4   Prospective Commander 38

Chapter 5   Taking the Helm .46

Chapter 6   The Fourth Great Ocean 57

Chapter 7   Periscope in Puget Sound 67

Chapter 8   Pointing North 75

Chapter 9   "You Are Going to Wreck This Program!" . . .83

PART II: DIVING BENEATH THE ICE

Chapter 10 To the Edge of the Unknown 89

Chapter 11 Collision! 106

Chapter 12 Good as New 118

Chapter 13 Bow to the North 126

Chapter 14 Lost Beneath the Ice 133

PART III: OPERATION SUNSHINE I

Chapter 15 Answering the Russians 145

Chapter 16 A Chance Encounter 154

Chapter 17 The President and the Admiral 161

Chapter 18 Poker Face 170

Chapter 19 Locating Leaks and Fighting Fires 179

Chapter 20 "Execute Operation Sunshine" 189

Chapter 21 En Route to England—Via the Pole 198

Chapter 22 Close Encounter 208

Chapter 23 Reverse Course .217

Chapter 24 Retreat to Pearl .227

Chapter 25 Preparing for "Panama" 234

Chapter 26 The Race Is On .243

PART IV: OPERATION SUNSHINE II

Chapter 27 "The Panama-Arctic-Pearl Shuttle" 251

Chapter 28 Where No Man Has Gone Before 262

Chapter 29 Point of No Return .272

Chapter 30 *Nautilus* 90 North .280

Chapter 31 "A Voyage of Importance" 283

PART V: WELCOME HOME, PANOPOS

Chapter 32 "Well Done" 297

Chapter 33 "The President Is Waiting" 300

Chapter 34 The Sun Shines on *Nautilus* 308

Epilogue 333

Sailing Rosters 339

Index 345

Acknowledgments 359

PREFACE

The talented and gentlemanly naval historian Clay Blair and I co-authored the book *Nautilus 90 North* shortly after the USS *Nautilus*, the world's first nuclear submarine, made her historic transpolar crossing in August 1958. That exploration, under my command, charted a top-of-the-world, under-ice passage between the Pacific and Atlantic Oceans by way of the North Pole. But our book was necessarily incomplete. Most of what actually happened remained hidden to public eyes—highly classified—for years afterward. Security concerns prevented us from revealing the most interesting features and capabilities of our nation's first nuclear submarine. We included very little background information on people and programs that were key in the development of *Nautilus*, her initial sea trials, and the under-ice explorations. Lacking also were details of behind-the-scenes events that gave impetus to the ultra-secret mission, some of which I only learned about years later.

Even though the book was essentially a restricted accounting of the historical voyage, it was a resounding success, climbing to the *New York Times* best-seller list in 1959. Before long, *Nautilus 90 North* was in print in a dozen or more different languages and distributed worldwide.

Over the years, however, it became more and more apparent that if viewed as a historical account, our book had significant shortcomings.

Now I am able to tell the full story about how *Nautilus* and her fine crew literally broke the ice on Arctic Ocean exploration by a nuclear submarine.

Our first under-ice excursions were in September 1957. Within weeks of that historic under-ice exploration, I had a once-in-a-lifetime opportunity to suggest that *Nautilus* explore and chart an ocean-to-ocean route across the top of the world, transiting the Arctic Ocean via the North Pole, completely under ice. If successful, the reconnaissance would immediately gain a strategic advantage in a part of the world that the Soviet Union considered their "backyard." At the time, the Soviets were our primary foe in the Cold War.

The suggestion that *Nautilus* was ready to make such a trip was of interest at the highest levels of government and the navy for many reasons, not the least of which was the fact that U.S. technology was viewed as lagging behind that of the Soviets. Their new Sputnik satellites were successfully circling the earth before our space rockets could get off the ground.

The person who ultimately made the decision—and the ultimate

Historic ship *Nautilus* at the Submarine Force Museum in Groton, Connecticut.

difference in the success of the secret mission—was President Dwight Eisenhower. As far as I know, he never received proper recognition for his strength and character in using the power of his office to sponsor a feat of exploration that was hailed as a technological victory in the Cold War— one that significantly boosted the sagging spirits of Americans as well as citizens of the free world all around the globe.

For years now, I have been introduced as "the fellow who took that submarine to the North Pole." Such a representation ignores the contributions of the many other people associated with *Nautilus*'s most well-known accomplishment.

I hope my *Nautilus* shipmates, and their families and loved ones, find pleasure as well as comfort in their story, as best as I can tell it, using available records, input from crew members, and honest recollections as my guidelines. In fact, I would like to think this story would fill with pride everyone involved with the navy's nuclear program as well as the captains and crews of all U.S. nuclear submarines. In particular I aim to honor those associated with the great ship *Nautilus*, from her designers and builders to the outstanding commissioning commanding officer, now-retired Admiral Eugene "Dennis" Wilkinson, his brave crew, and every crew thereafter. I also want to honor the personnel currently manning the *Historic Ship Nautilus*, now permanently docked and open to the public at the Submarine Force Library and Museum in Groton, Connecticut.

In telling this story, I am once again fortunate to have a talented and gentlemanly coauthor, Don Keith. Like Clay, he has authored several books about naval history and submarines, notably *In the Course of Duty*, a moving account of the World War II patrol of the USS *Batfish* when she sank three enemy submarines in three days—another incredible feat.

I am also fortunate to have had the support of family and navy and civilian friends. I thank them for never tiring of my requests for assistance on this project. My wife, Pat, especially has wholeheartedly encouraged and helped me. In addition to her concern and insight, she has done a tremendous job of organizing all manner of materials as well as assisting

Captain William Anderson.

with interviews and original research. I thank the family of John Krawczyk for allowing us to use many of John's wonderful photographs. In every way, John represented the best of *Nautilus*.

Hats off to the U.S. Navy, submariners, and submarine families and friends everywhere.

William R. Anderson
Captain, U.S. Navy (retired)
Commanding Officer,
USS *Nautilus* 1957–1959
January 2007

INTRODUCTION

he navy pier in Seattle was packed with people—a noisy, excited crowd that had begun gathering early for the scheduled arrival of what was almost certainly the world's most famous naval vessel, the USS *Nautilus*, the first—and at that time the only fully functional—nuclear submarine. People were grabbing the best viewing spots to watch for this spectacular ship, hoping to be the first to catch a glimpse of her as she approached the pier.

Though they had a clear view up Puget Sound, there was still no sign of *Nautilus*. Many in the crowd, especially those familiar with the ship and her stellar record of accomplishment, began getting anxious. It was not like *Nautilus* to miss a commitment or even to be tardy for one.

There was good reason why the excited crowd could not see the approaching ship. As the crew brought *Nautilus* closer to her destination—into the Strait of Juan de Fuca, past Whidbey Island into Puget Sound, and then the run down to Seattle—they knew they were entering some of the busiest waterways in the world.

"Captain, there's traffic everywhere," one of the crewmen noted. It was true. The radarscope was dotted with blips, big and small. Though it is quite narrow, the sound is also very deep.

"We can get in a lot faster and safer if we steam in beneath them,"

Eugene "Dennis" Wilkinson, the ship's skipper, decided and gave the order to take the massive vessel to periscope depth.

There they went, the bulk of the boat underwater, pulling down the periscope if necessary, headed for their waiting audience. The ship passed smoothly beneath sailboats, powerboats, and freighters, threading its way through the winding channel, generally with only the periscope exposed. It was likely none of those people on the vessels there had any idea what was sharing the water with them that day.

Meanwhile, those aboard *Nautilus* were getting ready for the arrival. The maneuvering watch (the crew members assigned to stations to help guide the boat into the pier) were on station and all line handlers were positioned at

USS *Nautilus* (SSN-571) surfaces at an unusually sharp angle during maneuvers. The ship outperformed even the expectations of her designers and builders.

the hatch nearest where they would be working once they were topside. The sonarmen were also carefully tracking other vessels in the area as well as the end of the navy pier, using the active sonar system to avoid collision.

Captain Wilkinson received a "mark" when *Nautilus* was eight hundred yards from the pier. He grabbed the number two periscope and began issuing the orders that helped maneuver the boat visually into precisely the right position. Only then did he give the command to surface.

As the unsuspecting but astonished crowd on the pier looked on, the massive hull of *Nautilus* suddenly shot out of Puget Sound like an unleashed whale, rising magnificently until her sail and decks were out of the water. With mouths open and eyes wide, the onlookers watched as hatches quickly flew open and line handlers emerged, the heavy ropes they carried at the ready; and then there were men visible on the bridge atop the sail, the highest point of the submarine. The big vessel eased smoothly up until she gently hugged the pier, and the well-trained crew had her tied off in no time.

Nautilus had made an entrance befitting the star that she was!

It was, indeed, a smooth and spectacular maneuver, and one that would only add to the lore already associated with the vessel. I was especially proud to be aboard *Nautilus* that day, observing the maneuvering for her auspicious arrival from inside her hull. I had only recently come on board, joining her while she was off the coast of California, and had ridden with her and her crew into Puget Sound, watching as she and her crew put on a show for the audience.

And it was there in Seattle, shortly after our spectacular appearance, that I relieved Captain Wilkinson and became the second skipper of *Nautilus*, thus embarking on a truly remarkable journey. Although I knew the capabilities of *Nautilus* as well as anyone by that time, even I could not have imagined what a spectacular and important voyage my new crew and I had just begun.

To be totally accurate, the adventure really started for me more than a year before, across the continent, on the Atlantic Coast, in the town of Groton, Connecticut.

Groton hugs the east bank of the Thames River very close to where it meets Long Island Sound. The town shares one of the finest natural harbors on the eastern seaboard of the United States with the city of New London, located on the opposite side of the river, making Groton perfect for its primary purpose. Today it greets its share of visitors with a large sign fashioned in the shape of a submarine. Painted on the conning tower is the number "571," the hull number of the USS *Nautilus*. From bow to stern, the sign reads "Groton—Submarine Capital of the World." And for many good reasons too, beginning with the fact that on the north end of town the U.S. Navy has a submarine base that is a moderate-sized city in itself. With berths for numerous submarines, the base serves as the navy's primary submarine training facility for potential commanding officers, line officers, and enlisted sailors from sub bases all over the country.

Three miles south of the base, the massive shipyard of Electric Boat Company is easily identifiable. Electric Boat's history can be traced back to John Holland, the man to whom, around the turn of the twentieth century, the U.S. Navy granted its first contract to design and build a "submarine torpedo boat." The Groton shipyard built its first submarine for the navy in 1931. In addition to building boats, "EB," as the locals call it, provides the navy with major upkeep and dry dock services and has operated for many decades as a wholly owned division of the giant defense contractor General Dynamics Corporation.

The deep-water channel on the Groton side of the river provides the ideal setup for submarines. They can maneuver easily between the naval base and Electric Boat for upkeep or continue to the nearby Atlantic for seagoing operations. This arrangement has kept submariners active in the New London–Groton area since World War I. But that is not the main reason Groton lays claim to being the "Submarine Capital of the World." This superlative stems from the fact that Groton is the birthplace of the first honest-to-goodness submarine, the USS *Nautilus*.

There have been submarines—or at least designs of submersible craft of one kind or another—for centuries, going back to Leonardo da Vinci.

Some three centuries later, during the American Civil War, the Confederate South's submersible *Hunley* became the first in history to sink an enemy ship, the Union's *Housatonic*. Unfortunately, *Hunley* also sank on the way back to shore and her entire crew perished.

The conventional diesel submarines that preceded *Nautilus* and were such factors in both world wars—as powerful and effective as they were—were really like surface

The world's first true submarine, the USS *Nautilus*, capable of staying submerged for an almost unlimited amount of time, unlike previous conventional submarines.

ships enclosed entirely within a pressure hull. While they had dive and submerge capability, they had to resurface, or at least come to snorkel depth, virtually every day to recharge the huge storage batteries. Also, within a matter of weeks, the diesel fuel that ran the engines that recharged the batteries had to be replenished. Thus, the range of the vessel was limited as was the overall length of time a submarine could be at sea without refueling.

The revolutionary nuclear power plant within *Nautilus*'s hull changed all that. It provided the capability to generate both propulsion and electrical power while the ship remained fully submerged. Theoretically, *Nautilus* could depart from the sub base in Groton, dive beneath the ocean's surface, circumnavigate the earth submerged, and with fuel (fissionable material) to spare, not surface until she got back to Groton. Her crew would remain comfortable and relatively safe for the entire trip.

As Rear Admiral John S. Thach, who once commanded the navy's antisubmarine development unit Task Group Alpha, jokingly put it, "Instead of a surface vessel that can submerge only temporarily, a nuclear submarine is a submersible that only has to surface temporarily—just long enough to reenlist the crew!"

The navy turned to trusted defense contractor General Dynamics Corporation, which owned Electric Boat, to build this unique vessel. With a very uncertain outcome in the eyes of many, construction officially began on June 14, 1952. That was the day President Harry S. Truman ceremoniously signed the keel, the central structure of the ship.

Nautilus began sea trials two and one-half years later. She exceeded all performance expectations from the outset. Moreover, the commissioning crew was so impressive that Groton's representative in the Connecticut General Assembly, Mr. Nelson Brown, introduced a resolution that hailed the *Nautilus* as "a mighty force for the preservation of peace . . . [and it is our] fervent prayer that God will pilot her and the country that built her." The measure passed unanimously.

Dennis Wilkinson was the perfect choice to command the world's first nuclear submarine. He was an experienced conventional submarine officer with an exceptional war record as well as a mathematics and technical wizard. He and his crew put *Nautilus* through demanding sea trial upon sea

President Harry S. Truman signs his name on the keel of *Nautilus* as construction begins on the revolutionary vessel, June 1952.

trial, pace after pace, without damage or harm to ship or men. He was not only a tireless worker but also a gracious and charming host to endless streams of visitors to the world's most extraordinary ship. He performed outstandingly, providing a service to our country that few could have come close to performing as well. He would be a hard act to follow. By the time *Nautilus* completed her initial sea trials, she had effectively rendered obsolete every other submarine in the world.

That was where I came in. I relieved Wilkinson as captain of *Nautilus* in June 1957 there in Seattle. As the second CO of this remarkable vessel, I believed I had the best job in the navy. I had already made plans, at least in my head, about what the greatest ship and crew in the world were going to accomplish. I wanted to be more than a second act to Wilkinson's spectacularly successful first one. *The Ice Diaries* focuses on the execution of the dreams I had for my command: under-ice exploration of the uncharted Arctic Ocean, using the first submarine truly capable of such.

Perhaps, I dreamed, it could come about that *Nautilus*, under my command, would be the first ship in history to reach the North Pole. I feel blessed that I was able to take those dream voyages and command that ship and crew on what would later be called one of mankind's greatest adventures.

This book is the story of how that adventure came about, complete with the details and scope that were impossible to include in any earlier recounting. I hope the reader will gain some sense of what it was like to be there and will understand how gratified we were to successfully take our ship on that important voyage.

PART I
A TRUE SUBMARINE

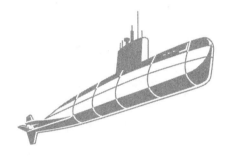

"[Putting a nuclear reactor aboard a U.S. submarine] sounds like something out of Jules Verne's *20,000 Leagues Under the Sea*."

—Vice Admiral Charles Lockwood
Commander, Submarine Forces Pacific Fleet, WWII

THE JOURNEY BEGINS

eactor critical is an atomic-age term akin to saying a powerful engine is running. Technically, it means that a controlled, self-sustaining chain reaction of nuclear fission has been achieved within the thick, strong walls of a reactor. Very simply, nuclear fission heats circulating water that makes steam that turns turbines that provide either propulsion or electricity—or both in the case of seagoing vessels. The production of energy by nuclear fission is commonplace today, on land as well as at sea, but it was only a far-reaching concept in 1939, the year I—a farm boy from Tennessee—entered the U.S. Naval Academy in Annapolis, Maryland.

Parallel to my first step toward becoming a naval officer, the federal government, under the auspices of the U.S. Navy, took its first step toward the atomic age by allocating the tiny sum of $1,500 to study nuclear fission and its possibilities. The study confirmed earlier speculation: nuclear reactors had the potential of providing the ideal power for naval vessels. Submarines in particular could benefit because reactors require neither oxygen nor exhaust, and the calibration of fuel, or energy reserve, could be done in years rather than days.

The demands of World War II, however, forced the navy to postpone its atomic dreams. The federal government channeled all nuclear research into the top-secret Manhattan Project, established in 1942 to develop super-explosive atomic bombs.

In the spring of that year, as the war raged in Europe as well as the Atlantic and Pacific Oceans, my classmates and I prepared for our graduation from the Academy. Under normal conditions we would not have completed our studies until 1943, but to help meet the war's need for naval officers, we remained nominally the "Class of 1943," but we actually graduated in 1942. Cramming a four-year program into three meant extended classroom instruction, reduced leave, and a big cutback of onboard ship training and summer cruises. Still, graduating a full year ahead of schedule agreed with most everyone. Spirits ran high despite the solemn reality that each of us would soon be receiving orders that would likely put us in the thick of war.

As graduation approaches, midshipmen traditionally have the opportunity to state their service or duty preferences. Some choose large surface vessels such as battleships, carriers, and cruisers. Others go to flight school or join the marines. I preferred the smaller vessels, such as destroyers, destroyer escorts, and submarines. At that time, though, submarine duty was not an option straight out of the Academy. Two years of experience on a surface vessel was a qualifying prerequisite. So I was surprised when my roommate, Dunbar Lawson, burst into our room announcing that forty of our class would be allowed to go directly into submarine service. The two-year service requirement had been temporarily lifted due to the demands of war.

I had never been on a submarine, but I rushed to sign up. I think I was the fourth person to do so. Turns out more than forty Academy graduates volunteered, and the navy accepted everyone who met the initial qualifications.

An aspect of submarines that I liked was that it was an all-volunteer service. I figured the commitment and character of the men on board submarines would be of the highest quality found in the navy. I was not wrong about that.

There were a couple of other factors as well. Submarine pay was slightly higher because it was considered to be more hazardous duty. I had also heard the food was the best in the navy.

But what I really liked about submarines was the small number of sailors comprising a crew. It stood to reason that an officer on a submarine would be given more responsibility at a faster pace than on a large vessel; overall advancement in rank usually would be in lockstep with responsibility. I was not wrong about this either.

So, after a sped-up graduation from the Naval Academy, I went directly to sub school in New London. It was there where I boarded my first submarine, an old boat that was being used only for training.

Sub school was also hurried up. Everyone worked seven days a week. Even the married students had to stay on the base every other night. Six months of training were compressed into three. I had excelled in academics during my three years of military school back in my home state of Tennessee before going to Annapolis. I think my class standing at the Academy, roughly in the middle of some five hundred students, however, reflected the attitude of a young man who was tired of classrooms and theories.

Sub school seemed to wake me up. I loved it.

The war in the Pacific gave me

Captain Anderson upon graduation from the U.S. Naval Academy in Annapolis.

plenty of opportunity to put my training into practice. My real education had just begun. I was lucky in every way, particularly in that I always had extraordinarily capable senior and commanding officers as well as shipmates. They set good examples of leadership and conduct that inspired me to do my best. That experience no doubt helped me the rest of my life, and certainly on our *Nautilus* missions beneath the polar ice.

My initial World War II assignment aboard *Tarpon* is a good example. After an all-night flight to Pearl Harbor, I reported aboard the submarine and was welcomed by her new skipper, Tom Wogan. *Tarpon* had already been labeled a "bad luck" boat. She had yet to sink an enemy vessel, even though she had been in the Pacific when the war began and this was to be her fifth official war patrol. Not long into my first run, the submarine's luck appeared to have changed for the better. We encountered a huge Japanese convoy, a long string of targets lined up in perfect position for us to attack. Before we could maneuver for an assault, the enemy apparently spotted our periscope in the calm sea. We were suddenly under a heavy depth charge attack from several destroyers. We managed to get away, but the targets were gone. The rest of the patrol proved equally fruitless.

When we returned to Pearl Harbor, we fully expected the worst. But Admiral Charles Lockwood, the Pacific submarine commander, once again demonstrated his positive leadership style, making a lasting impression on a young officer. Instead of relieving our skipper or castigating the crew, he expressed his confidence in us and told Captain Wogan that he and his crew—including me—had another chance to show what we could do.

Under way for *Tarpon*'s sixth patrol, I had the bridge on the eight-to-twelve watch one night when radar reported a large contact. The target ship appeared to be accompanied by only one escort vessel. I called the skipper to the bridge while I, as officer of the deck, ordered a course change so that the submarine would face the target in order to gauge its distance and course. While still on the surface, we hurried to catch up and then went to radar depth. We quickly lined up for an attack, a four-torpedo spread. Each weapon left our tubes ten seconds apart. This was a tactic designed to give the best possible chance of one or two of our torpedoes striking the target. To our amazement, all four of them exploded. We knew immediately that the vessel was much larger than we had thought, and we also knew that we had sent it to the bottom.

It turned out to be the *Tatsuta Maru*, an ocean liner that was being used by the Japanese as a troop ship. We also learned that she was bound for the island campaigns with as many as three thousand enemy soldiers aboard.

We sank a second vessel later on that same run, and the combined tonnage made that the best of any submarine patrol in the war to that point. Tom Wogan's perseverance and Admiral Lockwood's faith in him and his crew had paid off handsomely. That was a valuable lesson to observe firsthand.

When we returned to base, Lockwood told Wogan, "Captain, you can have anything you want." Our skipper quickly responded that what he wanted was for as many of the crew as possible to have shore leave back in the States. The admiral obliged.

That reward proved especially fortuitous for Reuben "Woody" Woodall, another Academy graduate aboard *Tarpon*, and me. We were both in love with our Academy sweethearts and wasted no time getting back to the States to see them.

I had met Yvonne "Bonny" Etzel of Newark, Delaware, through roommate Dunbar Lawson. She soon became my steady date. She was a loyal, charming, and beautiful young lady who on many occasions made the three-hour trip from her school, the University of Delaware, to Annapolis just to be my date at a dance or other Academy event. We quickly fell in love.

After her graduation she became an airline stewardess. At the time that profession required flight attendants to be single. A silly rule at best, it was probably broken many times, including by us. On that short leave to the States in 1943, Bonny and I met in Kansas City, where she was based at the time, far away from family and friends. There we were secretly married.

Reuben went straight to Washington, D.C., and married Peggy Johnston, daughter of Captain Donald H. Johnston, Naval Academy Class of '22. Reuben, a fine gentleman and officer, and I crossed paths many times during the war and have remained lifelong friends, but we were never shipmates again.

Upon my return to Hawaii, I was surprised to find that I had been transferred to *Narwhal*, an older and larger boat, one of the four submarines that were at Pearl Harbor when the Japanese attacked on December 7, 1941. Her commander—and my new skipper—was to become another strong influence. His name was Frank Latta.

A versatile man and exceptional leader, Latta was well respected by everyone in the submarine service and was very popular with his crew. Since he was a motorcycle enthusiast, the crew members stored a dismantled bike aboard, keeping it serviced and ready to put back together so the skipper could ride it when we arrived in port.

Since *Narwhal* was larger than most other submarines of that time, we had a special job to do. We were detailed to haul supplies to Philippine guerillas, including guns, ammunition, medical supplies, food, and even counterfeit Japanese invasion currency, an attempt to disrupt the economy of the occupied nation. We also took along ten men, commandos sent to assist the resistance.

At one of our unloading stops, three destroyers surprised us while we were at the dock. With shells from their cannon splashing all around us, we quickly tossed overboard the stores on deck and got out into water deep enough to submerge and attempt to hide. After a rattling depth-charge attack on us, we decided the enemy warships had moved far enough away that we could risk making a run for it on the surface. The Japanese spotted us, though, and quickly gave chase. Latta ordered full speed.

Narwhal was not the fastest submarine in the fleet, and after an hour of getting all we could from her diesel engines, the enemy ships were still in hot pursuit. Our chief engineer, Jake Plummer, not fully aware of our situation, called up to the bridge, "Captain, if we keep up this pace, we won't have any engines left back here!"

Latta's reply was immediate: "If we slow down, we won't need any damn engines!"

Somehow we coaxed a few more turns from those big diesels and managed to get away.

Frank Latta was later assigned to put in commission *Lagarto* (SS-371), a new submarine under construction. Before he left Hawaii for Wisconsin, where the boat was being built, Frank asked if I would be interested in following him to his new command. I thought the world of Captain Latta and enthusiastically accepted his offer

About three weeks later, however, I received a note from Latta saying that he had asked the navy to assign me to *Lagarto*, but they had been reluctant to do so. Orders had already been written to another officer to fill the number-three slot on the new boat. The other officer had received those orders. To change them at that time would be extremely disruptive. Captain Latta noted that he had reluctantly withdrawn his request. Tragically, on her second war patrol, with Frank Latta at the helm, *Lagarto* was lost in the Gulf of Siam with all hands, May 3, 1945. Had fate not sent me in another direction, I could easily have been aboard *Lagarto* that night.

After my secret marriage in Kansas City, I did not return to the States again for about a year, staying in New London just long enough to help put the USS *Trutta* (SS-421) in commission before returning to combat in the Pacific. In August 1945, while I was on my eleventh war patrol, two of the atomic bombs created by the Manhattan Project were dropped over Japan. World War II ended abruptly.

Almost immediately Manhattan Project officials turned their focus to other uses of the atom by inviting representatives from the army, navy, and certain defense contractors to assemble at Oak Ridge, Tennessee, the "secret" city where development of the bomb was based. The hope was that this group effort would produce a practical, functioning reactor that could be used for peaceful purposes.

Vice Admiral Lockwood, a man I greatly admired, had risen to command the entire Pacific submarine fleet during the war. He recounted years later of attending one of the Oak Ridge status briefings where he heard words that "sounded like something out of Jules Verne's *20,000 Leagues Under the Sea.*"

Also at one of those briefings was another navy man, a wiry engineering officer by the name of Captain Hyman G. Rickover. He was inspired by the possibilities of nuclear energy and saw early on that, as far as the U.S. Navy was concerned, a submarine would be the perfect application. He and members of his loyal group promoted the idea that the navy needed such technology, that it was the future of sea warfare.

It would not be easy. This would be the most difficult application to accomplish. Not only would a reactor have to be designed, it would have to be crafted to be small enough to fit within a submarine's hull. Moreover, the first steam plant to ever propel a submerged vehicle had to be built. Hardly any item or material needed for the job could be purchased. It all had to be developed. Moreover, there were huge maintenance and safety issues that would have to be resolved down the road.

Not to worry, Rickover must have thought. He was an engineer and in his mind enough was already known about the science or physics of nuclear fission; additional theoretical study would accomplish very little. He felt the time was right to define the objective and turn the task over to engineers, allowing them to begin the project in earnest.

Just what was the task? Build a true submarine, the ultimate stealth man-of-war, unencumbered by the limitations of conventional diesel submarines. This ship would not need to surface for months on end. Refueling worries would be a thing of the past. The nuclear reactor would provide virtually unlimited power as well as maintain an atmosphere within the boat that would ensure the safety and health of the crew. It would be a marvel, a real-life energy system that would rival Jules Verne's fantasy.

Rickover worked doggedly for the next six years lining up the political forces and engaging the scientific and engineering talent from civil as well as military sources. They completed the initial crucial steps of that task: development of a reactor by, it turns out, Westinghouse Corporation;

authorization from President Truman for a ship to put it in; and an agreement with Electric Boat in Groton to build it.

By the time construction began on *Nautilus*, I was at the Portsmouth Naval Shipyard, 150 miles north of Groton, focusing on the construction of another submarine, the conventional diesel submarine USS *Tang* (SS-563). I was her executive officer (second in command, "exec" or "XO" for short). My job was to check out the boat, monitor the correction of problems, equip the boat with supplies and necessary gear, and assemble and train the crew. I had plenty of help, of course.

It was exciting to read the news accounts of the fanfare surrounding the events on June 14, 1952, the day President Truman laid the keel of the *Nautilus*. But, very frankly, the promise that nuclear power held for the navy—or me—was not in the forefront of my mind. More urgent and worrisome was the fact that it turned out that I had not been readying *Tang* for routine, peacetime exercises. By then our country had been at war with North Korea for two years, and I was headed for potential conflict in the Pacific once more.

My primary missions in the Korean theater were reconnaissance patrols and training of U.S. antisubmarine forces. The fighting, if not the war officially, ended in July 1953, a few months after I took command of the USS *Wahoo* (SS-565). She was my first command and I loved every minute of it. Having held every officer's job aboard a submarine, I state with some authority that the skipper has it the best!

I had relieved Dennis Wilkinson, whose tour on *Wahoo* was cut short to allow him extra time to prepare for his next assignment as—you guessed it—first commanding officer of the USS *Nautilus*. With a link between *Nautilus* and me now established, I began following her progress, beginning with her launching, an event covered extensively by the newspapers and newsreels and the fledgling television networks.

It was on January 21, 1954, a cold, dreary, overcast day. More than fifteen thousand people stood either on grandstands and various platforms at Electric Boat's construction site or along the riverfront. The official program stated that *Nautilus* "will be listed in the eternal annals of man as the first practical demonstration of his ability to curb the destructive force of the atom and turn it in a positive direction."

The navy band played stirring patriotic music, the chief of naval operations and the chairman of the U.S. Atomic Energy Commission made speeches, and officials from General Dynamics and its Electric Boat Division distributed specially minted bronze coins that commemorated the grand occasion.

Captain Hyman Rickover, dressed in his navy uniform rather than the civilian attire he usually wore, seemed almost cheerful. Dennis, I believe, proudly rode *Nautilus* as she slid down the ways into the Thames after the ship's sponsor, none other than the First Lady of the United States,

First Lady Mamie Eisenhower breaks a bottle of champagne against the bow of *Nautilus* as she christens the ship. To her right is John Jay Hopkins, chairman of the board of General Dynamics, parent company of Electric Boat Company, builders of the ship. To her left is Commander Edward L. Beach, who was at the time the naval aide to President Eisenhower.

Mamie Eisenhower, smashed the traditional bottle of good-luck champagne across the bow of the half-completed submarine.

Newspaper accounts stated that as the 320-foot-long black hull splashed into the water to the sounds of the cheering throng, the sky opened up, some clouds disappeared, and the sun suddenly burst on the scene. What a day!

I wish I could have been there.

Barely eight months later,

USS *Nautilus*, the first nuclear-powered vessel, slides into the waters of the Thames River at Electric Boat Company in Connecticut, after her christening.

September 30, 1954, *Nautilus* was commissioned. There was more work to be done, but exactly in Rickover's scheduled delivery month, *Nautilus* was complete, ready for sea trials, on January 17, 1955. Based on accounts, *Nautilus* Chief Engineer Les Kelly reported to Commander Wilkinson, "Reactor critical." The engine, so to speak, was running. Shore power was cut a few minutes later and the lines pulled in. At precisely eleven o'clock, *Nautilus* began moving, cautiously at first, away from the EB pier into the Thames. At that moment, she became the first ship in history "under way on nuclear power," the now-famous message sent by Wilkinson to *Fulton*, a nearby submarine tender.

Reportedly, Commander Wilkinson did not baby the new submarine. She was steaming at a brisk twelve knots on the surface before she got out of the Thames channel, a pace, incidentally, that exceeded the posted ten-knot speed limit. The trip down the river lasted about twenty minutes. Casual observers, unaware they were witnessing a historic event, noticed nothing unusual about the boat with "571" painted on her sail. She appeared to be just another submarine heading for the Atlantic. But *Nautilus* was not like other so-called submarines. She was a true submarine, an entirely new weapon that the navy was just beginning to accept and understand, the first in a revolution of nuclear-powered ships.

In a demonstration of her worth and power a few months later, *Nautilus*, designed to steam faster submerged than on the surface, cruised from New London to San Juan, Puerto Rico, a distance of thirteen hundred miles, in ninety hours. This was—by a factor of ten—the greatest distance steamed totally submerged by any submarine. Her average speed was about 16 knots (about 18.4 miles per hour), the first time any submerged combatant submarine maintained such a high speed for more than one hour. Not surprisingly, this was the fastest passage ever made between New London and San Juan by a submarine of any type, traveling either surfaced or submerged. As a result of this cruise, the navy realized it must recalculate the length of time required by submarines to reach distant patrol areas. The navy's books, literally, had to be rewritten.

"New weapon" indeed!

Another marvel associated with *Nautilus* went almost unnoticed: the fact that development and delivery of the ship, from concept to sea trials, took only six and one-half years. That was an amazing accomplishment given that the navy normally requires three years to get a new uniform approved. *Nautilus*'s continued safe operation and spectacular performance ensured a place in history for Rickover, the man now known as "the father of the nuclear submarine." Wilkinson also has a well-deserved place in history. Not only was he the first commander of the world's first nuclear submarine, but later he was the first commander of the navy's first nuclear surface ship, a cruiser christened the USS *Long Beach* (CGN-9).

It seemed everyone was upbeat, including me. To begin with, our country was at peace and I was no longer separated from my family. Bonny and I were living in military housing near the sub base at Pearl Harbor with our first son, Michael, born in March 1945, while I was on patrol aboard *Trutta*. Our second child was expected in May 1955. Though I was still CO of *Wahoo*, with another six months remaining on a tour that kept me at sea a great deal, this sailor's life was relatively normal. It was about that time that I received orders for my next assignment: Head, Submarine Tactics Department, U.S. Naval Submarine School, New London, Connecticut.

The thought of leaving Hawaii was difficult. I could not have been happier with, or more proud of, my beautiful wife and our two sons. My new job was a good one. But leaving my assignment based at Pearl Harbor and the sub base that had sustained my fellow submariners and me for more than ten years evoked deep emotions. There was another, very personal reality. My seagoing days were probably ending. I was headed for shore duty and, from that point on, more and more teaching or "desk" jobs were likely. I cannot explain why a country boy from a landlocked state loved the sea so much, but I did. And whether it was flat calm or raging storm, we got along well together. From New London, there would be no more sailings—departing for faraway destinations and missions—and no more returns as part of a victorious crew.

That was the reality. Or so I thought, as my family and I left that beautiful, peaceful place.

2

AN AUDIENCE WITH
THE ADMIRAL

n early 1956, just about the time my family and I had
settled into the routine of living in Mystic and my teaching at the navy's sub school in New London, I learned that
Captain Wally Schlech, the officer in charge of the school,
wanted to see me. Long ago I learned that when your superior
officer summons, waste no time. I immediately straightened
my tie, put on my uniform jacket, and headed down the hall
toward his office. He and I were not buddies in any sense, but
he had been a skipper in the Pacific during World War II and
we got along well. I liked him also because he had helped
greatly with my transition from sea to land duty.

"Come in, Andy," Captain Schlech said in response to my
tap on his open door. "Admiral Watkins wants to see you this
afternoon." He seemed as surprised with Watkins's somewhat
urgent request as I was. "I have no idea what this is about, but
I'm sure the admiral will tell you."

Again, I wasted no time. Admiral Frank Watkins, the top
submariner on the East Coast, was in charge of all submarine
operations and support activities for the Atlantic Fleet, includ-

ing the sub school. His official position in navy circles was ComSubLant, the acronym for Commander, Submarines, U.S. Atlantic Fleet.

While I walked the short distance to his headquarters, I recalled exchanging salutes with Admiral Watkins when we had occasionally crossed paths, but I had no reason to think he would pick me out by name from any of the other commanders at the base. But I certainly knew him, and not just because he was the overall boss. He had a very good reputation among World War II submariners, particularly those who served in the Pacific. Watkins had been a submarine division commander, in charge of five or six submarines. Not long into the war, he appealed to his boss, Admiral Lockwood, to allow him to go on a war patrol as skipper of one of the boats he oversaw because he felt it would make him a more effective division commander. It was a highly irregular request, and Lockwood did not want to risk losing in combat such an excellent and valuable division commander.

Nevertheless, Lockwood agreed—making Watkins, at age forty-five, the oldest submarine skipper in the Pacific as well as the only division commander to take a boat on patrol. Word gets around about a man who risks his neck alongside his men in an effort to make himself a better, more effective leader. Watkins and his men sank one enemy ship and damaged another on what turned out to be the sixth war patrol of the USS *Flying Fish* (SS-229). He was awarded the Bronze Star and went on to become one of twelve World War II submarine skippers to make the rank of vice admiral.

Watkins's cordial handshake and invitation to pour myself a cup of coffee and take a seat put me at ease somewhat. But let's face it, for a lieutenant commander like myself, there is no such thing as being "at ease" in an admiral's office. He called me by my navy nickname, so I assumed he had been talking to someone about me. There was still no hint why, when he opened the meeting with an unexpected question.

"Andy, how do you like serving as head of the tactics department?"

I told him I liked it very much. I did not hide the fact that I missed sea duty, but I really appreciated the time to spend with my family.

He asked about them.

I told him Bonny and I enjoyed duty in Hawaii and that our second son, William, was born while we were there. We were sorry to leave but liked the idea of living on the East Coast, much closer to our respective parents. It was our first son, Michael, who had a tough time adjusting to the move. Fortunately we were able to lease a wonderful old house on High Street in Mystic that was the perfect size for us and within a block or two of Mystic Harbor. Michael loved that and began to cheer up with the idea of getting a boat of his own.

The admiral and I chatted about the war. He had obviously reviewed my military record and was familiar with highlights of my personal history: born and reared in Middle Tennessee; graduated from Columbia Military Academy in Columbia, Tennessee; graduated from the U.S. Naval Academy; eleven World War II war patrols; Korean War noncombat missions; and commanding officer of *Wahoo*.

Then, almost abruptly, he got to the business at hand.

"Andy, there is someone coming into town who wants to meet you. Where can I reach you this evening?"

"I'll be standing by at home, sir . . . or anywhere I need to be," I replied and gave him my telephone number.

"Fine, thank you."

And that was it. No hint of who or when or why. I never even considered asking.

It was hard for me to think about anything else for the rest of the afternoon. Who was so important that they would ask an admiral to set up an appointment with me? I went home early that day and stayed close to the telephone. Finally, in late evening, it rang.

"Andy, Admiral Watkins here. I'm sorry to say that the person who wants to see you won't be able to do so on this trip. His schedule is tight and he is already running late."

"I understand, sir," I replied, hoping he could not detect the disappointment in my voice. "Thanks very much for letting me know."

Before I could say another thing, he began speaking in a lowered, secretive tone.

"Look, don't say anything about this. The man I'm talking about is Admiral Rickover. There's an important job coming up and you are being considered for it, along with some others, of course. Nothing is confirmed yet."

"Yes, sir, Admiral. I understand completely."

He made it clear that orders for me to go to Washington to interview with Rickover would be arriving soon. With that, he said good night and hung up.

I was stunned as much by the way the news was delivered as I was by the news itself. Rickover! I had no idea what he had in mind or what I could contribute to the navy's nuclear program, but I knew for sure his shop was the hottest area in the U.S. Navy. Working with the people who created *Nautilus* was bound to be interesting and challenging, not to mention an exceptional opportunity for a career line officer like me.

As I awaited my orders, *Nautilus*, still the only nuclear submarine operating on the high seas, made headlines again on February 4, 1957, as she logged sixty thousand nautical miles. Every news reporter who could be jammed aboard *Nautilus* was on hand for the momentous milestone as she surpassed the fabled twenty thousand leagues achieved by Jules Verne's *Nautilus*.

Still without requiring her first refueling, she kept right on going. This made her even more popular. Commander Wilkinson and his crew continued also as hosts to navy brass, politicians, scientists, technicians, and hundreds of other people who managed to wangle a spot aboard *Nautilus* for a short cruise. It was a most sought-after ticket.

Meanwhile, other nuclear ships were being developed. The USS *Seawolf* (SSN-575) was launched and the keel for the USS *Skate* (SSN-578) was in place. Things were changing quickly in the submarine service.

Several weeks later, orders that sent me to meet with the most well-known personality in the navy arrived. My appointment was set for 0800 on a Saturday, at the main navy building, Rickover's office in Washington, D.C. An early Saturday morning meeting confirmed the rumor that Admiral Rickover worked practically all the time.

Before this meeting I vowed to learn as much as I could about the development history of *Nautilus* and her first year at sea, plus anything related to nuclear energy and Admiral Rickover. Fortunately, the base library had a number of reference books, navy publications, and press releases. Periodicals like *Time* and *National Geographic* had run feature articles on *Nautilus* and nuclear energy. Clay Blair, a *Life* magazine reporter whom I eventually came to know well, had written a book on the subject, *The Atomic Submarine and Admiral Rickover*. I became a regular at the library and read late into many evenings.

As I studied and made notes, Rickover's character and personality began to emerge. No doubt he was a visionary. He was also a patriot who worked long hours and practiced what he preached: fiscal economy on behalf of the navy. He was decidedly independent and did not care whether he was liked or disliked. In fact, he seemed to almost enjoy being difficult.

It wasn't easy to prepare for an interview with such a man. He could make or break a person's career. I tried not to worry about that side of this great man. I am a straight-forward guy and had no notion of attempting to out-fox him. I simply prepared to answer questions Rickover might ask about my background, *Nautilus*, or my ideas on the rapidly growing nuclear navy.

I took the train down to Washington the day before my scheduled meeting. My plans included staying the night as the guest of one of my former skippers, Commander Enders P. Huey, and his wife, Jane. I had served with Huey on *Tang*, which he had commissioned. He was an interesting fellow and I always looked forward to spending time with Jane and him.

I had given the Hueys' telephone number to Admiral Rickover's office, just in case something came up. Sure enough, only minutes after I arrived at their home, the phone rang and it was for me.

The voice on the other end identified himself as a naval officer who worked for Rickover.

"I am sorry to report that the admiral will be busy most of the day on Saturday," he stated. "There is no need for you to come in at eight in the morning. I would suggest that you come by late in the afternoon instead."

"Very well. Thank you," I responded. But as soon as I hung up, I regretted not asking more questions. I worried that the call may have been a trick. Perhaps Rickover was testing to see how I responded to a stranger calling me up and, essentially, changing my written orders. From the stories that circulated about Rickover, that sort of thing, or worse, had happened numerous times. His approach to testing a candidate's response to the pressure of an interview with him as well as his ability to think quickly on his feet could take any form. There was no way to out-guess him. He seemed to be looking for opportunities to find fault and attack.

A good example of that is the story about Rickover inviting a young prospect to lunch. The interviewee proceeded to put salt on his corn before tasting it.

"I will not have you in my group!" Rickover said abruptly. "You did not properly assess the situation before you took corrective action."

That was the end of lunch, the interview, and perhaps the young man's nuclear career. Rickover's tricky questions and abrasive style were certainly not mine. On the other hand, he was an admiral and he was the acknowl-edged "father of the nuclear navy." You have to admire the fact that there were many times he stood absolutely alone in his belief that nuclear reac-tors provided ideal propulsion for submarines and that a combination of navy engineers and civilian contractors could make it happen. He became scientist, financial officer, politician, contract negotiator, and lead engineer in order to produce *Nautilus*, an acknowledged miracle. In the process, he relished keeping people on their toes.

Furthermore, no one argued with Rickover and won unless he had the facts as well as the grit to stand up to him. He spoke and wrote elegantly and eloquently. He had no time to waste on interviews. He quickly and efficiently, but sometimes quite unfairly, sent someone he thought was a dull thinker on his way. He insisted on being surrounded by quick-witted, loyal people.

As I sat there that night in Commander Huey's living room, half-listening to the pleasant conversation, I thought about the telephone call and that it was probably meant as a courtesy on Rickover's part. But I wanted to take no chances. The written orders in my briefcase clearly stated that I should report to Admiral Rickover's office at 0800 and that, I decided, was the best thing to do.

I showed up at the N Building of the Navy Annex on Constitution Avenue (where the Vietnam Veterans' Memorial now stands) precisely at 0800. The aide who greeted me was cordial but noncommittal. He simply took me to an office down the hall from his boss's and told me to wait there.

It might have been a Saturday, but that section of the Navy Annex was full of "Rickover's people" and appeared to be operating full tilt. There were serious, concerned looks on all their faces. I could feel the excitement—quite different than the somewhat relaxed atmosphere at the sub school.

Just after lunchtime, one of the admiral's secretaries stuck her head in the door.

"You may want to run on down to the cafeteria and get a bite," she suggested.

"No, thanks. I'll just wait here."

I had been cautious so far. Why change tactics now? Besides, what if the admiral's schedule cleared up and he decided to meet with me, only to find I had gone out for lunch? As I sat there waiting for the interview of a lifetime, listening to the thunderous growling of my stomach, I wished I had been practical enough to bring a sandwich with me.

Finally, the admiral was ready to meet with me. It was late afternoon, just as promised by the previous night's caller.

With my hat in my hand I stepped into Admiral Hyman Rickover's office with no idea why he wanted to see me or what questions he might ask. Not knowing what to expect was torture for a submarine skipper like me, an officer who thrived on preparation and planning, practicing and exercising, being ready for whatever might come my way. Walking into Rickover's office seemed every bit as hazardous as negotiating a minefield. I hoped for the same good luck I experienced during the war.

White-haired, short, and slender, dressed in a civilian business suit as was his custom, Admiral Hyman Rickover was pacing back and forth behind his desk as he talked on the telephone. He stopped to jot down notes, taking no notice of me whatsoever. He gave orders to someone on the other end of the line and scribbled more notes on papers strewn about his desk.

I merely stood there fiddling with my hat, allowing my eyes to wander around the room. I had never seen an admiral's office that looked like this. There was no big desk or stuffed leather chairs. There were no oriental rugs, only a bare linoleum floor. Books were everywhere. The walls seemed to be covered with them. Side tables were also stacked high with papers, more manuals, and ship models. I cannot remember gazing over a more disorganized-looking work area.

As Rickover wrapped up the telephone call, he motioned for me to have a seat in the only other chair in the room. I was relieved that its four legs were all the same length. I had heard that he had a chair with sawed-off front legs, a ploy to keep a person, literally, on edge during a meeting.

But at that moment as I sat there before the admiral, I was extremely nervous and almost weak from hunger. By comparison, uneven chair legs would have been easy to overcome.

He banged the phone down and fixed his fearless gaze on me, but did not say a word or make a motion for a bit. I could almost feel how he turned that pause into his power. Then, just as I was about to break the silence by saying something like, "Hello, Admiral. Thank you for asking me in," he spoke.

"Where did you go to school?" he asked with no fanfare or preliminaries.

In an effort to answer fully and completely, I began by stating that my family moved frequently during the Depression and I attended a string of schools. Rather deliberately, I began to recount them, from Missouri to Kentucky to Alabama, then to Tennessee.

"Anderson, I don't need to know your life history," the admiral cut in. "I just want you to tell me where you graduated high school."

Despite all my determination to do otherwise, I had apparently annoyed or somehow disappointed Rickover. Things were not going well. I tried to recover my composure as I told him about Columbia Military Academy and, at his urging, briefly ran through my time at Annapolis and my naval career thus far.

Then he said, "Name the books and tell me their authors that you have read in the past two years and give me a one-sentence summary of each. Don't tell me about anything that you have read within the past thirty days because you knew then that you were coming down here. Those don't count."

The admiral's question caught me completely off guard. My mind went absolutely blank. I could not think of a single book I had read, much less the author or a summary sentence. Still, I read regularly and never dime-store novels. I wanted him to know what I had read, but as I tried to organize an answer in my head, I realized there was no way I would be able to extemporaneously spiel off a satisfactory answer. From early childhood, my dad emphasized taking a little time to think before responding to questions. Under the stress of Rickover's steady gaze, thinking was impossible. I could not utter a meaningful word about my reading. It was as if I had been struck in the head and suddenly rendered mute.

Rickover, well-known as a man of few words, had exactly one for me. "Good-bye."

I was so devastated, I do not know how I stood up and walked out of his office. I do not remember leaving the building or hailing a taxi for Union Station. You cannot imagine how awful this grown man felt. I called Bonny before boarding the train home.

"I don't think it went very well," I told her. "I'll be late getting back to New London so I'll take a taxi home from the station. We can talk about it in the morning."

I was wracked with depressing emotions as I watched the lights of the towns hustle past my train window on the ride back up to Connecticut. The truth was that being considered for a job in the nuclear navy and then not getting it could be a real blow to an officer's future. Though I had not talked to anyone about my interview with Rickover, things have a way of getting around. If Rickover passed me over, my career could well be derailed.

"You want to talk about it?" Bonny asked me the next morning.

"Not much to talk about. It was a disaster," I told her, and described what happened in the admiral's office. "I don't know what job he had in mind for me, but I do know it's a lost cause. I may as well forget it."

"Don't give up just yet," she said. "I've never seen you quit anything because the going got tough."

I suppose that was what was really galling me. Rickover dismissed me before I ever had a chance to think and respond.

Later that day I saw Bonny standing in front of our bookshelves, studying the titles on the spines of the volumes we kept there.

"Here's one you read. Remember, you told me about it and how much you liked it." She ran her fingers along the books and stopped at another one. "Here's one I know you took with you on *Wahoo*. And this one too."

Before long she had stacked up on the floor about fifteen books I had read, representing at least 90 percent of my reading for the previous two years.

"I see them here, I remember them well, but why couldn't I think of them when I needed to?" I asked her.

"Andy, how many people would be able to do that in that situation?" she asked. "Why don't you just write to Admiral Rickover and give him the answer to his question? Maybe it wasn't a trick. Maybe he really wanted to know what books you had read."

I considered her idea for the rest of the day. It might be a useless gesture. Still, what harm could it do?

To this day I am thankful to Bonny for that suggestion and glad I had sense to follow through and write the letter to Admiral Rickover listing the titles and a summary. I also stated frankly my desire to work for him and be a part of the modern nuclear navy.

I was never told directly that my letter influenced Rickover's decision to bring me on board. But a couple of months later—with absolutely no advance notice—I received official navy orders to report to Admiral Rickover for duty at his headquarters in Washington, D.C.

There was no way I could have ever imagined the amazing journey I had just begun.

3

GIVING MYSELF A JOB

My move to Admiral Hyman Rickover's Naval Reactors Branch (NRB) in Washington, D.C., became effective in July 1956. I went ahead to start my assignment and left Bonny with the job of packing up and making the move as easy as possible on the boys. Navy people move often. It is, depending on how you look at it, a good or bad part of navy life. Good in that we had the opportunity to live in some interesting places. Bad because we could never put down roots, like the ones from which I had prospered while growing up in Tennessee.

Leaving Mystic and changing schools and friends was especially difficult for our son Mike, who was then eleven. During the preceding school year, he had made the adjustment from school in Hawaii to school in Connecticut. Now here was another big change. Though only a few hundred miles, the relocation may as well have been halfway around the world again. His little brother, William, went cheerfully. Home for him was still wherever Mom was.

We rented a house just outside Washington in the

community of Falls Church, Virginia. The town came highly recommended by several members of Rickover's staff who lived in the same neighborhood. That is how I became a part of a most pleasant carpool. I still remember the interesting content of some of the conversations we had as we negotiated Washington rush-hour traffic.

On my first day at NRB, as best as I could determine, I was the only submarine ex-skipper on board. I was assigned a small office in the old, battered temporary building that served as the headquarters at NRB. I unpacked my few personal items and prepared to go to work. The only thing was, I still did not know what my "work" was.

It was a strange beginning. People were friendly, but no one seemed to be able to tell me what I had been hired on to do. It is expected that one has to break into new assignments, but in this case, I had no assignment beyond orders to report by a certain day at a certain place.

Throughout NRB there were plenty of books and manuals to read, and I did. I really was not bored. Still, I wondered just why Admiral Rickover brought me to this place. I suspected that I was a prospective nuclear submarine skipper but never mentioned that possibility to anyone. After all, at that point in my career, my nuclear training was nil.

It crossed my mind that this was another of the admiral's tests, that he was going to watch how I reacted to this total lack of guidance and then judge me on that. If I did nothing, showed no initiative, would I be summarily shipped out? Or if I were too aggressive, would he interpret that as signifying that I was a loose cannon?

So I waited and studied and waited some more. Still no duties came my way. Each morning I showed up for work, went to my office, and read through the stacks of manuals on nuclear propulsion history, design, and operation. At night I took some of the books home and continued my ad hoc atomic power education there. I talked with the others in NRB and found them all to be bright, communicative, and more than willing to answer a neophyte's questions about nuclear propulsion, atomic physics, *Nautilus*, and other projects.

I did not, however, ask the one big question that nagged at me: What is my assignment here?

Finally, after a few weeks of this, my studies reached a critical point and I asked for an audience with Admiral Rickover. I decided to be straight with him. Such a strategy had stood me in good stead before.

"Admiral, I've spent all my time at NRB so far reading and studying nuclear propulsion," I politely told him. "I've been aboard for several weeks now and I was wondering if you could give me some guidance as to what I should be working on."

He did not have to think about his answer at all. It was almost as if he had been expecting my visit.

"Well, Anderson," he said, "suppose the first thing you do is write up a proposal about just what it is that you ought to be doing."

That was it. That was all the guidance I was going to get from him.

"Yes, sir," I said, and then I turned and left his office, as if his answer made perfect sense to me.

Back at my desk, I stared at the stack of manuals and textbooks and pondered the vague but rather interesting assignment the admiral had given me. Assuming that whatever he had in mind for me would require such knowledge, just what should a submarine line officer do to become familiar and qualified with nuclear power? I had a few ideas of my own, but I decided to see if I could get some direction from others, the ones who had been willing to talk to me already.

I spent the better part of a week visiting one at a time with Rickover's top people, which included Harry Mandil, Ted Rockwell, Bob Panoff, and Captain Jim Dunford. I asked many questions—some of them probably pretty dumb—but they willingly and patiently answered them. Then I sat down and composed a memorandum, based largely on the ideas they shared with me. My memo to the admiral suggested that I begin work on a comprehensive program to prepare prospective nuclear submarine officers for qualification, and that I begin working my way through that program as I developed it. He accepted my self-assignment with a nod that I interpreted as, "Proceed." So that is what I did.

Mind you, up to this point no one had yet identified me as a potential nuclear submarine skipper. At least not to my knowledge. Maybe I was simply moving from teaching tactics at the sub school in New London to teaching nuclear propulsion at NRB in Washington. Well, if that was the case, I meant to make the most of it. I would show Rickover that I could learn the ropes. One of the first things I learned was that the history of the man and his project had been a turbulent but fascinating one.

Hyman Rickover was born in the Polish village of Mekow, which at that time was part of the Russian Empire. His school records indicate he was born in 1898, but his official navy biography says 1900. His family immigrated eventually to the Chicago area and soon settled in a Jewish neighborhood. Rickover was a bright, diligent, and hardworking student. He received an appointment to the U.S. Naval Academy in 1918. This was a providential move for both Rickover and the United States of America.

He graduated from Annapolis in 1922 and served aboard several surface ships. He attended Columbia University in New York City where he earned a master of science degree in electrical engineering, then qualified for command in submarines and served aboard the boats *S-9* (SS-114) and *S-48* (SS-159), though never as a skipper. During World War II, he was head of the Electrical Section at the navy's Bureau of Ships (BUSHIPS), and there he began to attract top technical people to his staff. He also developed a knack for working with private industry to accomplish things that he felt were important, even if it meant circumventing navy procedure.

After the war, then Captain Rickover sought—with remarkable vision— a post at the Atomic Energy Commission's Oak Ridge plant. Three other naval officers, Lou Roddis, Jim Dunford, and Ray Dick, went along with him and were soon heavily involved with a technical attempt that would change the course of naval warfare forever. They became set on the idea of reducing the size of a huge nuclear reactor to make it small enough so it would fit into a ship. Not just any ship, though. They envisioned it being used to propel a submarine through the depths of the world's oceans with the ease of Jules Verne's imaginary *Nautilus*. Many who knew him say Rickover had decided as early as 1946 that a submarine was the perfect vessel for nuclear power. It is difficult in this day and age to imagine how wacky that idea seemed to most people, both inside and outside the navy.

In theory, Rickover and his core team suggested, an atomic-powered submarine could remain submerged almost indefinitely, running virtually undetected. Verne's dreams of a *Nautilus* that could steam twenty thousand leagues under the sea could come true! Hyman Rickover was determined that he and his carefully selected group would be the ones who would get it done.

What Rickover was proposing seemed impossible to nearly everyone at all levels of the navy. First, there was the problem of reducing the size of a nuclear reactor enough to get it inside even the largest of ships, let alone a submarine. There would have to be some kind of a system that would transfer the heat from the intensely radioactive, closed-water circuit that ran through the reactor and then would drive a steam-turbine system that provided electricity to run the motors. Inside the radioactive portion of the water system, pumps would be required that could operate indefinitely without breaking down.

Any submarine sailor knew the reason for that. Should there be a malfunction, there would be no way to repair the pumps at sea. If one of the conventional submarines had such a problem, the vessel could run on the other pumps while the broken one was repaired. However, while at sea, how in the world could a crew go inside a nuclear reactor to fix a broken pump?

Of course, there was also the inherent danger of radioactivity. Enormously heavy shielding would have to be provided for the reactor itself. Safety was paramount. Even small radiation leaks could cause long-term health effects that were not yet fully understood. One of Rickover's earliest demands was that the crew be exposed to no more radioactivity aboard a nuclear-powered vessel than were those crewmembers aboard a conventional ship. For three years he and his carefully assembled group, working from an office that was rumored to have been converted from a women's powder room, wrote letters, lobbied, maneuvered, and established contacts, all in an effort to advance his "impossible" cause. Somewhere along the way Rickover came to the conclusion that the only way to get things moving was to go to the top. He wrote a letter to Admiral Chester Nimitz, the chief of naval operations (CNO). In that letter he proposed the development of the nuclear-powered submarine. Chester Nimitz was a former submariner and, as the commander of the Pacific Fleet during World War II, a bona fide hero. He was also a man of great vision. Nimitz gave the project his blessing. With him, Rickover had finally found a sympathetic ear within the highest reaches of the navy.

Very shortly, and probably to his great surprise considering the cold reception his ideas were getting from most others in the naval establishment, Hyman Rickover was appointed to head a new section in the Bureau of Ships. It would carry the simple but all-encompassing moniker "Nuclear Power Division."

Next on the list of potential hurdles was the Atomic Energy Commission. The department, concerned about the spread of ominous nuclear capability among both friends and enemies of the United States, kept an extremely tight watch on all atomic energy matters. Despite its early promise, practical development of the generation of nuclear power was moving very, very slowly, mostly because of the AEC's cautious policies. Hyman Rickover did not want to move slowly on anything.

Rickover came up with a clever way to overcome the stifling bureaucracy. Somehow he was able to persuade the Atomic Energy Commission to create a division called Naval Reactors Branch. He was also able to get himself appointed as its chief while retaining his existing job with the BUSHIPS Nuclear Power Division.

As head of the two divisions of the same project—both the navy and the AEC—Rickover could, in effect, write himself letters or memos and get the instant go-ahead from the "chiefs" of the two key agencies. It no longer would be necessary to build a case, write it up, and send it up through the convoluted navy chain of command and then wait for it to come back down the tortuous Atomic Energy Commission bureaucracy. No, Hyman Rickover could simply have a meeting with himself, make the decision, and get under way with whatever it was, all within minutes.

With such power he was also able to cherry-pick the best and brightest minds to work on his project. It is reported that he interviewed hundreds of engineers, chose a few, and elected to start a school to train others the way he wanted them to be trained.

So, with the resources he needed and the skids adequately greased to get past traditional bureaucracy, the first designs of the radical, new nuclear engine began to emerge from Naval Reactors Branch. Unbelievably, a full-size, land-based prototype of what would become the *Nautilus* power plant was soon in operation.

It was installed inside an authentic submarine hull section that had been constructed in an unlikely place for anything nautical—at the Atomic Energy Commission's desert test center in remote Arco, Idaho, about sixty-five miles northwest of Pocatello and about six hundred miles from the nearest salt water. Such a land-based prototype plant was typical of NRB's brilliant ideas and its insistence on safety every step of the way in implementing its radical projects. What was learned in Idaho was used immediately. The web of bureaucracy was once again subverted, and the *Nautilus* propulsion system was already a well-improved product even before the ship itself was completed.

One of my first stops in my new job was at the reactor simulator in Idaho. Though Arco was a town of less than a thousand permanent residents at the time, I found the almost nine hundred square miles of Butte County where the test facility was located to be teeming with bright people, all bent on making the most out of the recently harnessed atom. At one time the area held the world's largest collection of nuclear reactors. But to verify that we were most definitely playing with fire there, it should be noted that the Arco facility would later be the scene of the first fatal nuclear accident—though not related to the submarine simulator—in 1961, when three people died.

Despite my fascination with what I saw and learned in Arco, the ship *Nautilus* was what interested me the most. All of it, not just the replica of her power plant. As part of my studies at NRB, I read the detailed notes of her first skipper, Captain Wilkinson, and spent considerable time with what the navy's operational experts had to say about her. I also spent time at Electric Boat in Groton, watching the other nuclear boats being built. The more I read and saw, the more impressed I was with *Nautilus* and her sisters.

Few events in history have had as much impact as the launch of this remarkable vessel. That sounds like an overstatement, but that one submarine literally changed everything about naval and nuclear warfare, about how nations defend themselves, about exploration of the earth's oceans. I maintain that this effect is not fully appreciated even today, maybe because of all the other technological developments that have occurred since in areas like nuclear energy, space travel, and communications. People now tend to take scientific breakthroughs for granted. But when the dramatic debut of USS *Nautilus* is considered in the context of the day and time, her military and scientific impact is stunning. I also contend that we are still reaping the benefits of what we learned from the construction and accomplishments of *Nautilus*, many of which occurred more than a half century ago, including our Arctic missions.

One point is beyond argument. When the world's first atomic ship slid down the skids and into the waters of the Thames River in Groton in 1954, it immediately assured the obsolescence for American, Soviet, and all other nations' diesel-powered submarines. Soviet military leaders began to openly discuss nuclear propulsion. Throughout 1954 and 1955, approximately fifty articles on the topic of atomic power appeared in the Soviet military publication *Red Star*. Those stories broke a long press silence on the subject. Additionally, Sergei Gorshkov, admiral of the Soviet Fleet and the man widely regarded as the father of the modern Russian navy, instantly accelerated his country's atomic energy programs after *Nautilus* went to sea, diverting money and assets from other military programs.

President Dwight D. Eisenhower, who came into office one year before the ship was put in commission, had some interesting initial frustrations connected with *Nautilus*. First, it was his Democratic predecessor, Harry S. Truman, who had the opportunity to sign his name on the keel the day work officially began on the vessel, placing his own mark on the ship. That event had been arranged by none other than Admiral Hyman Rickover and was calculated to show up those in the establishment who had been less than supportive of his high-profile project.

Then, a few days before the ship was to be launched—sponsored and christened by the relatively new First Lady, Mamie Eisenhower—the *Washington Post* ran a front-page article that claimed the submarine was little more than a lab project and not a serious military vessel. A similar story also ran in *Time* magazine. The story correctly reported that *Nautilus* would only have six torpedo tubes instead of the ten that were available on late-model conventional submarines, implying that lack of firepower prevented

Nautilus crewman David Greenhill on watch in the ship's torpedo room.

A *Nautilus* crewman stands watch on the bridge.

her from having any offensive capability. The reporter incorrectly claimed, though, that she had only one periscope, and that this submarine was really no more than a "test vehicle."

President Eisenhower was livid that *Nautilus* was portrayed in the *Post* as essentially experimental. He was especially upset about the timing of the article, just before the boat's christening. By seven o'clock on the morning the story appeared, the president was on the telephone to Secretary of Defense Charles Wilson, who had extended the invitation to Mrs. Eisenhower to sponsor *Nautilus*.

"What do you mean asking my wife to sponsor this . . . this . . . test ship?" he yelled.

Wilson did the best he could to assure the president that the submarine was much more than that. The launch went as scheduled, with the First Lady using two hands to break the champagne bottle across the ship's bow while proclaiming, "I christen thee, *Nautilus!*"

This would not be the last time an event connected with *Nautilus* gave Eisenhower heartburn.

On the first trial runs at sea, the new ship's performance astonished even the men who had designed and built her. She could travel at a sustained underwater speed above twenty-three knots (about 26.5 miles per hour), and she could do so more or less indefinitely. Never had a submarine had such power and range. Even the most advanced diesel submarines—and they were the most formidable war machines ever built by man in their World War II prime—could only manage one-fourth that speed while underwater, and they could only stay submerged for a maximum of about eight hours before they began to run out of oxygen and battery power.

It was not just about speed, though. She was highly maneuverable while under water. She could safely submerge to a depth of 713 feet, deeper by several hundred feet than her predecessors. During the next couple of years, she proved herself to be remarkably effective in exercises with anti-submarine forces, as well as in just about anything else she was called upon to do. She was a remarkably effective warship.

Needless to say, I was soon swept up in the program. I did not know exactly how this wonderful vessel would fit into my future. But that did not matter. I had already begun to wonder what spectacular feats *Nautilus* and other atomic-powered vessels that followed her might accomplish.

Professor Arronax, Captain Nemo's reluctant passenger aboard Jules Verne's fictional submarine, summed up my feelings very succinctly when he said, "Ah, Commander! Your *Nautilus* is certainly a marvelous boat."

4

PROSPECTIVE COMMANDER

dmiral Hyman Rickover is portrayed as an impatient, ruthless, and maddeningly tough-minded man. I certainly saw him in that way too. He could be irascible, mercurial, hard to please, and downright rude. But you do not accomplish what Rickover did without sometimes ignoring standard procedures or stepping on toes.

My tour of duty with NRB was immensely productive, even though he and I were about as different as two people could be. He seemed to go out of his way at times to be undiplomatic. I was the opposite, always trying not to cause hurt feelings if I could help it. Rickover had devised an audacious way to make himself head of two important government agencies, in effect becoming his own boss. I followed the more conventional route to accomplish my goals.

But we shared one important characteristic: nothing was more important than the safety and well-being of the men and women who wore a U.S. Navy uniform. Nothing. I admired that and I believe the admiral appreciated my stance. No one ever had any trouble with the admiral by putting safety first.

I recall hearing about an engineering conference called to solve the question about how to attach the closure plate to the body of the reactor pressure vessel in order to absolutely seal the whole thing. Should it be a gasket or should it be welded?

The expert on the gaskets just happened to be the manufacturer of the devices and stood to win a lucrative contract. Welding experts battled verbally with him for several hours. Finally, the assembled group yielded to the gasket expert and concluded that gasket seals had the advantage. They would make it easier to refuel the reactor. Easier and cheaper and faster than welding.

Near the end of the meeting, Admiral Rickover stepped in for a briefing. He listened intently to the summary report, then turned to the man who would manufacture the gaskets.

"Sir, suppose your son was a member of the crew on a nuclear submarine," the admiral said, fixing the man with his laser gaze. "Would you feel better that gaskets or welding had been used?"

Those in the room that day report that the man was visibly shaken by Rickover's hypothetical question.

"Admiral, welding would be safer," he finally conceded.

Gaskets, in this application, were never mentioned again.

Early in 1957, I finally heard the words I had been hoping for. Captain Jim Dunford confirmed that I was, indeed, being considered as a prospective commanding officer for a nuclear submarine.

"Which one, Jim?" I pressed. "*Nautilus*?"

His face gave no hint at all, and his words were carefully chosen.

"Andy, for the purposes of training, if I were you, I would assume it might be *Nautilus*," he answered. "But listen to me when I tell you that is far from a promise, understood?"

Nautilus or not, I was elated. As far as I was concerned, being the second person to command the world's first nuclear submarine, and easily the most famous vessel on the planet, was a dream assignment. I prayed it would be my next duty.

I later learned that there was quite a debate among Rickover's deputies over whether or not I was the right choice for that assignment. Some were convinced that I was too shy and soft-spoken for such a high-profile job. My father taught me to speak only when I had something well thought out to say, and then to do so politely, as all gentlemen are supposed to do. Rickover himself had once pointedly told me that I ought to talk more. Maybe that was his way of trying to get me to speak up, to counter the opinions of those who felt my quietness might be a sign of weakness.

Someone said that I have a swanlike demeanor—cool on the surface but paddling like hell below it. That might be somewhat true. I was confident that I was ready for this job and that everything I had done in my life so far had prepared me for it. From military school through World War II, during the Korean War and the Cold War up to that point, long before I was picked as a prospective commanding officer (PCO) in Rickover's shop, I worked hard to be ready when and if an important assignment came. Others had done likewise, of course. By that time, some worked within a few feet of me at NRB, all good leaders, excellent submarine skippers, and otherwise very capable, experienced, competitive men.

Regardless, and despite those reservations on the part of some, word finally came from Navy Bureau of Personnel on May 8, 1957. It was finally official. I was about to assume what I thought was the best submarine job in the world!

As confident as I was about my ability to do the job, I realized I would be standing in a very big shadow when I climbed up onto the bridge of that boat. Dennis Wilkinson had done a wonderful job of testing and demonstrating the ship. He had been able to handle the top secret drills and operations equally as well as the public relations that went with the command of a ship whose profile was meant to be highly visible.

I was about to take charge of a vessel that had been thoroughly shaken down, but one that was ready for many more adventures. Dick Laning would commission the *Seawolf*, and Jim Calvert would commission USS

Skate, the third nuclear boat to be built, and a vessel that would later figure, in an interesting way, into our polar efforts. Shannon Cramer, Dan Brooks, and George Steele were aboard as well, each of whom would command later models of the *Skate* class of nuclear submarines.

None of us had any appreciable background in nuclear power. Few people did. To make up for lost time, we agreed to pursue the same newly designated "chief operator," a qualification required of submarine engineering officers. The procedure for these officers was to attend a six-month course at Nuclear Power School, studying a curriculum that was being developed on the fly, based in part on the work I had been doing at NRB. It reminded me of the accelerated prospective submarine commander training during World War II when we were learning tactics from war-patrol reports fresh from the Pacific theater.

"Qualification" is a long-standing requirement in the submarine service. It has long been a necessity that everyone who serves on submarines becomes qualified in all positions on the boat, which means a torpedoman would be able to drive the boat if need be. Those who pass the submarine qualifying examination earn the dolphin insignia, signifying their qualification. Those who cannot pass have their navy careers redirected into another area of service.

The rest of the would-be nuclear boat skippers and I did our book training in Washington, then made many trips of two or three weeks' duration each to the Idaho plant. There we received hands-on training of what we were learning in the textbooks. To speed things up, we worked two full shifts, seven days a week, returning to Washington exhausted after a couple of weeks of that grueling routine.

Because of my electrical engineering training, the technical aspect of it all was not so daunting. It was the magnitude of all that we had to absorb, and in a branch of science that had hardly existed when I was at Annapolis.

After following the demanding routine we had assigned ourselves, we were all able to take and pass the final written and verbal exams leading to "chief operator" qualification. That was a happy day for us. Now no one would ever be able to say that we commanded a ship with a revolutionary power plant but had no idea of how the thing worked.

It was about that time that Admiral Rickover, who surprisingly had a keen sense of humor, began calling all of us prospective skippers "heroes." I suspect he made fun of us to dispel any cockiness among us. We even received memos from the boss addressed: "To: Heroes." He could put us in our place as effectively as he did any bureaucrat.

I was already doing a lot of thinking about exactly how I would make my mark as captain of *Nautilus*. The more I thought, the more my mind steered me northward, toward a most unlikely part of the world for a warm-blooded Southerner.

I began some of the most serious planning I had ever done. I was very much aware of the responsibility I was about to be handed. The commander of a revolutionary type of ship has the opportunity for an unusually large influence on that vessel's assignments and schedules. And *Nautilus* was not just revolutionary; she was *the* most revolutionary ship of our time. I also knew that I had to develop a purposeful vision of what I wanted this vessel to accomplish and then sell the plan to a complex, multilayered command structure. The marketing of that vision would be easier and more quickly accepted if I was able to describe how it would lead to an improvement in naval capabilities and national defense.

In their first two years, Captain Wilkinson and his officers and crew had done a superb job of testing, proving, and shaking down *Nautilus*. They had confirmed the safety of the Rickover nuclear propulsion design. At the same time, they had made their vessel a star. The ship's popularity was greater than that of a hit Broadway show. Anyone who wanted to be up-to-date wanted an appearance with the first atomic-powered submarine.

Simply being an adequate chapter two to Wilkinson's rather spectacular chapter one would not be enough for me. I could not merely sustain the laurels that had been showered on *Nautilus* so far. She needed to try something that would take her to a new level.

I really cannot say where or when the idea first hit me. Somewhere between the time I came to work for Admiral Rickover at NRB and the time I knew that I would most likely have command of a nuclear vessel, my thoughts, and those of several others around me, turned to the North—the Far North; the absolute Far North.

It seems natural in retrospect, but I am still not certain why it jumped to the forefront when I began pondering how I would put my own mark on my command of *Nautilus*. I am only grateful to God that it did!

At that time, in early 1957, I knew very little about the Arctic Ocean, certainly not the water depth at the North Pole or the ice that covered the ocean there. My only concept of submarines and polar ice was one of fantasy. As a boy I had been thrilled when I read Jules Verne's *20,000 Leagues Under the Sea*. I marveled as I read how Captain Nemo took his amazing submersible ship under ice to the South Pole. Or at least the South Pole as Mr. Verne envisioned it. He did not know when he wrote that book that the South Pole rests not on an ocean, as does the North Pole, but on a solid landmass. Mr. Verne had the right idea about submarines under ice but the wrong pole.

There had been surprisingly few submarine operations in the Arctic before our nuclear-powered *Nautilus*. The first and perhaps best known—though also unsuccessful—was led by Sir Hubert Wilkins in 1931. Ironically, he conducted his operation aboard an ex-U.S. Navy submarine renamed *Nautilus*.

Wilkins believed that there were enough leads (open expanses of water between large collections of ice) and polynyas ("holes" or areas of relatively thin ice) to enable even a limited-range submarine to make its way across the frozen ocean by steaming beneath the ice from one hole in the ice to another. Wilkins also believed that the underside of the ice would be smooth enough to allow the submarine to ride along just deep enough to push up lightly against the icy roof overhead, skating along on inverted skis mounted to the decks of his boat.

Mechanical problems plagued them from the start, but Wilkins refused to be deterred. He made several unsuccessful attempts to steer the submarine under the ice pack. As they persisted in their efforts, the crew noted a one-inch layer of frost on the inside hull of the ship. The interior of the submarine was not heated. The crew finally refused to try any longer. The North Pole remained far out of reach.

In a way, Wilkins finally made it to the Pole. He died in 1958. The next year, his ashes were taken to the area near the North Pole by an admirer, Jim Calvert, in *Skate* and scattered by her crew on the Arctic ice.

During World War II, reports indicated German submarines occasionally used the edge of the ice pack as a hiding place. Conventional U.S. submarines in the late 1940s and early 1950s had made brief excursions under the fringes of the polar ice, too, but they had to be very careful. Too many things could go wrong. Besides, almost all the sea bottom was uncharted and little was known about the depth and form of the ice. If something did go haywire, the length of time a conventional submarine could stay under water was limited due to necessity of recharging batteries. With no way to surface, no way to call for help, and no way to power the submarine to open water, the ship and its crew would simply disappear, never to be heard from again.

As I anticipated the move to my new ship, one question kept resonating stronger and stronger in my brain. *Could* Nautilus *make it to the North Pole? Could she confirm the existence of a totally submerged Northwest Passage between the Atlantic and Pacific?* The inevitable lure of the Arctic and the search for the elusive ocean-to-ocean route, the same siren calls experienced by explorers throughout history, were taking hold of me. I became more and more convinced that under-ice navigation was the challenge for which I had been looking. I had a lot of studying to do to get ready.

I soon found out that I was not the only one. Commander Calvert and a couple of the other prospective nuclear submarine skippers at NRB were also dreaming of the Arctic. Captain Wilkinson himself was talking about it. I decided to keep my ideas to myself. If there was to be competition—and anytime two submarine skippers are in a position to compete, you can bet there will be—then any obvious efforts on my part to prepare would only intensify the whole thing.

There was one other consideration. I suspected that Admiral Rickover would reject the thought of taking a nuclear ship under ice so early in the nuclear submarine era. As it turned out, that suspicion later proved to be correct. At any point in our preparation, with simply a casual comment, Rickover could have stopped the whole plan cold. It is to his credit that he did not, but I am convinced he came close several times.

Keeping my early Arctic exploration ideas from my colleagues and my own boss—and even from my wife—I began to thoroughly investigate the possibilities. I checked out relevant books from the Navy Department library and took them directly home and studied them without drawing attention to what I was doing. Anytime I had texts or maps of the Arctic region in my office, I made sure they were equaled by material detailing other spots on the globe.

I made a point of not talking to anyone about the Arctic. If the subject came up, I would either say nothing or ease out of the conversation. As far as I was concerned, there was little indication that I had settled on Arctic exploration as a goal for *Nautilus*.

5

TAKING THE HELM

So it was in June 1957 that I once again hugged and kissed my family good-bye. Only this time I climbed aboard an airplane bound for San Francisco. There I was to join *Nautilus* at sea and ride with her and her crew to Seattle where the change-of-command ceremony was to take place. By this time we had also moved back to Mystic, to the same house we had left when I went to NRB. My family felt as if they had returned home.

There was no doubt in my mind that I was headed for what would become one of the greatest adventures any sailor could have. On the long transcontinental flight, with no snow in sight below us until we approached the Rockies, I could not help exploring in my mind the frozen Arctic. Of course, I knew that the immediate challenge was to relieve Captain Wilkinson, to integrate myself into the crew, and to gain their respect and confidence. Assuming command of any submarine is always something of a shotgun marriage. I have all the respect in the world for soldiers in foxholes and crew members of bombers, but no group of men is any closer than a submarine crew. They have no say-so in who their skipper will be, nor does a new commander have much initial determination in the crew members. They are stuck with each other, for better or for worse.

This could become an especially thorny situation if I did not handle it properly. I would need to tell the men of the possible under-ice exploration I was considering, and I would need to do it shortly after I took command of *Nautilus* if we were going to get moving on it before summer was over.

I tried to figure the odds of actually getting approval for a brief under-ice mission. They were far from certain. I had risked a quick conversation with Commander Robert McWethy, a fellow submariner who was then serving in the Pentagon, because I knew of his interest in exploring the world beneath the polar ice pack. He made it clear that there was strong and powerful opposition in Atlantic Fleet Headquarters to any such mission by *Nautilus*.

They felt that the world's most visible naval vessel should, instead, spend her time working with surface and air antisubmarine forces, anticipating the day when Russia would have its own fleet of nuclear-powered submersibles. There were some who considered exploration under the polar ice to be a foolhardy risk to our only fully operational nuclear submarine. Most were solidly opposed to taking a valuable asset to such uncharted waters and with such risky conditions. With everything else going on around the globe at that time, the loss of *Nautilus* and her crew would have been more than just a personal tragedy. Even the safe return of the boat but the failure of a high-profile mission could have negative political and military repercussions in the Cold War.

I understood those arguments perfectly. I still felt, however, that this country should take the leadership to explore that great unknown. The scientific and military benefits of under-ice exploration—particularly if approached cautiously—would far outweigh the risks.

The truth is, the reactions that I most worried about were those of the crew. How would they feel about taking "their" boat to such an inhospitable spot on the globe, particularly with a new skipper they did not yet know or have reason to trust? I would need them behind me, or any under-ice operations would be far more difficult.

Nautilus was at sea about forty miles off San Francisco. When I arrived with my sea bag at Mare Island, near Vallejo at the northeastern end of San Francisco Bay, arrangements were set to fly me out to the submarine by helicopter. It was not unusual for a relieving commander to join mid-cruise before assuming the helm. I was especially grateful for this opportunity with *Nautilus*. I had been aboard her several times before but remember vividly the special sense of exhilaration I felt as we thrashed our way out beyond Point Reyes and over the open Pacific Ocean. I also thought of Dennis Wilkinson. My arrival aboard would emphasize that his days as skipper of *Nautilus* were about to be over.

Then before I realized we were even close, we spotted the dark, sleek hull of *Nautilus*, bobbing on the surface of the ocean below us.

What a stirring sight! I could see several crew members topside, preparing for the helicopter at-sea transfer. The pilot eased down close to the deck and hovered there so I could descend to the ship in a sling apparatus that swung back and forth beneath the helicopter like a pendulum. The agile deck gang quickly steadied the sling and guided me safely down to the middle of the deck along with my gear.

Captain Eugene P. Wilkinson, the first commanding officer of USS *Nautilus*, the world's first nuclear submarine.

Before I knew it I was aboard *Nautilus*, and Captain Wilkinson was standing there smiling, hand outstretched, offering me a warm welcome aboard.

The helicopter headed back eastward, the decks were cleared, and

Ship's cook Roger Hall prepares another fine meal for the *Nautilus* crew.

shortly after my transfer, *Nautilus* submerged once again to her natural element, ready for the run to Seattle.

After being aboard *Nautilus* for only a short time, two things impressed me almost as much as Hyman Rickover's reactor. The first was her officers and crew. I had every reason to suspect that they would be top-notch, but once aboard, I knew immediately that these men were second to none. The second thing was something that would have been obvious to any old diesel-boat sailor accustomed to the tight confines of their subs—the comfort of the vessel—or "habitability," as the engineers insist on calling it.

As submarines go, *Nautilus* is a sizable vessel. She is 20 feet longer than a regulation football field—320 feet from bow to stern, about 10 feet longer than the conventional fleet submarine of the day—and her cylinder-shaped hull was 28 feet in diameter. In the center of the boat, or her "sail" section, she towers 52 feet from her keel to the top of her sail. She did not have to carry the traditional banks of heavy storage batteries or the great volume of diesel fuel for her engines, which took nearly half the total space inside the skin of conventional submarines. That made it possible to allot much more room for her crew's living and working spaces.

The wardroom, where the officers gathered for meals and a place usually used as a general-purpose meeting room, is nearly four times the size of one on the World War II diesel boats. The crew's mess is huge in comparison as well. Thirty-six men could comfortably eat there at one time. In about five minutes, the mess compartment could be turned into a movie theater that would accommodate as many as fifty men. The crew's mess also held an ice cream machine, a soda machine, and a jukebox that gave five plays for a nickel, a bargain even in 1957.

In addition, *Nautilus* was equipped with a heavy-duty automatic washer and dryer, a nuclear laboratory, a small but very well-equipped machine shop, a photographic darkroom, and a library that held about six hundred books. An interior decorator conceived the appointments and attractive color scheme throughout the boat. It was certainly different from my previous boats where the color was the traditional dull navy gray. I could not help but wonder what my old diesel-boat shipmates would have said about an interior decorator having anything to do with a submarine's furnishings.

Nautilus had many other amenities. In the tile-decked washrooms, there were individual small stainless-steel drawers to store the crew's toilet articles. Each man had his own bunk with a nice, comfortable mattress, another luxury diesel-boat sailors would have admired. On those boats, two sailors would often have to alternately share a single bunk as they went on and off watch, a practice dubbed "hot-bunking."

There was a reason for the more comfortable surroundings on this ship. Her crew would be spending days—and possibly months—submerged. It was important that it be as comfortable an environment as possible for them.

While *Nautilus* was on long underwater runs, a special "scrubber" removed carbon dioxide (CO_2) and other noxious gases from the boat's atmosphere. Oxygen was released into the ship as needed from a large bank of flasks installed outside the pressure hulls in ballast tanks. Later, oxygen generators were added, breaking even further the ship's ties to the surface. These devices would reduce water into its elements, with

USS *Nautilus* (SSN-571) makes a tight, full-speed turn. The maneuverability and underwater speed of this vessel astonished even those who conceived and built her.

the oxygen diverted into holding flasks and the hydrogen discharged to the sea outside. CO burners kept deadly carbon monoxide low. Air-conditioning units maintained the temperature inside the submarine at between sixty-eight and seventy-two degrees and kept the relative humidity at about 50 percent.

I struck up a conversation with one of the boat's enginemen, John P. McGovern, a Brooklyn, New York, native and a *plankowner*—a term meaning he had been aboard *Nautilus* since she was first commissioned. I was especially interested in the effectiveness of the vessel's air-conditioning system. The crew would learn soon enough the reasons for my curiosity on the subject.

"We've been close to the equator and we've been way up north, but the atmosphere inside *Nautilus* is always the same," he told me with pride in his voice. Several crew members told me that they had never worn a jacket while aboard the ship.

As McGovern described the comfort of the boat's environment, I could not help but think of the Australian explorer Sir Hubert Wilkins and his *Nautilus* and the frost on the inside of her hull when he dared to try to venture beneath the polar ice. I knew of my own experiences in the South Pacific during the war. A broken air conditioner could put a warship out of commission as surely as leaks or other depth-charge damage.

The auxiliarymen maintained the air-treatment machinery. The ship's doctor—Jack Ebersole when I first went aboard and later Dick Dobbins—was charged, along with the hospital corpsmen under his supervision, with keeping a careful check on the condition of the air inside the ship. These same men ran the radiation monitoring program. This was all as a direct result of Admiral Rickover's emphasis on crew safety. It was also in response to natural concerns about the possible exposure of the crew to radiation, working as they did in such close proximity to an active nuclear reactor.

So far, in the two-year history of *Nautilus*, the record of radioactive exposure aboard the ship had been wonderful. The men aboard had been exposed to less radiation than their counterparts on surface ships where they used conventional propulsion systems.

Each crew member was required to wear a film badge. Those were developed periodically so that individual exposure to radiation could be tracked. During a six-month test period in 1957, the average dosage received by individual crew members was less than 2 percent of the maximum allowable. Also during the entire test period, the maximum cumulative total dosage experienced by a member of the crew, an engineer who stood his watches in the engine room, was only 17 percent of the maximum safe allowable cumulative exposure.

In sharp contrast to what we were finding with *Nautilus* and her American siblings, there was evidence that Soviet submariners suffered serious problems with overexposure to radiation in the hurried first generation of their nuclear fleet. We can only assume they had no counterpart the equal of Hyman Rickover who demanded complete safety.

Another blessing aboard *Nautilus* was the presence of adequate fresh water. Thanks to nuclear power, there was the ability to distill pure water from seawater. The stills made plenty of water for anyone who needed it. Crew members could take a shower whenever they wanted, even every day. That sounds like a given, but it was not the case on conventional submarines. When they were on patrol, the suggested frequency of baths for crewmen was once per week.

Water from their stills was primarily intended for the banks of storage cells in the batteries below the decks. The joke, though too truthful to be funny, was that if the distilled water was clean enough, it went to the batteries. If it was not, it was used for cooking or drinking. There was rarely enough left over even for that weekly bath. The water produced on *Nautilus* was of sufficient purity for the reactor heat transfer loop or for make up water for the ship's storage batteries. There was plenty left over for such amenities as doing laundry, drinking, cooking, and bathing.

I quickly came to realize, though, that of all the assets of this wonderful vessel, the greatest was her crew of one hundred enlisted men and twelve officers. They were an all-star team of submariners, the absolute cream of the force. Each man had been handpicked and carefully trained. The average age of the crew was twenty-six, and most of them were already experienced submarine sailors before they came aboard this remarkable ship. Two-thirds of them were married. Each was a volunteer, just as American

Crew members on watch at the diving station aboard *Nautilus*. From left to right, LT William Cole, Chief Frank Skewes, Charles Black, William Brown, and Ray Kropp.

submariners always have been, but each had specifically volunteered for duty on this specific ship. While it is true that they received extra pay for submarine duty and the best food in any branch of the service, there was something else that attracted them to this particular duty station: the chance to serve aboard a very special ship, to experience that extraordinary *Nautilus* spirit.

Theirs had already been a unique ride. Before joining *Nautilus*, all officers and engineering ratings—regardless of their past experience in the navy—were required to study nuclear propulsion for a full year. The curriculum was made up of six months of academic work at the new Nuclear Power School in New London, then six months of operational training on the *Nautilus* land-based prototype plant in the Idaho desert. Of course, their new vessel served as a perfect advanced-learning module and the best place to get some serious on-the-job training. Of the 288 crewmen who had already served on *Nautilus* by the time I took command, 47 had been promoted to officer status or had entered programs that would eventually lead to commissions as officers. As good as submarine sailors are throughout the service, that statistic is impressive!

Nautilus had steamed well over 130,000 miles by the time I took command. She had called at a dozen different ports on both coasts of the United States and in the Caribbean.

As adept as the crew was at hard work when they were aboard, they were also skilled at having a good time while ashore. In ports away from home base, they did a great job of locating places where they could gather and enjoy a bit of local color. The special ship's spirit they had built carried over wherever they got together on liberty. Yes, they had a good time and blew off steam while ashore, but not at the expense of disharmony among shipmates or to the detriment of the ship's good reputation. To my knowledge, we never had a serious incident involving our crew members that might reflect negatively on our famous boat.

Since her commissioning two years before, *Nautilus* had become something of a floating exhibit of how nuclear power could be used to maintain peace in the world. Not surprisingly, considering the amount of publicity she enjoyed, many important people wanted to come aboard and see her in action. As best as they could be counted, it was determined that sixty-eight members of Congress, 186 admirals and generals, and various secretaries of the navy and other Defense Department brass had already signed her logbook by the time I came aboard.

So as we steered submerged toward Puget Sound and Seattle, I was even more elated at having been chosen to command this great ship and her

Commander Anderson speaks to a group of VIP visitors aboard *Nautilus*. Such visits were commonplace on the navy's most visible vessel.

extraordinary crew. I spent time on the run up the West Coast subtly finding out what these men wanted to accomplish that had not already been done with *Nautilus*. As proud as they were of their first two years, not one of them was satisfied yet. They wanted to write new chapters in the book of nuclear submarine operations. They made sure that their new skipper was aware that they felt they had only scratched the surface in the boat's two years of existence and were excited about whatever might come next.

I must confess, though, that I do not remember one of them mentioning the North Pole.

6

THE FOURTH GREAT OCEAN

At the Naval Academy we were frequently reminded that water covers 70 percent of the globe. Humankind was said to be separated by three great oceans—the Atlantic, the Pacific, and the Indian.

I received excellent instruction and a great head start on my military career at the Academy, but my instructors were incorrect about the three great oceans. There is a fourth, the Arctic Ocean, an oval-shaped body of water lying at the very top of the globe. Perhaps had it not been for the almost constant covering of pack ice, or the fact that its size is not accurately depicted on flat maps, it would have been on the list of the planet's great oceans well before. It was late in our planet's history, however, before humankind knew the body of water was constant, that the North Pole was not located on dry land that interrupted the ocean's expanse.

The Arctic Ocean is five times as big as the Mediterranean Sea. Like the other oceans on the planet, it separates great landmasses—in this case Europe, Asia, and North America.

Also like the others, the Arctic is, in the main, quite deep.

In *Nautilus* we were finally able to accurately measure major portions that had been previously inaccessible. For example, we found the water depth at the North Pole to be 13,410 feet. We also discovered a notable exception regarding the depth of the Arctic: it is relatively shallow when approaching from the Pacific side. This ice-laden stretch of several hundred miles would prove to be one of our greatest challenges, a very pronounced squeeze problem for an under-ice submarine like *Nautilus*, since she was fifty-two feet tall at her middle.

These submerged features remain mostly hidden by a more-or-less complete cover of sea ice. This ice varies in thickness and coverage. The deepest ice draft we measured in *Nautilus* was 80 feet, but we later learned that our limited instrumentation missed far thicker and more dangerous upside-down peaks of ice, and we were fortunate not to have learned of them in a more dramatic fashion. Subsequent voyages in the area have measured ice jutting as deeply as near 190 feet.

Oddly, if all the Arctic ice were flattened out like a pancake, it would only be about ten feet thick. The only predictable thing about sea ice is its unpredictability. It separates into chunks—some tiny ones called "brash," some block size, while others form floes that stretch from yards to miles across.

In some areas, the floes drift apart to form *leads* or *polynyas*—long, meandering "rivers" of open water or holes in large accumulations of ice, either of which might offer a patient submarine the opportunity to surface if need be and if they could be located in a timely manner. In other areas, particularly near a coastline, floes grind together. One side overrides another in a helter-skelter, building-block fashion, driving one plane downward and then freezes together to form especially deep ice. These can grow to a thickness formidable to any kind of submarine navigation, but especially if the water depth happens to be shallow as well.

By contrast, icebergs—formed by glacier action ashore—can reach depths of hundreds of feet. Fortunately it is very rare to find an iceberg in the Arctic Ocean.

In some regions, the ice is a blindingly pure white. In others, it is a cloudy gray. When the sun plays on broken ice, the edges can reflect a beautiful jewel-like blend of blues and greens. It is not difficult to understand the mesmerizing appeal of this strange region, a fascination that has drawn explorers for centuries.

There is life there. In a reconnaissance flight over the ice in 1958, I spotted what at first appeared to be a small, brown, dirt-covered island surrounded by the ice. But as our airplane drew closer, I could see dozens of walrus lazing on the edges of a particular ice floe. There are also polar bears and other smaller animals, and an amazing assortment of birds.

The top surface of the Arctic Ocean ice is reasonably regular, a factor of immense benefit to those who would proceed on foot or with dogsleds, or who would attempt to land a small plane. Some of the larger ice islands have even been used as more-or-less permanent bases for the military,

A view of the treacherous polar ice pack from the deck of USS *Nautilus*. The photo was taken during the second attempt to find a sea route beneath the ice from the Pacific to the Atlantic in the summer of 1958.

floating islands of ice that provide enough stability for the construction of buildings and even airstrips that accommodate relatively large aircraft.

But in looking at the floes from below, we found that the smoothness on top was greatly deceiving. A small ice hill only a few feet high as seen from above will magnify itself tremendously underneath with a keel five to ten times as great as its surface feature.

In subzero winter weather, the ice pack stretches far down the coast of Greenland on the Atlantic Ocean side and to below the Bering Strait, between Alaska and Siberia, on the Pacific side. Scientists are still studying the possible effects of global warming on this region, and there is evidence that the pack is receding dramatically. The ice floes are still there and still formidable, however, even if their coverage is not what it was five decades ago. I know from firsthand experience that they were something to fear and respect in the mid-1950s.

Native people have called the region home for centuries, and the first explorers approached the Arctic two thousand years ago. It has been of interest to adventurers and explorers ever since, but it was not until 1937 that some Russians landed an airplane on an ice floe near the North Pole. They drifted through the pack for nine months. Ultimately the ice sent them on a course toward the south. They finally reached open water near Greenland without any verification that they had actually reached the Pole.

Adolf Hitler and World War II temporarily delayed Soviet exploration of the Arctic, a major portion of which formed the northern edge of the union. More than one-quarter of Russia's territory is north of the Arctic Circle. Joseph Stalin, Russia's leader at the time, was convinced of the military significance of the region, especially as the aptly named Cold War followed World War II. As part of his program, a party of twenty-four Russians traveled in three twin-engine airplanes to the North Pole in 1948, landing on an ice floe somewhere in the area. Some say that was the first verifiable claim of attaining ninety degrees north latitude—the North Pole—but the claim is open to challenge.

Others maintain that it was Admiral Robert Peary, an American naval officer, who arrived there on foot and by sled in 1909. Though he claimed in his journal to have reached the spot on April 7, 1909, there is still doubt about it. Analysis of his calculations indicates that he was twenty nautical miles short of his lifelong goal. When he finally made it back to civilization, he learned that his former friend and fellow explorer Frederick Cook was claiming to have reached the Pole a year earlier than Peary. Cook's assertion, too, has been discredited.

Another naval officer, Richard E. Byrd, flew over the North Pole in 1925 but did not attempt to land there. His future explorations took him to the opposite pole, Antarctica, and his name is more closely associated with that end of the earth. I can recall back in the 1930s rushing home to listen for Byrd's periodic broadcasts from his Antarctica base, "Little America." The distance and the static of early radio made his voice hard to hear sometimes, but that only added to the thrill of being in touch with such a famous explorer.

Two U.S. Air Force lieutenants, Joseph Fletcher and William Benedict, landed a plane at the Pole in May 1952. Riding along was a scientist, Albert P. Crary, who would later play a key role in the International Geophysical Year observance, and would also make it to the South Pole. Those three individuals became the first humans indisputably verified to have set foot on the ice at the North Pole.

It was April 1968 before explorer Ralph Plaisted made the first confirmed surface trek to the Pole.

By 1956, though, the Soviet Union had sent hundreds of aircraft off to conduct landings and carry on exploration on the ice pack. Some of those probes were within two hundred miles of North America. It was not long before the U.S. military took notice of what the Russians were doing up there.

"If World War III should come, its strategic center will be the North Pole," declared General H. H. "Hap" Arnold, commander of the army air force during World War II. His warning came before the Second World War was over, before it was generally acknowledged that Russia would be the next great threat, and before most of the world knew much about the Arctic.

At Admiral Rickover's operation in D.C., and early in my studies of the Arctic Ocean, I felt the need to consult with someone who had actual experience in that region. This led me to two men who already possessed a strong vision of the potential for submarine operations beneath the ice-laden sea.

The first was Dr. Waldo Lyon. He was a physicist and at that time head of the Submarine and Arctic Division of the U.S. Naval Electronics Laboratory in San Diego, California. The other was Commander Robert McWethy, a fellow submariner recently assigned to an important job in the section of the Pentagon devoted to submarine matters.

Since Bob's office was just across the Potomac River from my own at NRB, I became a frequent visitor. He was always kind enough to give me time and to answer my questions in a straightforward way. As previously stated, he was also willing to keep me apprised of the attitude of those within the Pentagon who could have killed our under-the-ice venture at any point.

I did not know at the time, but Waldo Lyon would soon become an integral part of the *Nautilus* run to the Pole. By the time I made first contact with him, I was quite familiar with his groundbreaking work.

He got his start by making certain that a United States submarine was included in the Antarctic military exercise known as "High Jump," led by Admiral Richard Byrd just after World War II. That exercise was in Antarctica because having it in the Arctic region might have been too provocative to the Russians. Lyon's group at the laboratory had studied the relationship of the submarine to its environment—the sea—since 1940.

Somewhere along the way, Lyon and his team had developed interest in finding out what might happen when a submarine entered frozen waters. The Antarctic operation was conducted, a submarine was part of it, and Lyon returned to San Diego in 1946 even more interested in polar submarine operations. He was also convinced that the most effective region for such work was much closer to his home base in San Diego. That region was the Arctic. And that is when he suggested his branch be renamed "Submarine and Arctic Research Division."

A year later, in 1947, the U.S. submarine USS *Boarfish* (SS-327), with Dr. Lyon aboard, made a tentative trek beneath the Arctic ice pack, penetrating to a tense distance of only about six miles. Using what he learned from that trip, Lyon developed an inverted fathometer, which he planned to use to bounce sound echoes upward, off the overhead ice, instead of toward the bottom of the sea as with conventional fathometers. The object was to allow submarines to measure the distance below the ice pack, as well as to judge the shape of the underneath side of the ice and how much clearance the boat had.

Waldo Lyon deserves great credit for his foresight in seeing roles for submarines under ice in the Arctic. In retrospect, he may have been ahead of his time. It is clear that his early efforts received little support, financially and otherwise. It has been said that he built his laboratory with his own two hands, and that is likely no exaggeration. It is usually from such dogged determination that great things are accomplished, and I will always be appreciative to Waldo for his contributions to the success of what we did with *Nautilus*.

Commander Robert D. McWethy was an instructor at the navy's navigational school in Monterey, California, when, as the story goes, he noticed that his schedule called for lectures on Arctic navigation. Trouble was, he did not know much about it—just enough to know it was a tricky subject.

Navigating with magnetic compasses so near the magnetic North Pole created problems that so far had not been solved. Even the newly emerging gyrocompasses had problems at that latitude. McWethy knew that the air force had been working with some exciting new navigational techniques in the Arctic, so he requested time off and talked someone into giving him a ride in an air force plane across the Pole.

One of the first things he noticed as he flew over the ice floes—much as Hubert Wilkins had done before him—was the number of leads and polynyas in the otherwise unbroken ice.

One of the men on board the airplane asked McWethy the direct question: "Why can't you people operate submarines up here?"

"I don't know," was the commander's honest answer.

Again as it had with Wilkins, the idea of submarines operating beneath the ice soon became a near obsession for McWethy. Russia was the new threat. The Arctic region was in Russia's backyard. What better platform from which to stealthily operate and keep an eye on them than a submersible ship? They could operate freely beneath the ice, pop to the surface in a polynya, take a look around and radio back data, and then disappear again beneath the pack ice, the best cover on the planet.

In 1949, McWethy persuaded the navy's Bureau of Personnel to station him aboard a ship on which a submariner was most unlikely to find himself—the icebreaker USS *Burton Island* (AG-88). As the ship crashed through the thick ice between open stretches of water in the mostly frozen seas off the rugged coast of Alaska, McWethy pictured a conventional submarine easily ducking beneath these barriers. In 1950, Waldo Lyon did his own work aboard *Burton Island*. It was not long afterward that both men—for very different reasons—began to lobby the chief of naval operations, proclaiming the Arctic and its vast-covered seas as a prime submarine maneuvering area. Largely as a result of the influence of Lyon and McWethy, the submarine USS *Redfish* (SS-395), a World War II boat, was ordered to make an ice pack probe in 1952.

Equipped with Lyon's upward-looking fathometer, *Redfish* ducked beneath the pack, traveling a distance of more than twenty miles. She remained submerged under the ice for eight hours. Apparently the feat did not impress anyone in the navy command structure. There was no follow-up to *Redfish*'s probe, and it appeared top-level interest in polar operations for submarines was nil.

Neither Lyon nor McWethy was of a mind to let it lie. In late 1956, Commander McWethy had moved into an important Washington job, becoming a member of the staff of the chief of naval operations. He was placed perfectly to get things rolling. He happened to be there when the

CNO received a pointed letter from Senator Henry M. "Scoop" Jackson, from Washington State, a very powerful member of Congress and one who took special interest in military matters. Jackson had just returned from an Arctic tour with the air force and he got an idea while he was up there, surveying the intimidating ice pack.

Would it be feasible, the senator wondered in his correspondence, to operate a nuclear-powered submarine beneath the ice?

McWethy's boss passed the senator's letter to the submariner on his staff, assuming he would be the best man to draft a reply. It is easy to guess McWethy's answer.

Senator Jackson was quite perceptive, even though the nuclear submarine was only a recent phenomenon. In theory, such a vessel was an ideal platform from which to explore a region such as the Arctic.

As with any good sales pitch, there was no mention in McWethy's reply to Senator Jackson of the very real dangers involved, of the long list of unknowns, or of what might happen if a boat got into trouble up there.

Bob's letter sold more than just the senator. As he read the reply, Chief of Naval Operations Admiral Arleigh Burke decided to do more than merely mollify a politician.

He told his staff, "Let's really look into this."

Submarine exploration in the frozen seas of the Arctic had just heated up again.

Meanwhile I was deeply into my own studies of the region, spending my days at NRB cramming as if for the most important exam of my life. I needed to know much more about the ocean depths but soon realized that there were simply very few soundings. Most of the ones that did exist were widely scattered, taken by imprecise and unreliable means. Usually it was a plane landing on the ice, dropping a lead line from the edge of an ice floe. Even where data existed, it was often contradictory.

Ice thickness and draft figures were desperately needed. Would *Nautilus* be able to fit between the deepest down-thrusting ice keels and the ocean floor?

Was there any chance of icebergs drifting out into the ocean with their ultradeep, jagged, and deadly bottoms? I did not want to turn the world's first and only operational nuclear-powered submarine into another *Titanic*. Again I found little information available on the subject.

McWethy was one of the few people around who had appreciable experience in the Arctic. I was happy to have as many discussions with him as I could arrange. He was an outstanding submariner with a keen desire to contribute to the art of submarine warfare. We had a lot in common.

On my first visit to his Pentagon office, I found Commander McWethy busily working to gain support and enthusiasm for trying the navy's prize, USS *Nautilus*, under the ice. He seemed sincerely pleased that I, her prospective commanding officer, shared his enthusiasm and was ready to work quietly to set her on that northbound course.

But Bob was also a realist and understood what we were up against in trying to convince some people of the value of our plan. He recognized, as did I, that there were people in high places who would be opposed to what we wanted to do, which made a discreet approach advisable. I welcomed the strategy.

7

PERISCOPE IN PUGET SOUND

A nytime command of a submarine is turned over to a new skipper, a major part of the process is the briefing from the vessel's current commander. Captain Wilkinson spent as much time with me as he could as we moved up the coast toward Seattle, reviewing the activities of the past two years and the sea trials and shakedown that preceded active duty. He also talked about what the schedule ahead looked like. Most recently, *Nautilus* had been at sea, working with units of the Pacific Fleet, demonstrating to them the capabilities of a nuclear-powered submarine. There was no doubt that other navies—especially the Soviet's—would soon have their own nuclear boats, and the United States and our allies had to be ready for them.

On June 18, 1957, at the same dock in Seattle where *Nautilus* had so recently made her spectacular arrival, I spoke the words I had dreamed about for some time: "I relieve you, sir." With my salute and a handshake with Captain Wilkinson, the absolute responsibility for the performance and safety of the world's first nuclear submarine and her superb crew was mine.

I hope it does not sound egotistical or boastful, but I felt that day that I could do the job well, that I could take this magnificent ship to new heights. There was never a doubt in my mind. Much of that confidence came from knowing the capabilities of the vessel, the skill and dedication of the crew, and the knowledge that we all had the support of some very dedicated individuals at every level of the U.S. Navy. But I also knew that I had been preparing for that handshake and salute since I had those first dreams of exploring new worlds up north.

After my brief remarks, I turned to my executive officer, Lieutenant Commander Warren R. "Bus" Cobean, and asked him to make all preparations for our departure from Seattle. I did not have to say any more. Bus was another plankowner, having been aboard the entire period since *Nautilus* was put into commission, and I already knew him to be a superb

Commander Anderson officially becomes second captain of *Nautilus* in a ceremony on the ship's deck while berthed in Seattle. Captain Eugene Wilkinson, the ship's first captain, is at the microphone and Anderson is immediately to his left.

officer and cheerfully supportive of his skipper. He had earned his keep on this unique boat, beginning service as her first reactor control officer, then engineering officer and navigator before becoming second in command under me.

I soon shared with the crew that there might be a brief mission testing under-ice capabilities before a very important upcoming NATO (North Atlantic Treaty Organization) exercise, Operation Strikeback. I acknowledged that such a mission was not yet formally approved so our detailed planning would be deferred until and if approval came through. I emphasized that we should plan on getting ready for the Arctic and NATO as quickly as possible on our return to New London.

As we prepared to make our way back up Puget Sound, I reflected on what lay in store for my new command. The Pentagon had made it clear that *Nautilus*'s top priority in the months ahead was the NATO exercise. More explicitly, it had been faithfully promised to top NATO leaders that *Nautilus* would participate in what was to be the first such mission for a nuclear submarine. It was a command performance.

Strikeback was to be conducted in the North Atlantic and would involve six allied nations. Everyone was eager to see how *Nautilus* would perform against the largest striking fleet assembled in the twelve years since World War II. The British were particularly anxious to try their anti-submarine forces against *Nautilus*. They wanted to assess their own need to build nuclear submarines.

Of course, the crew and I were looking forward to the exercise as well. It would be an extremely important operation, and a chance for us to learn more about the capabilities of *Nautilus*. But I admit that from the very first moment I took command, my thoughts were elsewhere. As important as Strikeback was, my mind was on the possibility of a polar probe. I did not take the NATO exercise for granted, but I was comfortable that our submarine's speed, maneuverability, and expert crew would make a fine showing.

We made brief stops in Portland, San Francisco, and Long Beach, and a planned stop in San Diego to conduct exercises with surface fleet units

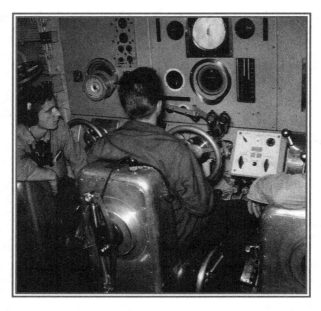

Crew member Roland Cave watches as an unidentified shipmate maneuvers *Nautilus*.

and, time permitting, some press and VIP cruises. After that, we were scheduled to head for New London, our official home base. That was when I
began preparations for the under-ice probe and Operation Strikeback.

Before we ever docked in Southern California, I caught wind of a disturbing rumor. Supposedly any attempt at an Arctic voyage by *Nautilus* had
been canceled.

I immediately called my boss, Captain Tom Henry, in New London,
to find out what he had heard.

"The probe is still a possibility," he reported, to my relief, but there was
a hesitation in his voice. "It looks like it's going to go through, but there
are some ramifications we need to talk about when you get back."

Time was growing tight. We were to arrive on station in the North
Atlantic for Strikeback on or about September 20. Our timetable, assuming rapid transits and a trouble-free refit at New London, left no room for

possible delays. We would have a maximum of ten days to spend at the ice pack in the latter part of August and the first few days of September and still be able to make our big appearance at the NATO event on time. Any thought of trying to go to the ice pack after the exercise was out of the question. It would be too late in the summer by then.

I took advantage of our stop in San Diego to visit at length with Dr. Waldo Lyon at the Naval Electronics Laboratory. He was already aware of my desire to explore under the ice, and he understood that he would be on board should the mission be approved. From his previous experiences aboard other submarines, Lyon was convinced that *Nautilus* could safely make a relatively deep and extensive penetration. The possibilities were exciting to both of us, but the longer we waited, the greater the ice buildup would be.

We never discussed going all the way to the North Pole on this voyage. This is an important point. The main objective, as we both saw it, was to cover a lot of territory and learn as much as possible about the Arctic ice and the ocean floor, about navigation and the operation of the submarine under such conditions, and do it all in the limited time available for the voyage before we had to head for our appointment at Strikeback. A run to the North Pole was never our goal on this mission.

Waldo and I put our views into a carefully worded confidential letter and mailed it to submarine headquarters in New London and to the naval command in Washington. The decision whether or not we could proceed with my plan for *Nautilus* rested with those commanders back east.

Before we left San Diego, I had an idea. To save time, we could go ahead and load most of Lyon's special upward-scanning fathometers (or "ice detectors") on board *Nautilus*. Waldo offered to send two men to New London to meet us upon our arrival to install and test the gear.

Meanwhile I asked Washington to have someone from the Navy Hydrographic Office meet us in Panama and to bring with him the latest Arctic charts, soundings, ice reports, and whatever other information was available. That would give me plenty to study as we made our way through the canal and up the East Coast.

I still did not know what Tom Henry's "ramifications" were, nor was our run to the ice anything close to a sure bet, but I wanted to be ready. When we arrived at the dock in New London, Waldo Lyon's men were already there, waiting to get to work installing the gear.

I was also thrilled to see Bonny and the boys waiting there for me when I stepped ashore. It had only been a little more than a month since I had left them, and I was anxious to hear how they had settled back in our old home and what they were up to. Mike was still pushing me to get him his own boat.

But I hardly had a chance to say hello before I received disturbing news. While we were making our way from Panama to New London, the polar expedition had very nearly been canceled. There was still a great deal of wrangling going on at the highest levels of the navy. Some were dead set against risking *Nautilus*. Others saw it as the perfect vessel for such a probe.

Captain Henry pulled me aside and said, "We need to talk."

Once in his office, he shut the door behind me and pointed to a chair.

"Okay, I know what the restrictions are now for the trip under the ice," he told me. I held my breath, ready for any possible deal breakers. "First, it will be necessary for a conventional submarine to accompany you and stand by at the edge of the ice when you take *Nautilus* under."

I thought to myself that there would not be anything the other submarine could do if we turned up missing.

"It's fine with me," I said. "Do we know who?"

"The *Trigger*."

"Is that Les Kelly's command?" I asked. Henry nodded. That was good news to me. I particularly liked the choice of Kelly, a fellow Tennesseean and a good friend. Besides, Les had been the chief engineer on *Nautilus* when she was commissioned. He knew our ship from stem to stern, and if anyone could be of help out there, it would be Les.

Then another thought struck me. "It's going to take *Trigger* twice as long as us to travel to the ice pack. She needs to leave right away."

We would be going to the edge of the ice between Greenland and Spitsbergen, and the conventional submarine was much slower than we were.

"We thought of that. She'll sail several days ahead of you so you can get there at the same time." Henry paused. "There's one other thing, Andy. Your operation orders will give a destination of eighty-three degrees north. That will be about two hundred miles inside the edge of the ice pack."

My stomach reacted negatively to this news. We had hoped to probe much deeper. Still, I agreed to that destination. Submarine skippers were usually granted quite a bit of freedom to improvise if they felt it was advantageous to the mission.

Back at *Nautilus*, I began to worry. The stipulated destination was much too restrictive. If things went wrong and we did not make it precisely that far, then the mission would officially be considered a failure.

But suppose things went really well and we wanted to keep going, maybe all the way to the North Pole? We had been, in effect, ordered not to.

I hurried back to Captain Henry's office, all set to put up an argument, to try to get the limiting portion of the orders stricken. On the way, an idea hit me.

"Captain, could you make a minor change to the operational orders?"

He looked at me sideways, cautious.

"Okay, what do you need?"

"Can you arrange to insert the word *approximately* before 'eighty-three degrees north'?"

He grinned, obviously on to me, and said, "Sure."

Not long before we sailed from New London, I asked Captain Henry if he had any thoughts on how I should interpret the newly added word *approximately* in our orders. He looked me squarely in the eye and said, "Andy, we know you will do the right thing."

Those simple words were an inspiration to me. There was no way I could have been given more leeway. My private personal hopes for reaching the Pole were alive.

Then he added, "You know, now there's only one person who can cancel *Nautilus's* Arctic work."

"Who is that?" I asked.

"You."

Reinvigorated, I almost ran back to *Nautilus*. On the way it finally hit me that after months of uncertainty, an under-ice probe was not only approved but defined in specific and official terms—a schedule, a duration, an "approximate" destination, and plans for a "buddy submarine" to stand by. It was time to tell my crew. I would no longer speak in terms of a possible Arctic cruise. It was time to be specific.

There was another reason for doing so. Should there be any member of the ship's company who preferred not to participate in the Arctic mission, he would have the opportunity to speak up and have duties arranged elsewhere, with no repercussions.

We were about to go where no ship had ever gone before under its own power and control. There was no room for reluctance or lack of dedication.

I identified with the sentiments of Jules Verne's fictional Captain Nemo in *20,000 Leagues Under the Sea* when he declared, "You begin to see the possibility—I should say the success—of this attempt. That which is impossible for an ordinary vessel is easy for the *Nautilus*. If a continent lies before the pole, it must stop before the continent; but if, on the contrary, the pole is washed by open sea, it will go even to the pole."

8

POINTING NORTH

T he team was coming together and we were fully involved with final plans for our trip beneath the ice. Commander McWethy had recently been transferred from Washington to a New London staff job. Dr. Lyon arrived from San Diego. Installation of his gear and other equipment aboard *Nautilus* was well under way. Very soon we were all involved in meetings with Rear Admiral C. W. Wilkins, Commander, Submarines, Atlantic (ComSubLant), and his staff. If there were any doubts about the magnitude of this mission or its importance to the U.S. Navy, all I had to do was glance around the table at those present for the meetings.

It was during one of those conferences where final plans were made for an event I had suggested several months previously: an aerial reconnaissance of the ice pack in or near the general area where we expected to be operating. I really wanted to see where we were going, albeit a view from the topside, and not from underneath.

On August 5, 1957, a group of us boarded a navy Super-Constellation radar-warning plane, and the pilot pointed its nose north. Along with me for the trip were Lieutenant Bill Lalor, my navigator on *Nautilus*, McWethy, Lyon, and Les Kelly from *Trigger*. Hours later we landed at Thule Air Force Base in Greenland. There we had to refuel and catch some sleep before beginning our flight just above the polar ice pack.

During the stopover, none of the submarine officers wore his dolphin insignia. We were deliberately not very friendly to anyone there either. We could not have anyone asking questions about why a bunch of submariners were way up in that part of the world. Our mission was classified, and we did not want to ignite anyone's curiosity.

Even in August the weather was quite cold, and the stiff wind blew up a surprising amount of dust. There is simply very little vegetation at that latitude, and without the winter snow cover, the land is similar to a desert. I remember the cold as we made our way to the plane the next morning. Soon we were taking off and once more headed northward.

In no time we were flying low over large patches of ice floating on the surface of the sea only six hundred feet below the fuselage of our plane. This was my first view of the formidable floes we would soon be dealing with, but our "view"—such as it would be once we plunged beneath the pack—was going to be from an angle 180 degrees from this one. I could not help but wonder what the underside of that stuff looked like, how far down it extended.

The ice looked cold and rugged, like a haphazard three-dimensional jigsaw puzzle. In some places the patches appeared to fit together perfectly, seemingly forming a solid layer with joints barely perceptible to the eye. I could easily imagine driving some kind of vehicle across it, dodging the hillocks, as if traversing a desert landscape. One could even forget that we were looking at frozen seawater and not some great, snow-covered, semi-flat landmass.

In many places, though, the surface seemed impossibly ridged and uneven, and in others, the puzzle pieces were missing altogether, as if they were yet to be laid into the frame. Imagine the most rugged, rocky terrain, broken by sharp, brittle non-eroded hills, but with no green trees or brown earth to break the constant white of the ice. In places, it seemed as if huge patches of ice had run together, shoving up small mountains, as if some tectonic force had been at work, slamming miniature continents together.

That was the landscape that rolled out beneath us and extended to the horizon in all directions. As we pointed the plane still farther north, I saw no evidence of its ending.

Sometimes we passed over sizable stretches of open water with a seemingly random mess of irregular blocks and white chunks of ice drifting about freely. The water was dark blue—almost black—in contrast to the ice.

It occurred to me as I looked down that there were far less expanses of open water, even at this latitude, than I had expected. What would it be like even farther north, where the temperatures never really moderated?

As the big plane's engines rumbled on, I kept my face pressed to a window with a movie camera against my cheek, trained on the ice below. I marveled at the mere idea of men setting out across that wilderness, using nothing but sleds pulled by dogs to transport provisions. What powerful impetus pushed them to brave such a harsh world, all for the sole purpose of reaching an unmarked geographical point on the treacherous ice, a spot beneath the North Star, ninety degrees north latitude? But I did not wonder for long. I knew that very same magnetic force was tugging me in the same direction.

I confess I was a bit disappointed when, after flying a thousand miles over the track of our proposed probe, we made a looping turn and once again headed south toward Iceland. There had been no plans to fly over the North Pole that day. Still, a part of me wished we had been able to ride on until we got there.

The next day we flew back to New London.

When I arrived at *Nautilus*, I found the ship filled with workmen. In addition to the usual refitting and repairs to our regular machinery, the installation of Lyon's five inverted fathometers was well along toward completion. The crew told me that we should be able to leave on schedule.

I turned my attention to my next concern, our compasses. The truth was that they would be the most critical instruments aboard *Nautilus* once we were running beneath the ice. Yes, we were counting on the fathometers to keep us from crashing into ice projecting from above, but we needed the compasses to make sure we went where we intended to go. And more important, we needed to be able to find our way back to open sea when the time came.

The ship was equipped with two types of compasses—one magnetic and one gyro—plus an auxiliary, or standby, gyro-type compass. Most people know that a magnetic compass does not, in fact, actually point to true north, the spot of the earth's northern axis, the geographic North Pole. Rather, it shows the way toward a hypothetical position known as the magnetic pole, which is located several hundred miles south of the true North Pole. Over most of the earth, this poses no special problem for travelers. But as one moves into the higher latitudes, allowances must be made for the difference between the magnetic pole and the geographic one. These corrections are called "variation," and they are typically plotted on navigation charts.

Assuming all corrections for local deviation are made, a navigator on a ship off the coast of Oregon, using only a magnetic compass and seeking a true, accurate northerly course, would most likely turn his vessel several degrees away from magnetic north, as his compass shows it.

A gyrocompass, though, is based on the gyroscope, which is typically a spinning wheel balanced on its axis, working in a vacuum. In non-extreme latitudes and if it operates properly, the gyrocompass always points to true north, or the geographic North Pole, as most sailors desire it to do. Ships of the United States Navy, as well as many commercial vessels, are typically equipped with gyrocompasses. Many other types of craft, from airplanes to the space shuttle, still rely on this method of navigation, even as many craft have added the capability to navigate by geo-positioning satellites.

The force that causes a properly operating gyrocompass to point to true north is the rotation of the earth. The axis of the rapidly spinning gyroscope tends, like everything else in nature, to follow the path of least resistance. In this case it is the rotation of the planet. This dependence on the earth's spin at its surface is greatest at the equator. It is zero at the North Pole. Because of this, even the gyrocompass becomes inaccurate when it is within a few hundred miles of either geographic pole.

So both the magnetic compass and the gyrocompass become less reliable the farther north a traveler ventures. Within a thousand miles of the magnetic pole, the magnetic compass begins to get more and more confused. Its needle is apt to swing wildly and to sometimes walk around in complete circles. Similarly, even the more complex gyrocompass loses stability as it approaches the true geographic pole, losing its focus as the earth's rotation at those high latitudes offers less and less pressure on the delicate internal mechanism.

These known problems posed a challenge for even as sophisticated a vessel as USS *Nautilus*. If the compasses were not reliable while we were following a virtually uncharted ocean floor, as we sped along beneath ice of indeterminate thickness in a world where we had no other reference points, we could easily become lost, and that would put us in serious trouble.

There could also be other forces at work, such as current, that could have the submarine drifting off in any direction with the crew unaware of what was happening. Errors can compound with amazing—and dangerous— speed, giving the navigator readings that are more and more flawed. The ship could easily end up heading toward a landlocked coastline or into the midst of much thicker, deeper ice, as she blindly steams along in mysterious waters. Or she could wander forever in circles. All the time, her crew might be unaware that the instruments were lying to them, that they were falling victim to what we called "longitude roulette."

In my studies I learned that the Sperry Corporation had designed a new compass, the Mark 19, which was supposed to be able to perform much more reliably in high latitudes. While we were making our way from Panama to New London, I called ahead a request for one of those instruments. During our refit period, the Mark 19 was delivered and installed on the ship. The crew also attended a class on its use and maintenance.

While I was appreciative of the quick response to my request for the new instrument, I was also aware that it carried a very low serial number, that it was still undergoing testing. We would be placing the success or failure of the mission—and our very lives—on what amounted to unproven technology.

Next we turned our attention to the other hazards we might encounter. Those included a submariner's worst fear—fire. Or the breakdown of some critical piece of machinery that would leave us immobilized beneath the pack, out of reach of any rescue vessel. At that time submarines could not communicate with the outside world while submerged. They had to come near the surface to use the radio, which is no problem in most of the world. But in the Arctic, at most points we would have a very solid ceiling between us and the surface.

Chief Engineer Paul Early and a group of the crew conducted a detailed tour of the ship, checking for any possible fire hazards. They dug into everything from fuse box connections with the nuclear power plant to the electric toasters in the galley. Even the smallest spark falling into something flammable could ignite a blaze, and even if the main result of such a fire was smoke and we controlled the flames, it could be disastrous if we were unable to surface and vent the smoke to the outside.

Every man aboard was asked to inspect and reinspect his gear. While we were under the ice—in effect voluntarily trapped, cut off completely from the surface—reliability of equipment, of systems, and of the crew members themselves would be as important as if we were at war and had taken our ship into battle.

I tried to imagine other possible emergencies that might befall a submarine while she was under Arctic ice. I was confident the crew was doing all that was humanly possible to prevent any problems, but should something arise, I needed to already have a plan for what steps to take to cope with a threat to the ship and the mission. I tried to visualize such extreme under-ice emergencies as losing propulsion under a pack too deep and compact for us to surface; cruising into shallow water overlaid with thick, dense ice, wedging the ship between the pack and sea bottom; running into a cul-de-sac and having the shifting ice shut off our retreat, effectively trapping us there; or the most likely hazard—a serious collision with the ice itself.

My strategy was to not allow any such catastrophes to occur. But if one did, I wanted it to be handled without fumbling.

I believed we could always reach the surface, even if we became hopelessly lost or had an onboard emergency. If we were not able to locate a handy lead or polynya, perhaps we could fire a salvo of torpedoes into the underside of the ice, blasting a way to the surface. Was I positive that would work? No, and I prayed neither *Nautilus* nor anyone else would ever have to try it and find out.

Even if we could not force the entire ship through a hole torpedoed into the ice pack, we might still be able to push up the sail, the housing for our periscopes, and radar and radio antennas. The sail on *Nautilus*, however, unlike those of her successors, was not made of tough, reinforced steel, in anticipation of such a maneuver. It was never intended for *Nautilus* to have to punch her way through ice using the sail. But still, if we could get our sail above the ice, we could abandon ship. For that eventuality we carried a large supply of cold-weather clothing, enough for the entire crew to be able to withstand the elements until a rescue team arrived.

The ship was becoming crowded. Along with all that heavy clothing, scientific gear, and special equipment, the cooks had stored away a ninety-day supply of food, which would last us through both the polar probe and Operation Strikeback.

We watched Commander Les Kelly and *Trigger* pull away from their berth well before we were scheduled to depart. Barring any problems, she would be on station at the outer edge of the ice pack when we showed up.

It was while watching *Trigger* pull away from the dock that the full realization hit me of how close we were to beginning our historic trip. I had every reason to expect that our eventual return to New London would be a triumphant one, whether we reached the North Pole or not. Once again the world would soon be amazed by the science-fiction-like capabilities of *Nautilus*. We would also be bearing a literal treasure trove of scientific and navigational information gathered beneath the ice.

I could not wait to steam down the Thames and out into the Atlantic.

But first I needed to pay respects to someone very important.

9

"YOU ARE GOING TO WRECK THIS PROGRAM!"

We were clearly on schedule to leave New London as planned, so I decided to make a quick one-day train trip down to Washington. I wanted to exchange some information with contacts at the Pentagon, bring them up to speed on our preparations, and see if they had any last-minute information for me. I also wanted to see if there were any other operational details I needed in order to get ready for Strikeback.

There was another stop I wanted to make while I was in Washington. I intended to pay my respects to Admiral Hyman Rickover and brief him on the ship's condition and what we had planned for her while we were under the ice. I suppose it was in my mind somewhere that I might gain his blessing for the probe.

When the secretary showed me into the admiral's office, I smiled and extended my hand, truly happy to see him again now that I was the skipper of "his" ship. I could tell at once that he was upset about something.

To my surprise and with no pleasantries whatsoever,

Rickover jutted out his jaw and, his eyes blazing, said angrily, "You're going to take that ship up there and get into trouble and you are going to wreck this program!"

My mouth fell open. I could not believe my ears. Astonishment is too mild a word for my reaction to his belligerent words and tone.

The admiral never interfered with the navy's operational plans. I heard him say many times that he was the engineer, the builder. He felt that it was not his role to tell the operator what to do with a vessel he had created once it was launched and placed into service. Quite to his credit, he stuck to his own self-defined responsibilities of dreaming, designing, building, and repairing revolutionary ships.

But he was certainly entitled to an opinion, and he had let me hear it—in no uncertain terms.

In the brief moment while I struggled to find a reasonable response to his emotional outburst, I realized that the polar mission I had fought so hard for was once again in jeopardy. I knew that all Rickover had to do to cancel it was pick up the telephone and call the head of submarine operations at the Pentagon and tell him the ship was not ready for Arctic operations. Or he might simply say the mission was premature. Had Rickover done that, it would have been the end of any under-ice exploration—at least for the foreseeable future and almost certainly for USS *Nautilus*.

I spoke carefully, hoping I could convince the admiral that I was not going to foolishly put the ship or her crew at unnecessary risk.

"Admiral, I appreciate your concern. You know me. You know that I am a step-at-a-time guy and I don't intend to put the ship or crew in danger," I said, hoping it did not sound like I was pleading. And hoping that he knew me well enough to realize that I was telling him the truth. "This mission has been planned not as a stunt but a test. We are intending only a brief, limited Cold War trip into a place the Soviets consider to be their private backyard. We have good reason for going there."

I explained to him that with missile submarines coming along soon, it would be crucial that we gather facts and develop our expertise about the

Arctic. I did not need to remind him that *Nautilus* was the world's first true submarine, that she was not only perfect but absolutely necessary for any under-ice test.

As I talked on, the admiral seemed to calm down. He eased back against his desk and listened without interrupting. Finally, when I had finished laying out my case, he paused a moment and then extended his hand to me.

"Anderson, call me when you need me."

I knew that was about the most ringing endorsement I was likely to get from him. I accepted his handshake.

"Thank you, Admiral," I replied and then turned and headed out the door.

I still do not know if he was truly against the first under-ice probe. It could well have been another test for me, just to see how serious and committed I was and whether or not I was adequately cautious in my preparations for the trip. I had seen him use just such a strategy in many other situations.

We will never be certain. However, we do know he made no move to stand in the way. If it was a test, I must have passed it.

When I got back to New London, only a few days before we were to leave, I received another shock. Rear Admiral C. W. Wilkins, ComSubLant, was stricken with a heart attack and rushed to the naval hospital in Portsmouth, Virginia.

This event deeply distressed all of us on *Nautilus*. Admiral Wilkins had been key in lining up approval for our mission, staunchly standing up against what we later learned was vehement opposition to the use of our ship in the way we intended. He was easily our most adamant booster. From what I found out after the fact, I believe without his vision and enthusiastic support for the mission, it simply would not have taken place.

Shortly before our scheduled departure, I received a truly inspirational letter from Admiral Wilkins. I immediately shared it with the crew. His words meant so much to us, especially because he had written them while still in the hospital recuperating from his near fatal heart attack.

I want to wish you and your people every success in the cruise ahead. There are those who look on this operation askance and with skepticism. I am not one of those. I believe it is a venture of great promise, in both the fields of national defense and science. I am sure the information you will collect will be of great value. The operation itself is one that appeals to the imagination and the venturesome spirit within men's souls. You will be pioneers and trail blazers. Your findings may lead the way to under-ice navigational capabilities for nuclear-powered submarines that may make it possible for them to go any place in the ice regions where the interest of national defense requires. I know you have done careful planning for this operation, that all foreseen hazards have been taken into careful account, and that every possible preparation has been made to insure a successful operation, which will add to *Nautilus*'s laurels and glories achieved by her officers and men.

PART II
DIVING BENEATH THE ICE

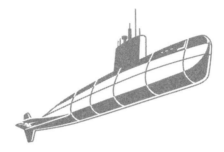

"I believe it is a venture of great promise, in both the fields of national defense and science. . . . You will be pioneers and trail blazers."

—Rear Admiral C. W. Wilkins, Commander, Submarines, Atlantic

10

TO THE EDGE OF
THE UNKNOWN

MONDAY, AUGUST 19, 1957

The entry in our logbook stated simply: "0620: Reactor critical."

Our power source was operational. The hundreds of checks and crosschecks had been completed. We were ready to attempt a voyage that explorers had dreamed about for centuries, one that had claimed ships and human lives even as it captured imaginations of far-thinking men everywhere.

Bonny dropped me off at 0700, kissing me good-bye outside the gates of Electric Boat. That is where my ship awaited, at the vessel's birthplace rather than at the sub base just up the Thames River, where she could get extensive upkeep and modifications for the missions that lay ahead of us.

Bonny sensed this was not a typical sailing. She only knew that I would be gone for about two months. The sea once again separated our family.

The rest of the crew, except for those who had spent the night on duty on the ship, went through a similar routine that morning. Most of them who had wives and children had relocated them to this area, and they seemed to take a bit of extra time saying their farewells at the gates, just as their skipper had.

When I got aboard, Bus Cobean informed me that all department heads had reported. We were ready to get under way. Bus also confirmed that Waldo Lyon; his technical assistant, Archie Walker; and another civilian, John Ropek of the Naval Hydrographic (now Oceanographic) Office, were on board and their gear stowed.

"0800: UNDER WAY."

On schedule, having already cast loose from shore power, we took in the mooring lines and backed away from the Electric Boat pier. There was no fanfare or ceremony. It appeared to be as typical as a departure could be. All hands worked quietly and efficiently at their assigned maneuvering stations. As we eased out into the Thames River, we executed a slow twist to line up with the deep-water channel and ever so deliberately headed out, bound for Block Island Sound and then the Atlantic Ocean.

As I had requested, a navy tugboat accompanied us down the river, just in case we needed a nudge or two to keep to the channel. We carefully maneuvered around dozens of fishing boats and pleasure craft that were already choking up the river. The crew on the main deck stowed the mooring lines and buttoned up the topside, ready to take the boat under as soon as we could.

I had been up and down the Thames on many occasions—as a passenger and at the helm of various submarines, including *Nautilus*—but this was my very first time leaving home port for an extended cruise as the skipper of the world's most famous vessel. As I stood on the bridge and watched the calm, well-practiced work of the crew, the responsibility of accomplishing two important missions crowded out any chance of my being sentimental over the occasion or nervous about my transit downriver.

Our orders were simple. We were to rendezvous with *Trigger* near the

View of the bridge of *Nautilus*.

southern edge of the polar ice pack, off the coast of Greenland and north of Iceland. There we were to trade turns exploring under the ice as we gathered information on the ocean, the weather, and the ice itself. After that we were to join up with NATO naval forces and assume a major role in Operation Strikeback. This was to be the first participation in a NATO exercise by a nuclear submarine. Everyone was extremely interested to find out if *Nautilus* would live up to her reputation. After Strikeback we would follow up with a few post-NATO-exercise operations, working with only British units. After a brief stop in Portland, England, we would return home.

That ambitious schedule left only ten days total for Arctic work. Coordinating with *Trigger* and providing her an opportunity for her own trials under ice meant at best we could count on only six days total under ice. In the back of my mind I knew full well that everything had to go like clockwork for there to be even one chance of getting to the North Pole, should we decide to make a try. I was determined to take the journey step-by-step. For the time being, we all remained focused on getting to the open sea where we could check out *Nautilus* and her newly installed equipment.

Some of the gear was experimental, including a Type VIII periscope—an intricate device that came with a heated air jet, designed for deicing and defogging. We also carried a LORATT long-range sonar communications system with directional and omni-directional hydrophones; a Mark 19 Sperry master gyrocompass, designed to work better and have greater accuracy at high latitudes; and several fathometers to take continuous soundings of the polar ice pack above us and of the Arctic Ocean floor beneath us as we steamed along. It was clear that the navy had bought into our polar exploration idea, and they intended that we make the most of it. It had been a busy stopover at Electric Boat, and now we had to be sure everything worked properly and that we were adept at using it.

We proceeded on the surface, making our way in the early-morning mist through Block Island Sound. The water there was still too shallow for comfortable submerged cruising. *Nautilus* reached the open ocean by noon. While still on the surface, we took about an hour to swing the ship in a large, looping circle to check the performance and errors of our magnetic compass, the backup to our two gyrocompasses. Everything seemed to be in order, so we again turned the bow of the submarine to the northeast.

As big a hurry as we were in, I did not begrudge the time spent checking the compasses. In the area where we were headed, there were no accurate charts illustrating ocean depths or sea floor contours. While beneath the ice pack, we could not even rely on observing celestial objects, the sailor's long-time navigational method. We carried a sextant, of course, but there would be few opportunities to come to the surface and "shoot the sun and the stars."

Additionally, we would be out of reach of the U.S. Coast Guard's low-frequency radio navigation system, LORAN (Long Range Navigation).

Long range or not, its signals would not extend to where we were planning on going. Once we ducked beneath the ice, we would be "exploring" in every sense of the word.

"1714: PASSED NANTUCKET SHOALS LIGHTSHIP ABEAM TO PORT 3.7 MILES."
"1822: SUBMERGED AT 40 FATHOM CURVE."

The late-afternoon summer sun still shone brightly, making the Atlantic waters green-tinged as we took our ship down, toward cold darkness.

Once under way, we were not surprised that we were already running into some minor problems. That was typical after extensive upkeep and installation of so much new equipment.

The diver's light flooded out almost immediately. This was a powerful lamp mounted topside, and we hoped to shine its light on the underside of the ice as we looked at it from the periscope. It would be of no use to us now.

The bathythermograph, an instrument used to measure the changes in seawater temperature, also went out of commission shortly after we submerged. Again, nothing crucial, but it would have assisted us in collecting important information.

In addition, we discovered that number one periscope had been improperly packed. It was very difficult to train, and its transmission of bearing was erratic. Besides, an annoying trickle of cold salt water ran down the back of my neck anytime I tried to use the thing.

As was typical, the crew did not seem discouraged by the problems. They saw them as obstacles to overcome with knowledge and work. If we were unable to fix them, as usual we would develop work-arounds. That was what we were trained to do.

The nature of our trip was not a surprise to our crew members. Although the mission was classified, I had specifically asked that every man aboard know where we were headed and that he have the opportunity to request leave rather than make the ice portion of the trip. No one did.

Not long after we submerged, Bus Cobean came to my stateroom. I could tell from the look on his face that he wanted to have a serious talk with me.

"Captain, some of the crew are somewhat apprehensive about our plans to go under the ice," he told me.

I appreciated his frankness. I was not surprised to hear it either. I admit that I had some apprehension myself. The difference, however, between my concerns and those of some of the crew was that I was the man in charge. I had control. I could regulate our every move and leave to chance a bare minimum of risks. Or I could plow ahead, assuming the attitude that we should take some calculated risks since the objective warranted a bold attempt on our part.

I rationalized to myself that part of the reason for the crew's doubts was their lack of experience with me—especially in challenging situations. All they had on which to judge my style was a routine transit from Seattle to New London, interspersed with a few short demonstration cruises and some routine operations with surface and air groups. They had no way of knowing how their captain would handle an emergency, or whether or not I would be inclined to take unnecessary risks to try to make a name for myself and my boat.

Once Bus let me know that there was some anxiety among the men over our mission, one fact was clear: any apprehension had to be countered. It was essential that I had the crew's confidence—in the ship, in the mission, in me as their captain.

With so much going on during our brief stay in Groton, there had been no briefing of the crew on how we would approach our Arctic work and what our goals would be. I blamed myself for this failure. With workmen on board *Nautilus* almost around the clock, it would have been difficult to conduct crew briefings. But with a special effort, we could have arranged a secure meeting room ashore for that purpose. I should have done so.

After Bus left my stateroom, I thought a bit. Concluding that this situation was worthy of my immediate attention, I decided to address the crew over the 1MC, the announcing system that carried throughout the ship.

I went to the Attack Center, lifted the microphone from its hook, pressed the button, and spoke: "All hands, this is the captain speaking. First, I want to thank you all for speeding up the loading and preparations for sea. I also want to thank you for pitching in to fix the problems that have come to light before and since we got under way."

I paused to get a new grip on the microphone. I could imagine the more than one hundred men up and down the length of that magnificent ship—men in the torpedo room, those driving the boat in the control room, others who were off watch having coffee in the crew's mess, all stopping whatever they were doing, pausing to hear what their relatively new skipper was about to tell them.

"For the first time, *Nautilus* has been directed to participate in a NATO exercise. This involves operations that are entirely familiar to almost all of you. The ship has made hundreds of similar simulated attacks against surface ships and other submarines."

It was a definitive first for *Nautilus*, but I knew everyone aboard was confident we would perform superbly. Only overconfidence, sloppiness, or mechanical failure could make it anything but a tremendous success.

"Prior to NATO, we will be joining up with *Trigger* under Captain Les Kelly, who will stand by while we explore under the polar ice pack . . . and vice versa. I want you to know that it is perfectly natural to be a bit apprehensive about going where no man has ever gone before. It is even more so when you and your ship are in the hands of a new skipper."

In the few minutes of rumination in my quarters, I had decided to address the issue head-on. These were bright guys, and they deserved complete honesty.

"I want you to know that I am a one-step-at-a-time kind of guy. In wartime it can be different, but this is not wartime—at least not the 'hot' variety. I want each of you to know that if at any time this magnificent ship and this great crew are headed into serious danger, this skipper will reverse course and reassess the situation.

"We are lucky to have on board Dr. Waldo Lyon, a man who knows

Dr. Waldo Lyon (far right with hands on hips), director of the Submarine and Arctic Research Division of the Naval Electronics Lab, briefs the crew on what to expect beneath the polar ice pack.

more about sea ice than any man on earth. I am asking Commander Cobean and Dr. Lyon to arrange a series of talks about what is known about the Arctic, its ice, and other characteristics. I want these to be scheduled so every single man on board will be able to attend."

I quickly thanked the men for their attention, released the talk button, and returned the mike to its hook. I had no way of knowing if my little speech had had any effect on the crew. But I got an indication shortly.

I stepped out of the Attack Center and headed toward the wardroom to get a fresh cup of coffee. Before I got there and before they knew I was approaching, I distinctly recall overhearing steward James Owens talking to another sailor, his assistant, Donald Wilson.

"Well, I've got faith in the captain," Owens proclaimed.

"I do too. But I'd still rather be back in New London," Wilson replied. They both laughed good-naturedly.

I immediately felt better.

We surfaced that evening to allow work on the leaky periscope. After inspecting the hull gland, we realized that a key that went between the periscope barrel and the bearing transmitter had not been installed. Fortunately, we had a spare. Once crew members replaced the key, put in new packing, and lubricated the bearings and glands with grease, the periscope was reassembled and tested. It worked much better, but when we tried to aim it, the training was still very stiff. We hoped that it would free up with use.

While we were performing those repairs on the surface, a naval vessel passed us close abeam and—as is customary—challenged us by searchlight. We responded in kind and provided our identification.

"Where bound?" they signaled.

For an instant, I considered answering with the destination that was most on all our minds aboard *Nautilus*: "North Pole."

I quickly decided that would be ill-advised. Instead, I told them we were bound for a classified mission to the north. It was, after all, the truth.

TUESDAY, AUGUST 20, 1957
"0624: WITH REPAIRS TO TYPE VIII PERISCOPE COMPLETED, SUBMERGED."

With the main problems with the periscope solved, we once again eased beneath the waves, returning to our true element, and resumed our north-easterly course, this time at high speed.

As we continued toward our meet-up with *Trigger*, we slowed only long enough to get the ship in proper balance for submerged cruising. After loading ninety days' worth of provisions and a large cache of other supplies and parts, it was necessary to adjust the amount of water in the variable ballast tanks to ensure the weight and distribution of the stores were properly compensated for. Those four ballast—or "trim"—tanks were located one forward, one aft, and two at midship, one on each side. The intent was to adjust buoyancy so we could maintain optimum control over the ship while submerged. And should we be forced to suddenly slow down, our control of depth and angle would not be lost.

After my little speech and the repairs on the periscope, life aboard *Nautilus* settled into a familiar routine, broken only by emergency drills. Those included one very special drill: a vertical, elevatorlike ascent that sent us straight up toward the surface. Submarines typically dive and surface while gliding forward, like an airplane taking off or landing. This different kind of maneuver would be necessary should we want or be forced to surface through a crack or a lake of open, unfrozen water in the midst of the ice floes. Our drill went well. We could only hope it would be as smooth should we have to do it in a hurry, amid ice that could also be moving at the time.

We also began a series of films, lectures, and briefings, telling the crew about our new equipment and about how we would need to operate in the Arctic. This instructional program seemed to help allay most of the anxiety about our upcoming polar plans. I even sensed a growing excitement among the crew members about the possibilities.

We also began using some of our new navigational equipment, including the untested Sperry Celestial Altitude Recorder (SCAR), which was to be used with the Type VIII periscope. This device was designed to permit taking star or sun observations while surfaced or even when submerged at periscope depth.

While all this was going on, I tried to find the time to refresh myself with the little information available on Arctic water depths and ice condition estimates. Meanwhile we cruised deep and fast, coming to periscope depth only occasionally to check navigation position by LORAN or to copy radio traffic via a long antenna or a raised whip antenna. Also, occasional trips to a relatively shallow depth were necessary for use of our garbage-ejector system.

THURSDAY, AUGUST 22, 1957
"2000: RECEIVED SPECIAL 30-DAY ICE FORECAST."

We received a message from the Navy Hydrographic Office indicating possible ice drift. We continued to conduct our training programs and emergency drills. We also carried out maneuvering tests to determine the rate of course changes for various speeds and rudder angles. I suspected that we might find ourselves in situations calling for fine-tuning our maneuvers.

Later it would become clear to me that I had not stressed this enough.

I also noted that apprehension about the nature of our mission had waned, now that we were into a routine of training, drilling, and standing regular watches. These fellows were professionals. As long as they were doing their jobs, and when they were assured every shipmate was prepared to do his, they seemed not to worry about things that might lay ahead for them.

TUESDAY, AUGUST 27, 1957

"1000: RECEIVED CINCNELM 270324Z LOCATING RUSSIAN FISHING FLEET OFF JAN MAYEN (ISLAND). WE WILL PASS 35 MILES EAST BUT BE ON WATCH."

"1902: PASSED LATITUDE 60N, THE POINT BEYOND WHICH OPORD REQUIRES THAT WE KEEP RADIO SILENCE AND REMAIN UNDETECTED."

We were past Iceland, northeast of the volcanic Norwegian island of Jan Mayen, and not far from our designated meeting point with *Trigger*. It was unlikely that *Nautilus* had been detected by anyone—friend or foe—since diving, having repaired our periscope and transmitted our last message. That was more than a week before off the East Coast of the United States. Still, we redoubled our efforts toward remaining clandestine by placing into effect special patrol routines that minimized the chances of revealing the vessel's presence. This included such things as limiting to a bare minimum putting a periscope or anything else above the surface. It also meant careful sonar watches and giving all contacts we might encounter a very wide berth. If it became necessary to use radar, the sweep was quick. Radio silence was the order of the day. Nothing was exposed above the surface if we detected anyone else using sonar. This status was maintained until a tracking solution showed the contact or contacts were far away.

Data collection procedures were ordered so the crew would arrive in the Arctic as fully rehearsed as possible. Among those was a careful recording of time versus ship's position, mean depth, under-ice drafts, seawater temperature, and weather conditions—when they could be observed.

WEDNESDAY, AUGUST 28, 1957

Nautilus was now cruising deep in seldom-traveled waters. Not long after midnight, while resting half awake in my bunk, I felt the ship heel violently and take on a sudden, drastic up-angle. I could hear loose gear sliding around and crashing to the deck.

I hurried to the control station.

"Solid sonar contact. nine hundred yards dead ahead," the conning officer reported.

To avoid hitting whatever lay directly ahead of our course, he had quite properly thrown the fast-moving *Nautilus* into a different course and speed, using full rudder and backing full. Unlike Captain Nemo's *Nautilus*, we had no large window at the bow of our vessel to see what was ahead of us. We had to rely on sonar for our eyes and ears, and an operator was always on duty, scanning ahead of us for obstacles in our path. In these remote seas, we never knew what manner of vessel, uncharted undersea peak, iceberg, or other obstacle might be out there in the way.

As he gathered more information, the sonar operator slowly and rather sheepishly realized that it was a very large fish, shark, or whale that had popped up on his equipment.

As the day wore on, we established several more sonar contacts with various types of aquatic life. Some we could detect as far away as four thousand yards—two nautical miles away. I cautioned the officers on watch to maintain constant vigilance, not only for whales or other large sea creatures but also for underwater obstacles like unreported icebergs or uncharted peaks along the ocean bottom.

A collision with any of those things could abruptly end the reign of Admiral Rickover's spectacular atomic vessel.

"2300: A LITTLE SURPRISED TO FIND A SHIP CONTACT 1000 YARDS ON STARBOARD BEAM."

Life at sea is seldom dull. Slightly north of the sixty-four-degree-north parallel, we went up to periscope depth to take a weather observation and to attempt to get a SCAR fix. Much to our amazement, we saw a well-lighted ship, estimated to be 250 feet long and about fifteen hundred tons. It was less than a mile from where our periscope poked above the surface of the sea.

The strange thing was that our active and passive sonar had failed to pick it up, and sonar could not locate the ship even after we had a visual sighting of it through the periscope. Though it was dark and overcast at the time—only an hour short of midnight—I concluded it was probably a large trawler, probably quiet because it was stopped, using no engines, maybe pulling in fishing nets.

I guessed our failure to detect the ship with our active sonar was because of poor listening conditions and the possibility the ship's hull was made of wood.

View of *Nautilus* from the bridge of USS *Trigger*. As a requirement for the okay for *Nautilus* to make her first under-ice explorations in 1957, the conventional diesel submarine *Trigger* and her crew were to accompany the nuclear vessel, stand by at the edge of the ice pack, and take turns making probes.

THURSDAY, AUGUST 29, 1957

"0515: CROSSED THE ARCTIC CIRCLE AT 23.5 KNOTS, AT TEST DEPTH (713 FEET)."

We went very deep and opened *Nautilus* wide open as a celebration of our crossing the Arctic Circle—sixty-six degrees, thirty-three minutes, thirty-nine seconds north latitude—for the first time.

We noticed sonar conditions had become quite poor. That was disconcerting because we were now in the area in which Operation Strikeback would be conducted following our polar exploration.

Shortly after crossing the Arctic Circle, we came to periscope depth to check the weather. Typical of the region, it was solidly overcast with heavy fog, limiting our visibility to about one mile or less.

FRIDAY, AUGUST 30, 1957

Near Jan Mayen, we made our first attempt to establish contact with *Trigger* using LORATT, our long-range sonar communications system. At 2239, we finally located her. She was precisely at the rendezvous point.

As senior officer, the first order I gave Les Kelly was, "Request you immediately head for the North Pole."

A keen-minded submarine officer, Kelly immediately realized I was not serious and promptly replied, "Roger. What speed?"

SATURDAY, AUGUST 31, 1957

We headed our respective ships to the north, and running in tandem, we began the last leg of our trip to the edge of the ice pack. My crew was operating as a perfect team, but *Nautilus*, from a purely technical perspective, was not quite in peak condition. The number one periscope remained balky, and various minor mechanisms were reported out of commission.

Of greatest concern to me was the CO_2 scrubber, the machine that kept carbon dioxide below harmful levels inside the ship. The thing had been having problems since we left New London. Despite constant repairs, it was still not functioning efficiently. Two shutdowns, both initiated to repair the device and keep CO_2 levels below 2 percent, cost us a seven-hour delay in starting our under-ice operations. However, we were determined to continue if possible. In the back of my mind was the nagging worry that something as basic as this machine could jeopardize our run beneath the ice. There was little time to spare. Our presence at Operation Strikeback was not optional.

And then, there it was. We had the ice pack in sight in the far distance. My first impression was that we had finally happened upon a long-sought friend.

SUNDAY, SEPTEMBER 1, 1957
"1250: SURFACED."

We had begun to notice many contour features on the bottom of the sea that were not noted on any of the available charts. It was no surprise but still a bit disconcerting to see the inaccuracies of our charts of the sea floor.

A favorite pastime of the *Nautilus* crew was watching movies.

South of the ice pack, we brought the submarine to the surface. We had traveled 4,040 miles, all without surfacing, over eleven days, twenty-two hours, and fifty-five minutes. This was the longest continuous submerged run for *Nautilus* up to that time. We had set another record without even trying.

We transferred some cold-weather clothing and other gear to *Trigger*. It arrived in New London after Kelly and his boat departed, and we were more than happy to deliver it to them. We also exchanged some movies. That was an old submarine tradition too. During World War II, submarine crews would sometimes risk attack in order to surface and swap movies with their sister boats. It was that important to keep fresh films available.

The deck gang under Chief of the Boat Larch used an ingenious way to accomplish the transfers. To go too close to *Trigger* would have risked damage to one or both our ships. I kept *Nautilus* about twenty yards from *Trigger* on a parallel course at matching speed. The deck gang had broken out our rubber raft and inflated it. Then a line-throwing gun was used to pass a line to the other submarine. This line was attached to the raft and another line was tied to the opposite end of the raft. Using these lines, the raft was passed back and forth between the two vessels, and in short order the transfers were made.

Remaining on the surface, we continued northward toward the ice.

Trigger was not equipped with the new Mark 19 gyrocompass, and her old-fashioned one—the same type being used at that time by almost every ship or submarine in the U.S. Navy—had already become erratic in these high-latitude waters. We were happy to give *Trigger* several course checks.

As I watched from the bridge, a small chunk of ice drifted past to starboard. Then there was another one, a bit larger, passing to port. I gave the order to slow down, and our ship coasted quietly through the cold waters. We carefully steered our way into the floating ice. We had finally arrived at the edge of one of our planet's last true unknown areas—the mysterious, daunting polar ice pack. It was lighted somewhat by a natural, yellowish incandescence called "iceblink."

The wind topside was surprisingly gentle. Wispy patches of fog floated past us, reminding me of the San Francisco Bay. The sea was benign. It was relatively comfortable on the bridge, not too much colder than on a stretch of the Thames River on a Connecticut winter day.

As I surveyed the ice that stretched before me, Admiral Rickover's angry words came to mind: "You are going to wreck this program!" I testify here that I was using that explosion from the admiral as a challenge, not as a hindrance. It would spur us on, not destroy our resolve. I knew we could safely complete our mission. And I was more confident than ever that we could possibly make our transit to the North Pole as well as across the Arctic the next great accomplishment for *Nautilus*, for the navy, and for our country.

From the bridge I could see *Trigger* lying nearby. I suspected that Les and his crew were anxious to do some exploring under the ice as well. Even though we had to share the precious under-ice time, I was glad after all that *Trigger* was there with us, each standing by to help the other.

We went first. The plan was to rejoin *Trigger* outside the pack in approximately twenty hours. I still anticipated a major journey for *Nautilus*, but not until we had familiarized ourselves with conditions and completed plenty of checking on our compasses. I had no intention of our getting lost at these high latitudes. In addition, we needed more experience using our special ice-detecting and measuring equipment. It was untested and unused, having been on the shelf for the past two years. Could we trust it?

Steven White, a Californian and an officer who looked young enough to still be in high school, was the conning officer that afternoon. He would be one of the *Nautilus* crew members who eventually retired at the highest rank, that of four-star admiral. I told him he could clear the bridge and submerge when ready.

At precisely 8:00 p.m. New London time, eleven days out of home port, *Nautilus* nosed under. Uncertain of exactly how thick the ice would be there at the edge, we descended to six hundred feet before we approached the floe. Then without hesitation we set a course due north, toward the North Pole, on a route where no man or vessel had ever been before.

11

COLLISION!

SUNDAY, SEPTEMBER 1, 1957
"2053: PASSED UNDER FIRST FLOE—ABOUT 160 YARDS WIDE,
6 FEET DEEP."

We proceeded cautiously, at speeds between three and a half and ten knots. *Nautilus* passed far beneath the edge of the ice pack for the first time. We soon determined that the thickness of the ice over our heads at this point varied from three to sixteen feet, about what we expected. Leads were also common near the edge of the pack, though they were already filled with brash (broken fragments of ice) and block ice.

There seemed to be little tension aboard our vessel. The men who had just gotten off the previous watch were enjoying dinner in the crew's mess, just as they had done so many times before, carrying on their usual good-natured banter. As I walked the length of the ship, I could hear music coming from the jukebox.

Though we were plowing along nose-first through deep,

cold water and there was a near solid blanket of ice over our heads and unknown territory in front of us, we were perfectly comfortable. Temperatures in most parts of the ship were fine for shirt-sleeved comfort. I wondered what previous Arctic explorers would have thought of such a thing.

MONDAY, SEPTEMBER 2, 1957
"0000: UNDER WAY SUBMERGED UNDER THE ARCTIC ICE PACK."

The Arctic has a long habit of dealing out stern initiation to those who would conquer. Our magnificent *Nautilus* did not get a free pass.

We began our first penetration with high hopes, diving beneath the pack, maintaining a deep cruising depth of 600 feet. We were concerned that there was a slight chance that an iceberg may have broken loose from Spitsbergen and drifted into the edge of the pack. After a few miles with the ice revealing itself to be more or less as we had expected, we came up to a cruising depth of 350 feet.

I had asked Dr. Lyon to be on the lookout with his upward-beamed fathometers for a surfacing possibility. The lesser cruising depth would allow his equipment to have a better view of what was above us. We also needed to give him a more realistic chance to map the undersurface of the ice. No one had ever had such an extensive view as we now had—electronic though it might be—of this side of the floes, mile after mile.

Essentially, we were entering an unexplored cave two thousand miles deep. There were no profiles to go by, no maps of either the ice overhead or the ocean floor below. We wanted to accurately measure and record both, first to show that it could be done, and second to insure that the data could be used by future spelunkers, including us. Every foot we charted was an added foot's worth of knowledge about this last frontier.

Soon Lyon's sonar equipment told us enough that we were able to form a good picture of the underside of the ice. Or at least that is what we believed at the time.

We found the ice pack to be broadly diverse. In places it consists only of small blocks and brash—which the crew called "B & B"—that could be easily penetrated by any strong ship. Most of the pack is made up of irregular ice islands, however, ranging in size from a few feet to a half mile or more across. We also soon verified that the underside of the ice is not smooth and flat as others had believed, but rough and uneven.

As we had observed from the air, the ice is broken by leads (open water) and polynyas (thin ice) in great numbers. But we also noticed that very few of them were large enough to fit a submarine of our size into them, nor were

Archie Walker (assistant to Dr. Waldo Lyon) and Philip Boyle study the equipment that gave *Nautilus* crew members a picture of the ice under which they were passing.

they numerous enough to attempt a puddle-jump as Sir Hubert Wilkins had envisioned.

So it was that we steamed along happily, our ship running smoothly, recording our version of the ice pack. Only later would we discover that we were not getting a true picture. Dr. Lyon's equipment, though gathering meaningful data, was not always giving us an accurate look at the ice above us.

Crewman Al Charette checks the printout from an unusual device used in the first under-ice probe by *Nautilus*. It is an early fax machine that was modified to be used as a depth recorder.

There were two recording pens on the modified equipment. One obtained its information from our depth gauge, which indicated as precisely as it could the surface water level. We were able to see how accurate it was as we crossed short stretches of open water. We were relatively comfortable with the line it drew on a continually unspooling piece of recording paper.

The second pen hooked up to one of Lyon's ingenious upward-scanning fathometers. Its job was to draw a picture of the underside of the ice as it related to the water-level line. Working in unison, the two pens were theoretically drawing a profile of the ice pack beneath which we ran.

Only on our next polar voyage a year later would we discover a serious flaw in this method. The rate at which the upward-scanning fathometer worked was too slow for the speed at which *Nautilus* was traveling. The scan return we were receiving was not nearly as accurate as we thought, and it did not really show the texture or the depth of the keels in the pack.

Put quite simply, at times the ice was much thicker and the pressure ridges were deeper than we knew. But we were unaware, and so we sped on.

I wanted to take a look at the ice. I ordered the ship brought up closer, and then I carefully raised one of the two periscopes. The view I had into that world was astounding.

The water was a gray color. The early-September sunlight filtered nicely through the ice. I cranked the field of the periscope up and—by virtue of magnification—looked at the underside of the sea ice from the equivalent distance of a few feet.

The effect was a bit unnerving. I remember the chunks of ice above us had every appearance of low, dark storm clouds passing overhead. I knew it was the motion of our ship that gave that impression.

It occurred to me that I was seeing something few men had ever seen before. Maybe a brave U-boat skipper or one of the U.S. or Russian conventional submarine captains who had dared to venture beneath the ice pack had raised a periscope and seen this. But certainly not with the clarity I had. Nor with the illusion of passing clouds produced by our ship's amazing submerged speed.

There was another problem with monitoring the ice from below. I should have been smart enough to predict it, but I did not think of it. I was one of the submariners who had the opportunity to fly over the ice pack prior to this voyage. From the high altitude air above, one seldom goes very far without seeing what appears to be a good submarine surfacing opportunity. From below, however, with the type of crude experimental under-ice fathometers available to *Nautilus*, we could pass right by a fine opening just a few yards to one side or the other of the ship and not even realize it was there. Our gear only saw what was directly overhead.

Likewise, a good surfacing opportunity could be missed because the ship's course took her quickly across the smallest dimension of the polynya. A severe form of tunnel vision hampered us.

At that time, because of the limited knowledge of ice conditions and the restrictions of the sonar equipment, finding a good place to bring the submarine to the surface required considerable maneuvering and patience.

Heaven help us if we had to go up in a hurry!

"0512: IN THE VICINITY OF A LEAD."

Much quicker than any of us wanted to, we reached the point where we had to return to meet again with Kelly and his boat or there might be general panic over our possible fate. Shortly after hitting the point where we had to turn and start back, Lyon reported that his overhead sonar indicated a lead, almost directly above our position.

As badly as I wanted to quickly surface and look around, I elected to proceed cautiously. After considerable maneuvering and measuring, the river of open water appeared to be about 400 yards by 1,400 yards. Since part of our mission called for the development of surfacing tactics in these conditions, I decided we might just as well try it then and there. I was confident we could handle the vertical ascent with ease. We had practiced it on the trip up there, and everything had gone very well.

We maneuvered *Nautilus* around the opening at various depths and courses to determine if it was fully clear of ice, as it appeared to be on Waldo's equipment. It was still a relatively small opening for a vessel our size to ease through, a bit like tossing a basketball through a hoop from behind the three-point line. My officers and I felt we could get a good-enough view of it with the sonar and should have no problem squeezing at least our sail up through the opening in the ice.

"0621: MADE VERTICAL ASCENT FROM 120 FEET."

Our position was eighty-one degrees, two minutes north, six degrees east. The SQS-4 scanning sonar and the upward-beamed fathometers showed us a picture of clear water directly overhead.

All the time I was on number one periscope and had the optics tilted upward. The view was not perfect. I could not tell visually if what I was seeing was open water all the way to the surface or not. The transmission of light through the ice surrounding the lead and the cloudiness of the water at this depth were such that I was mostly seeing into a nondescript grayness. It could be open water or solid ice.

I made the decision to rely on the sonar and fathometers. They still showed a clear path to the surface.

We used high-pressure air to put an estimated three-thousand-pound bubble in a ballast tank. This was calculated to give us six thousand pounds of positive buoyancy as the sail reached the surface. We only wanted to go up enough so the sail poked through the hole in the ice. We certainly did not want to bob up and down too much.

I requested a vertical ascent rate of about three inches per second, but something did not feel right as *Nautilus* began to head toward the surface. It quickly became obvious that we had overshot. We were coming up at about four times that rate—at a foot per second—due to the effect of the water's frigid temperature!

Still should be okay, I thought. *The periscope will break the water surface any moment and I will have a clear view of miles and miles of ice in all directions.*

I kept my eye on the eyepiece, the periscope turned northeast so I would not be looking directly into the brilliant Arctic sun when we rose clear of the icy surface. Then, at a distance later calculated to be four feet— about four seconds' worth of vertical travel between the viewing window of my periscope and what should have been open water—my field of view was filled with what appeared to be solid ice.

Solid ice!

I instinctively braced myself and shouted the order to flood the negative ballast tank, the quickest way to take on weight and stop our ascent.

"Flood negative!"

Even as I heard the *whooosh!* of seawater rushing into the ballast tank, I felt the ship shudder sickeningly. The deck lurched beneath my feet. My periscope optics turned black as night.

It would not have surprised me at all if a torrent of ice-cold seawater rained down through a massive rent in our sail—if the ship had heeled over, its superstructure breached, and she headed on an uncontrollable dive for the bottom of the sea, taking all of us with her.

But except for the disconcerting shudder and the blind periscope, everything appeared normal as we dropped down again away from the surface. We headed down from a depth of 58 feet at the time of the collision with the ice, going deep, and then leveled off at 250 feet.

"Number one periscope has had it," I told my diving officer.

I almost hated to ask the question, dreading the answers I might get back, but soon I was on the 1MC, requesting all compartments to check for and report leaks. One by one, each reported no apparent problems.

Satisfied we had no major structural damage, we set course due south, back toward the edge of the ice pack to where *Trigger* awaited our return. With no hesitation, we began to look for another opportunity to once again attempt to surface and survey the damage.

But when we went up to 120 feet to begin to look for another hole in the ice, we discovered, to our dismay, that our number two periscope was out too, optically useless. Though it was fully housed at the time, it was obvious that it also had been damaged in the collision with the ice.

We were blind.

We forgot about trying to surface. I ordered a return to cruising depth and a course south for *Trigger*. We would need to get out from under the ice before we could surface safely and look at the topside damage.

"0902: AT CRUISING DEPTH 300 FEET, SPEED 12 KNOTS."

The trip down to the rendezvous point provided several hours for me to try to figure out what to do. I went to my stateroom and sat at my little fold-out desk, thinking.

What if the damage was such that we would not have time to fix it before the operation was scheduled to begin? It was made very clear to me that by far the greatest priority for this deployment was the NATO exercise.

How could we participate in the largest NATO naval battle problem in history with no working periscope?

I decided to wait and see what we were up against. Maybe the damage was minimal, something we could quickly fix and get on about our business.

So we ran on to open water.

"1407: SOUND CONTACT ON TRIGGER, SNORKELING."
"1452: RENDEZVOUSED WITH *TRIGGER*."

Using the underwater telephone, I told Les Kelly about our predicament—that we were virtually blind for the moment. I asked him to check and see if it was clear to ascend.

He confirmed it was.

"1512: SURFACED."

When we emerged onto the bridge, we were sick. We found a mess. I later summarized what I saw for my official report:

> Examination of the sail revealed that both periscopes had been bent backward: #1 by about 3 inches at the top, #2 with its smaller neck, perhaps 6 inches. #1 was intact. #2 had its upper window shattered and gas was escaping. The barrel is undoubtedly flooded. The top of the sail forward of the BPS-1 radar well had been mashed down by varying amounts up to 6 or 8 inches. Both periscopes now housed above the top of the sail where before #2 had been housed fully. The bridge was somewhat smaller due to the upper two feet of fairing being torn and pushed inboard. The bridge gyro repeater stand was bent and bridge gyro flooded but it was subsequently dried out and repaired. All other masts and retractable devices were tested and it was determined that except for the superficial sail, the net loss was two periscopes. The deformation of the aluminum

sail showed that only the forward half of the top had made contact with the ice and that the under surface of this particular block was irregular. It was probably also somewhat plastic because no scratch marks or sharp indentations were apparent.

Why the incident had happened, or even exactly what had happened, I did not know just then. My immediate thoughts were on fixing either or both of the periscopes and getting ourselves back into the ball game.

Later, Lyon stated that he thought we must have collided with a small block of ice that had floated over the top of us while we were ascending. Based on the violence of the shudder we experienced with the collision and the damage to the ship, I felt that it was more likely a major floe, and the upward fathometers had simply missed it. Unluckily for us, it struck the most sensitive spot on the submarine.

When we came to that abrupt halt upon striking the ice, we came to rest at a keel depth of fifty-eight feet. From the keel to the top of the sail is fifty-two feet. This indicates that we were up against ice with a draft of six feet (fifty-eight minus fifty-two). With a draft of six feet, the likely thickness of the ice we struck would be at least eight feet, and possibly a foot or two more. Actually, with number one periscope raised and striking the ice, the distance from keel to ice bottom would have been more than six feet. The more I thought about it, the more convinced I was that we collided with ice that was between eight and ten feet thick. No wonder it bent our periscopes and wrecked our bridge!

Obviously I disagreed with Lyon's assessment that we had hit a relatively small "block" of ice floating in the polynya.

I had to concede that we would not be able to take part in the NATO exercises without a working periscope. There was no time to conduct any other under-ice operations and still have time for repairs. We would have to cancel our ice-pack exploration and depart immediately for Scotland, where our tender repair ship would be located, waiting to support U.S. submarines, including *Nautilus*, that were taking part in the crucial drills.

After months of preparations, the collision with the ice was a disheartening turn of events.

Of greater importance, this would mark the first time that *Nautilus* had failed in an assigned mission—in this case, a failure that could dampen what little enthusiasm there was for future under-ice exploration.

And it had happened under my command.

For the first time in my career, I was beginning to have doubts about myself and my ability to take this amazing vessel to where she needed to go. I felt I had let down my crew too. After convincing them that I would not unnecessarily take them or *Nautilus* into harm's way, I had very nearly ruined her in that lonely polynya near the top of the world. It appeared Admiral Rickover had been correct. I may well have "wrecked the program."

On further reflection, I realized that I had made several serious mistakes.

First, I got into too much of a hurry. In the back of my mind, I wanted to complete our first under-ice penetration promptly so we would have plenty of time for a really deep second excursion—maybe all the way to ninety degrees north, the North Pole. I was simply rushing things.

Next, when we searched for a good surfacing opportunity and tested the opening for its suitability as a safe way up, I should have used more time carrying out the evolution. Even if it took a full day or more, that would have been a small price to pay.

Likewise, I should have carried out more practices in making vertical ascents. Control of the rate of vertical ascent is different during an open-ocean drill than it is under ice. This is because of the probability of a positive temperature gradient in that chilly water. In other words, the water in and under the ice will likely be colder than the water deeper down. This means that the rate of ascent will tend to accelerate as the submarine rises into the much colder water, it being more buoyant than the deeper, warmer water. In this case, though we had come up within regulations, we had obviously come up faster than we should have, which is why we hit the ice so hard and did so much damage to our ship.

I now knew that the sails of submarines would need to be redesigned for under-ice work. They had to be much stronger. They would also need to be reshaped from their flat top to a somewhat rounded shape. Then sensitive periscopes and masts would be housed well inside the top of the sail so they would survive a reasonable amount of pressure when the ship collided with ice.

And as tempting as it was to want to look up at what was above us while we were on the way up—water or ice—both periscopes and all masts should have been down and fully housed during the last stage of the ascent. In studying the damage, it would have been easy to assume that both periscopes were up and in use during our ascent. In actuality, only number one periscope was raised. If number two was elevated at all, it had been raised a few inches inadvertently, or it had crept up because of a hydraulic leak. Fully housed, it still took a severe blow because the top of the sail gave way when we hit the ice so hard.

My biggest error in judgment, though, was that I put too much faith in relatively untried equipment. The upward-beamed fathometers were designed for slow-moving conventional submarines. They had too slow a cyclic rate and did not have the option of bringing in the beam width for a detailed examination of an opening that was chosen for surfacing.

If there was any consolation, I had learned a lot, and learning was definitely one of the goals for being in that brutal part of the world.

While I was looking for positives, I finally found another one. We had traveled 150 miles beneath the polar ice pack. Before we wounded our magnificent ship, we had achieved still another record.

But at what price? At what price?

12

GOOD AS NEW

MONDAY, SEPTEMBER 2, 1957
"1512: THOUGH THE ODDS WERE 100 TO 1, CHIEF ENGINEER EARLY,
ENSIGN (LAURENCE) MCNAMARA, COB LARCH, KRAWCZYK,
MCGOVERN, SCOTT, BEARDEN, KURRUS, KROPP, YOUNGBLOOD,
REECE AND HOLLAND TEAMED UP TO PUT US BACK IN BUSINESS
PERISCOPE-WISE."

The miraculous repair of our periscope is a stirring story, even if it might seem to lack the flair or drama of the rest of our missions. It may not be clear to some why it was even necessary, why it was so crucial that those brave crewmen quite literally risked their lives to get a damaged periscope back in service. Could we not have simply canceled our plans for more exploration beneath the ice and headed on down to rendezvous with the tender, get our damaged sail and periscopes patched up or replaced, and make our date with NATO?

Those who ask that question do not understand duty or the importance of following orders and completing a mission.

Nor do they comprehend the significance of our doing what we were sent to do.

I think the timbre of the times is also lost on many people today. We had come through a horrible world war, repelling strong, well-equipped enemies at a high cost. Then we had suffered through the non-war of Korea, a "police action" in which we were denied a clear-cut victory, despite the heavy price we had paid seeking it. In the mid-1950s, the Soviet Union posed the most serious threat to our country, to our democracy, that we had yet seen in our history. Technologically they seemed to have surpassed us on several fronts, and they appeared destined to do so militarily as well. They had atomic power, just as we did, and they were successfully testing truly frightening weapons. We also had intelligence that they were quickly developing the means of delivering those weapons to American soil, using rockets.

Nautilus was not sent under ice as an idly chosen destination, nor were we merely on a publicity-seeking lark. The Arctic was a strategic target in the middle of a hostile geographic area, a region that could well determine the victor in the next war, should there be one. We knew it was more likely that there would be such a war if our country did not appear strong and technologically advanced enough to prevent it. We simply had to establish some history there, to increase our knowledge of the place. We had to show the Soviets, their friends, and our allies that we had the equipment, the desire, the knowledge, and—most important—the resolve to operate there.

If we failed in our attempt, not only would we have not fulfilled our mission, but we would also be signaling to the world that our capabilities, military and scientific, were suspect. The Soviets could make much of such a failed effort.

One of the central characters in our periscope miracle was Chief Fire Control Technician John Krawczyk. On a submarine, "fire control" refers to firing torpedoes, not fighting fire, and since one of the uses of periscopes is to identify and pinpoint targets for torpedo attack, periscope upkeep and maintenance are a responsibility of the chief fire control technician. John was talented on several fronts, including serving as our unofficial ship's photographer. He came to be known as "Mr. *Nautilus*" because of his more than nine years of service aboard the vessel.

As soon as we had returned to open water and it was safe to do so, we brought *Nautilus* to the surface and Paul Early as chief engineer went topside to assess the damage. With him was a small survey party consisting of Krawczyk and a couple of New Yorkers, Auxiliaryman John McGovern and Seaman Robert Scott. A submarine's sail is the smooth, rounded, streamlined enclosure designed to house and protect two radar masts, two radio antennas, and the two periscopes from being damaged by objects floating in the water. The sail also provides a cramped bridge for the conning officer and lookouts during surface operations.

The damage party quickly ascertained that number two periscope was beyond repair. It was bent severely, the viewing glass was smashed, the viewing glass hold-down frame was fractured, and the periscope was flooded with seawater.

Number one periscope seemed to be physically intact, although it was bent backward at about forty-five degrees from the vertical. And when we collided with the ice, we shoved the forward part of the sail enclosure downward about six to eight inches, making the already small bridge even smaller.

Paul Early took a long, hard look at the number one periscope. He decided that there was an outside chance that it could be bent back vertical. There was no way to know, though, if that would restore alignment of the complicated optics inside. The survey party also quickly determined that some work would have to be done on number two, even though there was no way to put it back in service. We would have to weld a cover plate over the smashed viewing glass port. Otherwise there was a threat that the ship could be flooded through the periscope barrel. That could be disastrous if we had to go deep or were beneath the ice and unable to surface. If we could not make number two reliably waterproof, we probably would have to remain on the surface until we could rendezvous with the submarine tender, where we could get it patched up.

"Captain, I think we can do some good on number one," Early reported when he returned below. "It's a long shot, but I think it's worth a try."

"Permission granted to give it a try," I said, without hesitation.

There was one more complicating factor. When we first dived beneath the ice, the weather had been relatively calm, with only some fog to ruin our view. When we surfaced, the damage assessment team opened the hatch to a freshening gale. By the time the party went up to begin an attempt to repair the periscopes, the icy wind was howling.

Early and Laurence McNamara, an engineman, headed the project, and they were joined on deck by Krawczyk, McGovern, and Scott along with Raymond Kropp, a seaman from Coaldale, Pennsylvania. The men determined that they would work on both periscopes at the same time. One team would attempt to straighten and seal number one in the hopes that was all it would take to get it back in service. The other men would drain and flush number two, fabricate a cover plate, and seal the viewing glass port. It could be repaired later, in a submarine periscope shop.

The cold wind was brutal, biting at the exposed skin of the men's faces as they hauled up and positioned on the bridge two hydraulic jacks and four blocks of wood. As they worked, the gale seemed to grow even stronger, and the crew members had to take precautions to try to keep from being blown overboard. Perched on the slick deck of the pitching bridge, surrounded by the sharp-edged, jagged metal at the damaged top of the sail, the men set to work jacking the periscope toward the vertical.

Using the blocks of wood for bracing, the four-man work party wedged their jack between the bent number one periscope and the aluminum superstructure. They hoped that would provide a backstop for the jack. Then very gently they began pumping the jack, applying pressure against the bent periscope. Its strong, stainless-steel barrel remained rigid and unyielding. Instead, the aluminum backstop bent. They would have to find something else against which to brace the jack.

After several hours of maddeningly slow experimentation in the rugged weather, they found their new backstop: the number two periscope. Fortunately, both periscopes were installed on the ship's centerline, with number two about four feet behind number one.

Meanwhile the ship's two stainless-steel welders, Richard Bearden and John Kurrus, came to the bridge to see if they could fashion a metal cover plate to replace the broken viewing window on the number two periscope. They made several trips to the top of the sail, armed with pencils, cardboard, and scissors with which they made a template for the replacement cover plate. They also assisted Krawczyk, Kropp, McGovern, and Scott in trying to build a backstop that would be strong enough to support a jacking system to straighten number one periscope.

Now once again they were ready to apply pressure with the powerful jack. As the jack gently expanded, the bracing held, and little by little the barrel began bending back toward the vertical.

"Looking good, guys," Krawczyk reported down to us. "She's straightening. Keep pumping!"

It appeared the procedure was going to work. But just then, above the roar of the gale, the sailors on the bridge heard a pronounced, brittle *crrraaack!*

The tapered portion of the barrel had split open at the point of the original bend, about two feet below the viewing window glass at the top of the instrument. The crack was about four inches long, and the dry nitrogen gas inside the periscope was hissing out into the wind. With the pressure released, total clouding of the internals was inevitable. And, of course, the periscope would flood on submergence and be a possible pathway for a dangerous seawater leak.

The men came below—tired, cold, but determined. They congregated in the operations compartment, each warming up with a hot cup of coffee.

Early turned to Bearden and Kurrus.

"Do you think you could weld that crack?" he asked them.

"We'll sure try!" they answered in unison.

I gave permission to proceed. They got busy assembling the necessary equipment to do the repair job.

Even under ideal conditions, stainless-steel welding is a precise and exacting operation. I was amazed that Paul would even suggest such an attempt. The temperature was near freezing, the wind chill below zero, and a gale howling. Obviously at that point in time, I did not fully know the strength and depth of determination of the typical *Nautilus* crewman. Repairing a periscope in an Arctic gale was not what those men had trained for, but *Nautilus* sailors were versatile and tough.

Bearden and Kurrus again pulled on their foul-weather gear, got their equipment together, and without complaint headed back upstairs. As part of the attempt, they would have to lay out more than 150 feet of heavy welding cable to reach from the midpoint of the engine room to the top of the sail. Adding to the difficulty factor was the need to run the cable through bulkhead doors that are normally kept clear as part of the "Rig for dive" and emergency procedures.

"Rig for dive" allows the ship to be secured with minimum effort, in the shortest possible time, to guarantee its watertight integrity. We were supposed to always be ready to submerge immediately if we needed to. Permission to break "Rig for dive" is not something that skippers treat lightly, but it was necessary if we were to run welding cable and pneumatic hose through the ship.

Again I gave permission, but with the proviso that a crew member be stationed at each bulkhead door and hatch to disconnect the weld cable and pneumatic hose so the doors and hatches could be shut in an emergency. The two ship's welders set to work in those horrible conditions topside. The ship was rolling continuously, and the men had little way to brace themselves. One of them had to hold on to the other, keeping him upright and preventing him from slipping overboard.

When the men reached the bridge, the wind had become so fierce it literally tore the welding masks off their heads. Bearden's mask skittered along the deck and blew into the sea. Another one had to be fetched. This one was tied to the bridge, just in case it blew off again.

"It was blowing about thirty to forty knots by the captain's estimate," John Kurrus later recalled. "I don't remember the exact temperature, but I can confirm that it was damn cold!"

The frigid wind was so strong that it was difficult to hold on to the welding rod, much less exercise the control of it that was necessary to get a solid weld. The first crisis came when the men could not maintain an arc in the thirty-knot winds. A full-length foul-weather overcoat was hung over the periscope to form a rough windbreak, but it proved to be too confining. The men retreated once again to the warmth of the crew's mess to think about developing a better windbreak enclosure.

No one suggested giving up and heading for the tender.

Dutch Larch and Arthur "Gunner" Callahan listened to the welders' tales and came up with a plan. While Kurrus and Bearden gripped warm coffee mugs to get the circulation back into their fingers, Larch, Callahan, and Ray Kropp carried armfuls of canvas, several mop handles, and quantities of white line through the hatch and up the ladder to the bridge. In short order they created a workable tarpaulin over the area. Amazingly, it held up in the fierce winds.

With a reasonable shelter in which to work, Bearden and Kurrus resumed their formidable task of closing the four-inch crack. At the same time, the work on the number two periscope continued so that the device would not leak. Work continued for about twelve hours—twelve hours in the middle of an Arctic storm. The welding rods sizzled, sparks flew, the welding machine hummed reassuringly, and little by little the crack in the periscope's barrel was filled in with good solid weld.

Finally Kurrus and Bearden successfully closed the gap and mounted the cover plate. When the two men staggered down from the bridge, I met them in the Attack Center. They were two of the coldest, most tired-looking men I have ever seen. Dr. Dobbins was on hand and gave them a quick look-over.

"Captain, I believe a prescription of medicinal brandy would be good for what ails these two," he said.

"Absolutely!" was my reply, confirming Doc's prescription.

We had already determined that the number one periscope appeared to be straight enough to be used. The weld seemed to have sealed the crack too. But we were not finished yet. We still had to evacuate the device, removing all moisture that had seeped in when the gas leaked out. Next we had to find a way to create a vacuum and recharge the periscope with dry nitrogen. If we could not do that, upon submerging in the frigid water the optics would immediately cloud and the periscope would be useless.

Crew members Jimmy Youngblood and Thomas Reece came up with an ingenious solution to the problem. For our onboard steam plant to work, it was necessary that the steam be exhausted into the main condensers. These operated with a thirty-inch vacuum for efficiency so the steam could turn back into condensate. Youngblood, who was assigned to the engine room, suggested that we run a noncollapsible hose from one of the main condensers up through the ship's passageway to the periscope. In that way we could use the steam vacuum and its strong suction to pull moisture out of the cloudy periscope barrel.

The crew quickly rigged a hose, snaking it through the open doors. The suction was applied, and almost instantly the periscope was rid of the moist air. A charge of dry nitrogen gas was shot through the periscope fitting. Then, just to be sure, the whole operation was repeated. Finally, the nitrogen fitting was sealed off.

After fifteen hours of muscle-numbing hard work, our number one periscope—though banged and bent—was functionally almost as good as new. The crew stored all equipment, and we returned to "Rig for dive" conditions.

This was the most amazing repair job at sea that I had ever observed. Or ever heard of, for that matter. There was heaven and a great crew to thank for a near miracle. With the periscope back in service, we could continue our under-ice exploration and still arrive ready for the make-believe sea battle of Strikeback.

The North Pole was still a possibility—at least in my mind!

13

BOW TO THE NORTH

TUESDAY, SEPTEMBER 3, 1957
"0105: SENT *TRIGGER* EXCURSION TWO MESSAGES."

A s soon as I could, I relayed the good news about our repairs to Les Kelly, letting him know that we would continue operations as scheduled. According to plan, *Nautilus* would submerge for a second time at 0800 and proceed beneath the ice to eighty-three degrees north, and perhaps farther.

"Approximately 83N," was the destination specified in our operation orders.

I told Kelly that we would be gone between two and five days.

"How far north does this imply that you might go?" Kelly shot back. I imagined the grin on his face.

I thought for a moment. I had not told a soul on the ship—not even my XO—but following our first excursion under the ice and after the periscope had been repaired, I had privately worked up a set of figures pertaining to speed, distance, time, and course that would take us to the North Pole. It was, at that moment, 630 miles away, under ice. I figured that if all went well, we could make it there and back in four and a half to five days.

If we could make a start soon, my intentions were to make a run for the North Pole.

I did not want to divulge even that tentative plan. I feared that if we fell short of the goal of reaching the Pole, it would be many people's perception that we had failed the entire mission, and that most definitely would not be the case.

"Do not know how far north we will go," I replied jokingly to Kelly's query. "But we might get close enough to talk to Saint Nick."

We had already lost most of a day fixing the periscopes, which left very little leeway for such contingencies as surfacing and coping with navigation difficulties, equipment failures, or other slowdowns. I had already increased my earlier calculation of ten knots average speed to twelve knots. This was right up against the upper limit of what we thought were good pictures from the upward-beaming fathometers. Clearly this would have to be a very rushed trip.

For coordination between our two submarines, Les Kelly and I had set up a simple procedure. We would take turns making excursions under the ice while the other stood by. The excursion submarine would specify the position of the next rendezvous, plus the time window within which it would occur. The departing submarine would also specify the number of hours after the rendezvous window had passed before the standby submarine would become concerned and think about reporting the under-ice partner missing. I expanded this from the twelve hours used for our first excursion to sixty hours. I did not want to be within miles of the North Pole and have to swing back south just to meet an arbitrarily narrow time slot.

In addition, there would be a schedule for the dropping of a practice depth charge by the standby submarine. The idea was that the two submarines could precisely synchronize their chronometers, the shipboard clocks used for navigation. Following an exact schedule—generally every six hours when we were within twelve hours of rendezvous time—the standby vessel would drop a practice depth charge over the side. Exact timing of hearing this small explosion would tell the excursion submarine its distance from the standby vessel, using the 4,800 feet-per-second rate at which sound travels in seawater.

Of course, the last thing Kelly and I wanted was a situation where the standby submarine would feel compelled to report an emergency. That possibility made us very meticulous when we prepared these arrangements on each excursion.

"0720: SUBMERGED FOR SECOND CRUISE UNDER PACK."

We discovered that the repaired periscope had its field tilted up about six degrees. This caused the view to be cut in half in low-power magnification. In high power it was less noticeable and completely useful. It was still, as before, hard to train. Our emergency repairs had had no effect on that nagging problem.

We submerged a bit ahead of schedule and went deep under the pack, traveling considerably faster than we had on our first probe. This time we were less concerned about the dangerous deep ice than we had been on our initial penetration. Soon our equipment would be tracing the sea floor in this part of the world for the first time in history.

WEDNESDAY, SEPTEMBER 4, 1957
"0021: WE HAVE YET TO FIND ANY OPENING."

Ice conditions above us were about as expected, with drafts varying from a few inches to twelve to fifteen feet. A few pressure ridges projected downward as much as forty-eight feet from the surface, but there was plenty of water below us should we need to go lower to duck beneath the deeper plunging stalactites of ice.

"0545: SOUNDING DECREASED TO 1300 FATHOMS."

The ocean depth suddenly had decreased, the bottom rising up forty-two hundred feet in fifteen minutes. The only chart we had to go by was a very rough Soviet contour chart of the Arctic Basin. It did not show this geophysical feature at all. Nor did it indicate many others we encountered. Most of the bottom contour information was based on unreliable predictions, extrapolations, and estimates. We were blessed with precision instruments and vastly greater mobility than were those few who had preceded us to this region, so we were continually adding to future charts. The Soviet chart on board, unreliable as it was, was still the best we could lay our hands on.

"1429: LOST 400-CYCLE ELECTRICAL SUPPLY FOR ABOUT ONE MINUTE."

Just before we reached the eighty-sixth parallel, I was informed that both gyrocompasses were acting abnormally. I raced to the control station, dreading what I would see on the instrumentation.

It had happened so abruptly that we stared at the indicators, not quite believing what we saw. Then we quickly realized that something other than the high latitude had caused the gyros to stop working.

We found the cause of the trouble a few moments later. A circuit breaker had tripped. The power supply had failed at the worst possible time, causing loss of both gyrocompasses. In an instant our most reliable navigational aids had become useless, and all because of the equivalent of a blown fuse.

Even at lower latitudes and even with power restored, it would take awhile to get the compasses stabilized and back online. At eighty-six degreees north, so close to the North Pole, there was a strong probability that even the Mark 19 would not settle enough to become useful again.

Fortunately Paul Early and his electricians quickly analyzed the problem. Through an incredible bit of bad design, the compasses were fed by the same circuit as one of our regular water transfer pumps. The pumps, operating in colder water than they ever had to before, had overloaded the circuit and tripped the breaker. We now know that the design violated all the rules of required redundancy in submarine systems, particularly in such a vital one as the navigation instrumentation. There are usually at least two separate ways to do most tasks on a submarine, and certainly two power sources for crucial systems. Not this time.

Paul and his guys got the compasses back online and took steps to protect the circuit. We turned off any other items on the same circuit that were not essential to navigation. The magnetic compass seemed to mock me, to be wagging a finger in my face as it swung back and forth through a lazy arc of sixty degrees, trying to show the way.

Or was it simply saying, "I've told you a thousand ways, Captain. The Arctic is not to be taken for granted?"

With restored power supply, we watched and waited to see if the gyrocompasses might settle down and give us useful readings. When a gyrocompass is shut off in normal latitudes and then turned back on, about four hours are required for it to begin to give reliable readings. Since no one had ever tried to restart a north-seeking gyrocompass way up there at the top of the globe, we did not know how long it would take. For all we knew, it might never do so.

Meanwhile Chief Quartermaster Lyle "Doggie" Rayl plotted our course as best he could by averaging out the magnetic compass swings. His challenge was to steer for the midpoint of the metronomelike gyrations. Christopher Columbus had better control of direction back in the fifteenth century than we did that under-ice day in September 1957. Rayl was known for his great attention to detail in maintaining the plot of the ship's position, and he remained at the chart table the entire time we ran beneath the ice, noting the smallest detail available to him.

There was no cause for panic, but we were quickly aware that we were almost certainly accumulating a sizable error as we continued in a direction we thought was north. My guess was our navigational variance was probably about twenty miles, having accumulated at the average rate of two to three miles per hour.

We considered making a 180-degree turn and trying to steer back down our own wake. There was one consideration, though. Making a sharp turn would only disturb the restarted gyrocompasses, causing them to take even longer to settle. We continued on our best estimate of a northerly course, assuming our bow pointed roughly toward the Pole. It would not take much of an error to throw us into a game of "longitude roulette." It was a real possibility that we could be led toward the wrong ocean. Or even worse, we could run up against a rugged and dangerous ice-locked coastline.

As skipper I faced another reality. My personal objective was the North Pole. Steering for eight and a half hours, however, following a compass that was swinging a dizzying sixty degrees and gyrocompasses that might never recover from their hiccup, covered by thick ice overhead that shielded us from any view of the guiding stars, I, William R. Anderson, and my trusted navigator had no earthly idea where the North Pole was. I was not one to claim we had gotten there when we really did not know where we or the Pole was located at any given moment.

"2016: MADE SLOW TURN TO THE SOUTH."

On the positive side, we surely had gained considerable knowledge on the problems of high-latitude and under-ice navigation as well as gathered a massive amount of scientific information. It was data that would prove very valuable only if we survived the trip and took it back with us from beneath the pack. We had found no attractive surfacing opportunities in an area where we were told they would be abundant, so we had no immediate chance to share our experiences with the rest of the world.

The restarted Mark 19 gyro now appeared to be fairly well settled, but we still considered the data to be suspect. Shortly after we passed latitude eighty-seven degrees north, about 180 nautical miles from the North Pole (an estimate we were later able to confirm), I gave the order to execute a sweeping, gradual turn back to the south.

It was not an order I issued lightly. We were, in effect, giving up on the undeclared goal of our mission: making an under-ice run all the way to the North Pole. And we were only about the distance from Nashville to Louisville from that goal. I deeply regretted we had not reached the Pole but considered that to go any farther would expose the ship and the crew to undue risks. I had vowed not to do that in my promise to my superiors, to Admiral Rickover, and to my crew.

Reluctantly—more reluctantly than anyone could ever imagine—I decided to give up on the Pole—at least for this trip.

If there was any comfort, it was based on our having set a new and impressive string of records. We had proceeded 240 miles farther into the ice pack than our eighty-three-degree-north target destination, the goal specified in our operational orders. More important, we had gone farther north under our own control than any ship in history. From any perspective, *Nautilus* and her crew had greatly exceeded our mission requirements. It was a success!

I had no way of knowing then that others would soon claim our trip anything but successful, a dismal failure. And that once more, any chance of *Nautilus* journeying to the top of the world would become a remote one.

Even before I could face that turmoil, there was one other challenge occupying my mind. We were not safely out from beneath the ice yet.

In fact, we would soon come to realize that we were just plain lost.

14

LOST BENEATH THE ICE

THURSDAY, SEPTEMBER 5, 1957
"0000: CRUISING AT 350 FEET BENEATH THE ARCTIC ICE PACK."

We had no choice but to put some faith in our gyro-compass now that it seemed to have found itself. Twice during our movement toward open water, we came upon leads or openings in the ice that appeared to be promising surfacing opportunities. If we could get to the surface, we could "shoot the sun" and confirm where we were and which direction to go.

But after making vertical ascents, we found the first polynya filled with large, heavy blocks of ice, and the second one turned out to be not an opening at all but a solid ceiling of ice. It was a bit disconcerting that the upward-beamed sonar kept reporting open water. We slowly ascended. At the suggestion of Steve White, we were using the retractable whip antenna as a guide. We could view it from the periscope, and if it started to bend, we knew it had bumped into something overhead.

It started to bend! I immediately gave the order to flood

negative and get back down to cruising depth. Each attempt ended in a narrow escape.

The operator on the upward-beamed sonar thought the ice that bent our whip antenna was only about three inches thick. Even ice that thin would have been too much to risk our already damaged and depressed upper sail structure. Moreover, our lone remaining-but-repaired periscope projected up enough above the sail to be wrecked once more on contact with ice of any substantial thickness. As badly as I wanted to get to the surface to check our position, I had to keep in mind that the primary reason we were scheduled for this part of the world was to participate in Strikeback.

It was a real morale-breaker for us to take two hours to determine that what the ice sonars were reporting as clear water was really a sheet of thick ice. I made a mental note that aggressive refinements to our ice monitoring sonars were very much in order. I did not blame anyone, particularly Dr. Lyon. We were there to learn.

"0300."

It had been apparent for several hours that we were definitely not on the reverse of the track we had made northward—the only track that would lead directly back to *Trigger* and hopefully get us there before Kelly reported *Nautilus* missing beneath the ice. Based on the information available on water depth, bottom contour estimates, water temperatures, and estimated currents, we thought we were traveling east of our original track to the north.

"0327."

To compensate for the estimated eastward error in our direction of travel to the south, I ordered a thirty-degree course change, from 180 to 210. I held on this course for six hours. At twelve knots, this meant six nautical miles per hour westward made-good, or a total of thirty-six miles. We would later learn that this put us thirty-six miles in the *wrong* direction.

At a time when we should have observed the ocean plain becoming deeper beneath us, leading us into the open waters of the Greenland Sea, we suddenly happened upon shallow water. We noticed that the ice was much thicker above us, and that it extended deeper, squeezing down disturbingly close to our ship. The water temperature was much colder than we had anticipated too. We quickly deduced and were later able to confirm that we had come close to an ice-locked coastline, that of northern Greenland, only two to three nautical miles away.

Once again we were lost. It was either turn left or turn right. Straight ahead was no option. Neither was "reverse full." In my gut I favored turning left, and it was my call. I ordered a ninety-degree turn to the left, toward the east.

What seemed like hours passed. Then we were—thank heaven—in deep water once more, and things had begun to check somewhat with our expectations. It was a frightening experience for captain and crew, but I heard no one express any doubt or fear. I know each man was likely doing exactly what I was: envisioning our driving right into a coastal inlet, filled with deep, ridged ice, then finding ourselves trapped there as if we had walked into a dark alley, with no idea of how to get back out.

And with all that ice overhead, surfacing was never an option either.

FRIDAY, SEPTEMBER 6, 1957
"0500: THE SEAWATER TEMPERATURE SHOWED US THAT WE ARE PULLING INTO AN OFFSHOOT OF THE GULF STREAM TONGUE."
"0930: LEFT THE PACK AND ENTERED CLEAR, OPEN WATER."

You could almost hear the collective release of held breath throughout *Nautilus*.

We were submerged under the ice for more than seventy-four hours and had covered a distance of almost a thousand miles. I could only hope Les Kelly had not yet reported us late, even though we were already fourteen hours past due.

No, we had not made it to the North Pole as I hoped. We believed the high-latitude navigational knowledge we had gained, however, would be of far greater value to other nuclear submarines that would soon venture under the ice—ours and those of our allies when they had them—than whether or not *Nautilus* reached the Pole. We had gone farther north than the ice-locked *Fram* (in the 1890s) and *Sedov* (in the 1930s) had as those ships drifted at the whim of the floes. And we had traveled much farther north on the planet than any ship had ever gone under its own power.

On the not-so-positive side, working backward we computed that we had amassed a total navigational error of forty nautical miles. We felt that was not so bad, considering we were for about half a day forced to rely on a wildly swinging magnetic compass to show us the way.

"2325: EFFECTED RENDEZVOUS WITH *TRIGGER*."

Though a bit concerned about us, Les Kelly had not yet reported our late arrival, which was his call. We did not discuss the North Pole at all. I assumed he knew we would have let him know had we gone there.

SATURDAY, SEPTEMBER 7, 1957
"0740: *TRIGGER* SUBMERGED."

After we made contact with *Trigger*, she got a turn to cruise under the pack. After resting and relaxing while she steamed sixty miles under the ice for roughly half a day—a considerable and record-breaking achievement for a conventional submarine, by the way—we got under way for a third trip of our own beneath the ice.

"2008: MADE 1000TH DIVE."

The honor of handling this meaningful dive went, quite rightly, to Bus Cobean, the senior member of the remaining commissioning crew aboard

Nautilus. Such a large number of dives so relatively early in the ship's history can be attributed to the many short demonstration cruises she had made, trips in which *Nautilus* was up and down like an elevator for the benefit of her passengers.

Everyone aboard was in good spirits. We had done more than our mission called for, and we had overcome some serious and dramatic obstacles to do so.

SUNDAY, SEPTEMBER 8, 1957
"1158: ENTERED UNDER PACK FOR EXCURSION 3."

We took our time on the third under-ice voyage. The pressure was off. We steamed back and forth in that odd, frigid world, allowing Dr. Lyon to gather a continuous record.

"1633: STATIONED POLYNYA PLOTTING PARTY."

When the day was half gone, we found a good-sized polynya and decided to surface and take a look around. We commenced detailed evaluation of the lead. It appeared to be about 150 yards by 100 yards and seemed clear of floating ice. However, it was also continually changing shape with the drifting floe.

We maneuvered *Nautilus* carefully beneath the opening and then inched our way up, being ever so careful. Continuing to follow Lieutenant Steve White's suggestion, the retractable radio whip antenna was raised. I could see as we came up that the antenna tip broke water without bending. Next the periscope pierced the surface, and I was able to inspect visually a scene few men had gazed upon from surface level.

Broken, jagged ice spread out to the horizon in every direction. Once again I felt an almost overpowering sense of awe at the majesty of it all. It was truly breathtaking. I longed for the giftings of a poet to be able to describe it adequately.

As it turned out, the polynya that looked so large to our instrumentation was just large enough to hold us when we fully surfaced. The water was calm, almost placid, and though the ice moving all around us was strong enough to do us serious damage, we were not worried in the least.

Three *Nautilus* crewmen in a rubber raft at the edge of the ice pack during the 1957 under-ice mission. The men are John Krawczyk, the unofficial ship's photographer, Chief of the Boat "Dutch" Larch, and Ray Kropp. Krawczyk was taking photos of the pack and the submarine from a distance.

If the floating ice pack closed in and tried to grip us, we would simply sound the dive klaxon and go back beneath it.

I suggested that John Krawczyk put over the side in a rubber life raft. I wanted to get some pictures, including some of *Nautilus* from a distance, showing us sitting there in the midst of the ice. Several crew members volunteered to row for John as he snapped away, but the honor went to Dutch Larch and Ray Kropp.

As I stood on the bridge, watching the raft bobbing gently in the dark, cold water, I had an odd thought. Had we been so equipped (and had we been so ordered), we could have fired a number of guided missiles from this patch of icy water. We were close enough to the Soviet Union to do some serious damage too. Ours was a peaceful mission, but we never lost sight of the military implications of our ability to operate a nuclear submarine in this region. The Russians would recognize that as well.

Our ship had opened up a new chapter of exploration and naval warfare. This cruise had demonstrated from a military standpoint that nuclear submarines could operate in this region in relative safety and comfort once navigation and ice sonar problems were solved. And at least for the time being, we were completely unopposed by hostile naval forces. We even had relative immunity from air attack. If we saw aircraft on the radar while on the surface, we could easily disappear beneath the best cover on the planet.

We knew (and the rest of the countries of the world, friend and foe, correctly suspected) that the U.S. Navy already had several revolutionary nuclear-powered missile-launching submarines in various stages of development. Admiral Rickover described them as "underwater satellites," and I can think of no better description. They would be capable of unleashing a withering attack against any enemy that might decide to launch another war against us or our allies. This new exposure of three thousand miles of their previously inaccessible coastline must have been quite a shock to the Soviets.

My crew and I are still proud of the role we played in making this awesome deterrent to war a reality.

"1928: SUBMERGED VERTICALLY."

After about an hour and a half of activity in our icy swimming pool, we submerged while drifting slightly toward the starboard side of the lead. We saw no more openings in the ice that looked particularly attractive, so we stayed down.

MONDAY, SEPTEMBER 9, 1957
"2100: THIRD EXCURSION COMPLETED."

This time we had steamed 293 miles in thirty-three hours and successfully completed one in-ice surfacing. These rather timid results were my doings. With Strikeback looming around the corner and for the sake of my own crew's morale, I was determined to do no further damage to *Nautilus*. The one unspoken objective that had eluded us—reaching the North Pole—was not going to be possible this trip. It was more important to gather what information we could, to learn everything about operating beneath the ice, partly for our future benefit should we have the opportunity to try another run for the Pole. It was also for other vessels that would certainly follow us to this place.

"2315: ARRIVED RENDEZVOUS POINT, COULD NOT FIND *TRIGGER*."

We searched the vicinity of the rendezvous point, but there was no sign of Les Kelly and his boat. I became concerned.

TUESDAY, SEPTEMBER 10, 1957

At 0224, we surfaced to optimize radio and radar coverage. We promptly found ourselves in the middle of another Arctic gale. Seas were state "5" with wave troughs running up to about forty feet, which only increased my concern for *Trigger*. Unlike *Nautilus*, she could not dive deep and stay down until the storm blew itself out.

Two hours later we obtained a radar fix on Spitsbergen. It confirmed that we were within five miles of our dead-reckoning position. We were where we were supposed to be, but where was *Trigger*?

There was one possible answer to our sister boat's whereabouts. We saw some sizable ice blocks near where we were supposed to meet. For such contingencies, we had arranged for an alternate rendezvous point, a spot more distant from the ice pack. Had Kelly decided to play it safe and gone to the alternate? I had to make a quick decision. I ordered the ship to submerge and proceed to the alternate point at high speed.

When we arrived, there was still no sign of *Trigger*. And still no ability to raise the submarine on any sonar, radar, or radio channel.

Now I was really worried.

Finally, at 2134, not long before we would have reported Kelly and his boat as missing, we heard something. At first it was difficult to tell exactly what it was, but then we decided it was the distant keying of *Trigger's* underwater telephone. Again, the sigh of relief was almost audible up and down the length of *Nautilus*. Realizing the possibility of a huge navigation error, Kelly had wisely made a high-speed submerged run close enough to get his own fix on Spitsbergen. Then he hurried back to the original rendezvous point. We had missed each other in the interim. Soon we were back in communication.

Two days ahead of schedule, we set a submerged course for Scotland to see if we would have time to replace our periscopes. We wanted to be in excellent shape for Strikeback if possible. We learned that our tender, the *Fulton*, had periscopes on board. I was not surprised at the thoroughness of her preparations, but I was further relieved that the damage to our periscopes would have no impact on our primary mission with the participants in the NATO exercise.

As our ship headed toward warmer waters, we felt a strong sense of achievement at having expanded man's scientific knowledge of the Arctic area.

And we were excited about writing the next chapter—whatever it might be—in the remarkable story of *Nautilus*.

PART III
OPERATION SUNSHINE I

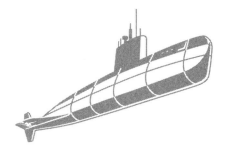

"I want no one—I mean no one—to indicate the success
or failure of this attempt until I, personally, indicate
where and when the announcement will be made."

—President Dwight D. Eisenhower, referring to Operation Sunshine,
the run to the North Pole

15

ANSWERING THE RUSSIANS

OCTOBER 5, 1957

The *New York Times* announced an amazing event from the previous day in an unusual three-column headline, a distinction usually reserved for the deaths of world leaders or the beginning of war. The Soviet Union, at 7:30 p.m. local time on October 4, launched a rocket carrying an earth satellite. Two hours later they proclaimed that the Soviet Union had led the world into the Space Age.

Only about the size of a basketball and weighing 183 pounds, *Sputnik I* took about an hour and thirty-eight minutes to circle the planet. It flew at an average altitude of 370 miles. The satellite passed over some portion of the United States at least seven times per day.

Sputnik I was fifty times the weight of the proposed American Vanguard rocket payload, which still had not been able to get off the ground. Many in the United States recognized that if the Soviets could put a satellite into space, they might soon be able to send a ballistic missile armed with a nuclear weapon to any city in America and certainly to any European capital.

For the first time in history, someone would have the capability of attacking the United States quickly and without warning, and there was not a lot the military could do about it. The United States had no similar response ready. As a prelude to their spectacular satellite launch, the Soviets had already announced the successful test of an intercontinental ballistic missile and of a hydrogen bomb.

A more realistic, immediate concern was that the Soviet Union appeared to have edged ahead in the technology race when they hurled that steel basketball into space ahead of any American satellite. The space race was on, and the United States appeared to be stuck at the starting blocks.

In Little Rock, for the first time in days, there was no headline on the front pages of the morning *Arkansas Gazette* or the evening *Arkansas Democrat* newspapers about the tumultuous events surrounding the integration of the city's Central High School and President Eisenhower's efforts toward that end. That story was replaced with the news of the Soviet Union's Sputnik launch.

Meanwhile, with the successful participation of *Nautilus* in Operation Strikeback and the maneuvers with the British navy behind us, we headed back westward toward home. Our triumph in Strikeback was, of course, kept strictly under wraps. It would be a full year before reporter Jack Anderson broke that story, telling how *Nautilus* "theoretically sank almost the entire British navy" three times over while hiding beneath an aircraft carrier.

During our trans-Atlantic crossing, I put a lot of thought into what we had learned in the Arctic and what the next steps in that area should be. It was at this time that one key point became crystallized in my mind: our primary goal should not necessarily be to reach the North Pole. There was a far greater—and much more ambitious—objective that we should pursue in that harsh region.

As I mulled the possibilities, I was torn between two approaches to follow-up explorations. I made sure both options were expressed in my official report of our under-ice mission. On the one hand, I suggested future Arctic operations be built around a series of deliberate missions—each more aggressive, each building on the one preceding it—and carried out over a period of years. On the other hand, I strongly expressed my conviction that the transpolar submarine was by no means a fantasy.

Man's old dream of a Northwest Passage beckoned the nuclear submarine. If Pacific submarines could join their Atlantic sisters, and vice versa, by moving freely across and throughout the Arctic Ocean, and be able to reinforce each other wherever the battle might be, then U.S. naval strength would be measurably enhanced at relatively little dollar cost. At the least, the Panama Canal and far more distant routes from one hemisphere to another would be virtually removed from the equation.

As we steamed submerged back toward New London, and with those thoughts in mind, I spent considerable time looking over our Arctic Ocean charts, contemplating an ocean-to-ocean trip all the way across the top of the world. Limited as they were, those charts confirmed that while the approaches to the ice pack from the Atlantic were very deep, those from the Pacific side were discouragingly shallow.

For a more detailed study, I asked our navigator, Bill Lalor, to go over all the navigation information we had on the Pacific approaches to the Arctic Ocean and let me know how he felt about an ocean-to-ocean transit—submerged, of course—across the top. After his experiences trying to guide us safely from beneath the ice pack with the wildly swinging compasses, it was reasonable to expect that Lalor would be cautious. He reported a day or two later that he felt such a venture was not advisable at that time, that perhaps it could be accomplished in the future. The water was just too shallow, there were few accurate depth-soundings, and data on the ice thickness was practically nonexistent, especially in regard to the Pacific approaches. Bill told me there would certainly be a "squeeze" problem—maybe an impossible one.

I largely agreed with Lalor's findings, and I put the concept of a Pacific-side approach to the North Pole on the back burner. Nevertheless, regardless of the exact plan, I was determined to gain support for some type of follow-up mission for *Nautilus* that would enable us to take advantage of the hard and nerve-wracking lessons we learned during mission number one. As I talked with other members of my crew, I realized that our ideas for better equipment and improved procedures for operating in that environment would have filled a book. To a man, the crew members were ready to apply those ideas to a practical, workable plan to conquer the Arctic.

None of us had any concept of the charged atmosphere we were about to sail into as we approached Block Island Sound and prepared for the north turn up the Thames toward home.

OCTOBER 10, 1957

As his advisors gathered in the White House for a hastily called meeting of the National Security Council, President Dwight Eisenhower wore a grave expression. They knew full well that Sputnik had far greater value for propaganda and perception than it did for any practical warfare application.

Undersecretary of State Christian Herter told the group that now, more than ever, the United States had to assure "even the best of our allies" that we had not been surpassed scientifically or militarily by the Soviets. The initial foreign policy reaction to Sputnik had been "pretty somber."

"We will have to do a great deal to counteract them and, particularly, to confirm the existence of our own real military and scientific strength," Secretary Herter declared.

Another member of the panel, G. Edward Larson, an assistant to presidential advisor Harold Stassen, wondered if the United States had adequate plans to counter the Soviets.

"If we lose repeatedly to the Russians as we have lost with the earth satellite, the accumulated damage would be tremendous," he noted. "We should accordingly plan to accomplish the next great breakthroughs first." He paused for effect and then asked, "Do we have any such plans?"

The pointed question left the room silent for a moment. Finally, the president responded.

"I agree with your assessment, Mr. Larson," he said. "But we can't possibly set up a whole vast scientific program of basic research in areas about which we don't know anything, and then attempt to outdo the Russians." He was getting tired of failures. People were blaming him, a lame duck president, for all that seemed to be going wrong from outer space to Little Rock. Hell, they were even blaming him for Elvis Presley being drafted into the army the year before! Looking at the group around him, the old general became a field commander once again. "We must, above all, still seek a military posture that the Russians will respect."

Several ideas were tossed out for discussion, but none resonated. Meanwhile at the head of the table, the commander in chief was only half-listening. Instead, he was quietly considering some other possibilities for bolstering the American spirit and showing the Soviets that the technology race was not quite over yet.

LATE OCTOBER 1957

Nautilus arrived in the home waters of Block Island Sound in her usual way: quietly, stealthily, submerged, and hidden. When we were just a few miles away from the point at which we would surface for our final approach to the sub base, as was my habit I got on the ship's announcing system and went over the plans for our stay in port. I pointedly reminded the crew not to talk to anyone—and I meant *anyone*—about what we had been doing. Our missions—both beneath the ice and with Strikeback—were classified confidential. I was confident they got the message. These guys were used to keeping the business of submarine operations to themselves.

Shortly after hanging up the microphone, I received the report that we were into the shallow waters of the Sound. I gave the command to surface the ship.

As usual at homecoming, everyone was in high spirits. As soon as our radio antennas dripped dry, one of the crew tuned in a news program on the commercial broadcast band and a group of crew members who were off watch gathered in the crew's mess to catch the latest news and sports scores.

To my astonishment, one of the lead stories in the newscast was about *Nautilus* and our "secret" mission up north!

The report came loud and clear: "The USS *Nautilus* will shortly return home to its base in Groton having for the first time operated extensively under the polar ice pack."

I was horrified, to say the least. Only moments before I had told the crew to keep silent about our exploits. Now a newscaster on the radio was telling everybody listening precisely what we had done!

I was angry, but little did I realize what a blessing this unexpected announcement would turn out to be. The release of the information about our polar ice exploration would help change my life and those of my officers and crew forever. And it would elevate the legend of *Nautilus* to an amazing level.

I learned later that a senior Pentagon official had pointedly disclosed news of our under-ice trip in a speech. A reporter seized on the story, and other media quickly realized the news value in such a thing. Never mind that it was supposed to remain secret. As embarrassed as I was, however, someone much higher up was even more disturbed by the premature announcement of our high-latitude operations. That someone was in the White House, behind the big desk. The timing of the whole incident was especially unfortunate in the eyes of the president of the United States.

According to the Navy Department, which released a follow-up official press statement on October 29, not long after our return home, the 1957 under-ice voyage of *Nautilus* was "one of the most incredible adventures in naval history." That seemed like a bit of an overstatement to me. Nevertheless, hyperbole or not, the press seemed to pay little attention to the delayed formal announcement. The truth is that we were knocked out of the news by Sputnik's launch by the Russians. Waldo Lyon may have put it best when he later wrote that our accomplishments on that first venture beneath the ice were "lost in Sputnik's shadow."

The ramifications of placing that satellite into orbit cannot be overemphasized. It set off a groundswell of alarm within the United States not seen since the Japanese attack on Pearl Harbor. President Eisenhower termed it a "wave of near hysteria."

The rhetoric coming from the Soviet Union was ominous. The leaders indicated that their country was now in a political "position of strength," that the launch of Sputnik demonstrated their lead in intercontinental ballistic missile (ICBM) development. Nikita Khrushchev, the Communist Party leader, said that world peace now rested on Moscow and Washington, and he emphasized that the two nations would have to either talk things out or fight them out.

With *Nautilus* at sea most of October 1957, we were not aware of the furor set off by Sputnik. Not long after we returned, I heard a strong rumor that President Eisenhower was furious that the Pentagon had revealed our first Arctic mission and at the way it was handled. He felt that the Pentagon should have deferred to him—the commander in chief—for such an announcement. I later learned that he complained loudly and long to his naval aide and others that with the Russian Sputnik overhead, the word of our accomplishments was mishandled miserably, the impact smudged out by the excitement surrounding the satellite.

"If ever there was a time that I need to talk about something positive in American technology, it is now," Eisenhower raged. "And here they let this extraordinary *Nautilus* news dribble out."

Now we know that it was the anger of the president that ultimately sent *Nautilus* and her crew across the top of the world on our historic mission.

NOVEMBER 3, 1957

The Soviet Union announced the launch of *Sputnik II*, just a month after their first astounding feat. Not only was this satellite six times the weight of the first, but it also carried a unique, warm-blooded passenger—a dog named Laika. Even though the former Moscow stray died a few hours after launch, the cachet of such a thing captivated the world's imagination even more, and it easily dominated its front pages.

EARLY NOVEMBER 1957

We had been back home only about a week when I was summoned to Washington to brief the staff of the chief of naval operations at the Pentagon. They wanted to hear about Strikeback and the subsequent exercises with the British navy, but they also had interest in our Arctic work. Or at least some of them did. My official scientific report on the ice probes had already been filed, so I assumed they had seen by now my recommendations for a deliberate but concentrated approach to further under-ice operations.

In a forty-five-minute meeting with about fifteen navy operations officers, I outlined what we had accomplished in both the NATO and Arctic missions. I also attempted to promote future voyages below the Arctic Ocean ice pack. I emphasized the scientific and strategic military value of further exploration in this unfamiliar and daunting region. I reminded them that from the fringes of the ice pack just east of Spitsbergen, it is only 420 miles to Murmansk, 1,200 miles to Leningrad, and 1,440 miles to Moscow. Nuclear submarines could cover the Russian northern commercial sea route that extends just off the coast of Siberia. We would be able to operate silently and safely in the big ocean that the Russians had long considered to be their own private domain.

To my dismay, few—if any (except for the submarine officers present)—of the group showed much interest in our under-ice accomplishments. They clearly did not see much point in continued submarine exploration in the Arctic.

The predominant reaction seemed to be, "What have we lost up there?"

There was little consolation in how impressed the naval leaders were with our exploits in Strikeback. On the contrary, what we did in the NATO drills only made them more adamant that *Nautilus* and her crew should be focusing mainly on involvement in antisubmarine warfare exercises akin to that one.

It was almost nightfall when I left the Pentagon. I confess that my mood was growing as dark as the Washington night sky. I was especially discouraged because I felt I had not persuaded to my way of thinking the people who could make or break our plans for further Arctic voyages.

I was not looking forward to the train ride back to New London, and it was taking me a long time to flag down a cab. It appeared that even the taxi drivers were conspiring to deny me a ride.

But then, on the steps of the Pentagon's Mall, in the midst of all the busy comings and goings, I spotted a friendly face.

And the man was headed my way, a smile on his face, his hand outstretched.

16

A CHANCE ENCOUNTER

had met Captain Peter Aurand, President Eisenhower's naval aide, six months earlier when he paid a courtesy call on Admiral Rickover while I was still training in nuclear propulsion. Now here he was, on the steps of the Pentagon, once again offering his hand.

"Where you headed?" he asked.

"Union Station, then back to New London."

"Look, I'm headed back into Washington. Let me give you a lift."

It was typical rush hour, and the knotted-up traffic gave Captain Aurand and me a chance to talk. As we crossed the Potomac, he casually asked me what *Nautilus* had been up to lately.

I told him about the NATO exercise from which we had just returned, and I also told him about our probe under the Arctic ice pack. Along the way, I highlighted the fact that we had come within about 180 miles of the North Pole, and that we had surveyed ice and sea bottom throughout 1,400 miles of under-ice travel.

Aurand was, of course, aware of both the exercise and the under-ice work, but he seemed especially interested in the details of the trip up north. As we eased past the Lincoln Memorial, he suddenly glanced over at me and asked me a question that took me by total surprise.

"Commander Anderson, could you postpone your trip home, stay overnight, and come to my office at the White House first thing in the morning?"

I did not hesitate in my answer.

"I will." He asked me not to mention our meeting to anyone.

Today as I look back on that chance encounter with Captain Aurand, I have to say that the hand of the Almighty must have been involved. That random meeting on the Pentagon steps on a dark, cold November afternoon would begin a remarkable chain of events that made history and at the same time changed my life and the lives of my entire crew.

The next morning I walked the few blocks from my hotel to the White House. I assumed there would be an involved routine at the gate, but the guard stated that Captain Aurand was expecting me. Another uniformed guard escorted me to the naval aide's office.

After a quick exchange of pleasantries, he got right to the point. He spun his chair around and pointed to a large world map that covered a good portion of his office wall. He lowered his voice to confidential level.

"Would you be able to take *Nautilus* all the way around the world in one continuous, submerged transit?" he asked.

As I sat there, staring at the map, considering a response to his question, two and two began to add up to four. On our ride in from the Pentagon the previous day, Aurand mentioned the president's anger at not being able to announce our record-breaking under-ice penetration. I knew it was the timing of the thing that had the president so upset. He was catching heat from the press and political foes after the Russians launched Sputnik, along with other things that were happening with his administration.

Captain Aurand's surprise question about a submerged circumnavigation of the world brought it full circle to me. The White House was interested in some kind of demonstration that would counter the perception that America's lead in science and engineering was lagging behind the Russians. And what better way than with our nuclear submarine, *Nautilus*, which was certainly capable of such a display?

I answered Aurand's question decisively.

"A submerged trip around the world would be feasible. It would be only a matter of time and fuel," I told him.

I did not share with him the thought that was in the back of my mind, that such a transit would be downright boring, no real challenge at all for *Nautilus*.

"There is another possibility," I told Aurand. "There is a more challenging and significant transit that perhaps could be made: an ocean-to-ocean voyage, under the ice, crossing the entire Arctic Ocean via the North Pole."

Aurand's face lighted up as he shifted his gaze to the very top of the huge chart. I could tell that he was intrigued by the idea of such a bold exploration.

As he considered the converging lines of longitude at the top of the world, I began to explain what I had in mind. If undertaken, the voyage should be from Pacific to Atlantic, which would enable us to get the most difficult part of the trip out of the way first. There were two reasons for this. First, it would eliminate the obvious risk of coming from the Atlantic side and not being able to exit on the shallow, uncharted Pacific side. Turning around and heading back would not be so bad per se, but given the risk of our navigational equipment being even slightly off, the farther we had to navigate up there, the greater the ultimate inaccuracy could become. I did not want to get lost beneath the ice again as we had on our first Arctic trip, and particularly in shallow water with its possible dead ends and "squeeze" problems.

Second, beginning the trip by entering from the Pacific side of the pack would minimize that very issue. In short, navigational readings would be the most accurate when we most needed them to be, through the shallow-water, deep-ice, narrow-channel hazards of the Bering Sea.

I also emphasized that the trip had far more important aims than merely reaching the North Pole. We could prove to the Russians our ability to work effectively beneath the ice. Every mile we operated only added to our knowledge of the region. That information would be invaluable as we made more strategic use of the Arctic. We would have finally shown the way for a sea-route Northwest Passage from one hemisphere to another, though hardly by any means that the early explorers could have anticipated or exploited.

I did not think I had to remind Captain Aurand of the boost the successful accomplishment of such a voyage would have on the country. After all, that was what he was looking for in the first place.

"Captain, let me work on this," Aurand said, still studying the very top of his wall chart. "But for right now, let's keep this between just the two of us. I'd rather you not even mention to anyone that you have been to the White House this morning."

I took his words seriously. He would not make such a request without good reason. I assured him that I would keep the visit confidential. I also told him I would further study the feasibility of such a polar crossing. We shook hands and I turned to leave. Just before I got to the door, he stopped me.

"Do you think you could come back down in a week or two and brief some of the White House staff on what you did in your first trip under the ice?"

I did not bother to consult my schedule. I replied with an enthusiastic, "Yes, sir."

I hailed a cab and rode toward Union Station, barely able to believe the turn of events and the possibilities that might lie ahead. My first thoughts were on what I needed to learn before I was completely confident such a mission should be attempted. Had I opened my mouth and bitten off more than I could chew?

There was another big question. What might I face in dealing in total secrecy with the White House, likely unable to tell even my bosses what we were doing? If one of them asked me about this trip to Washington, I would have to lie by omission, and that would be only the first of what could be plenty more.

Before I had even finished the trip to the train station, I concluded that such special risks and problems were well justified. I was already visualizing the charts I had tucked away in my safe aboard *Nautilus*.

I said nothing to anyone about my visit to the White House—not Bonny, not my bosses. Then two weeks later I was back in Washington. About fifteen members of the White House staff, including presidential counsel Sherman Adams and Press Secretary James Hagerty, were there for the briefing.

My presentation, in my opinion, was far from polished. Staff members were constantly entering the room, whispering messages to Mr. Adams and Mr. Hagerty and others. Despite the distractions I plowed ahead, trying to make my case, but I could see nothing in the faces of these busy, powerful men to indicate what they were thinking.

Afterward, Aurand motioned for me to follow him back to his office where for about an hour we again discussed possible future polar operations. We agreed that a journey from the Pacific to the Atlantic by the under-ice route would be more significant than a round-the-world, underwater "Magellan" cruise.

When I left his office, Captain Aurand once again cautioned me not to reveal the nature of our discussions to anyone, or even that I had been there. He also asked me to not discuss with anyone a possible transpolar trip.

When I got back to *Nautilus*, thoughts were churning in my mind. I could not discuss a trip with anyone. If the trip was approved, however, we had precious little time to prepare for it, to obtain better equipment than what we had on our first under-ice exploration. I soon decided that I needed the full efforts of my outstanding officers to get the ship and crew ready. I would not, however, divulge or permit the divulgence of the possible mission to the entire crew. That was not due to a lack of respect or confidence in them. It was merely a matter of numbers. The more people who know a secret, the more likely an inadvertent leak will occur. I knew that any leak would probably result in the operation either being called off or being dramatically changed.

Soon after I returned from the White House briefing, I called in my stateroom my trusted chief engineer, Paul Early, along with my new executive officer, a handsome, smart Mississippian named Frank Adams. I also called in my new navigator, Shepherd Jenks. (Former exec Bus Cobean had left *Nautilus* to become skipper of the conventional submarine, USS *Tiru* [SS-416] and later commanded three nuclear submarines—probably a record! Bill Lalor was now propulsion officer on *Nautilus*.) I gave Paul, Frank, and Shep a full account of what had happened in Washington.

They were thrilled about the possible adventure and eager to get going with preparations. Toward that end, I began a five-by-eight-inch secret notebook in which to address and check off essential preparatory steps. Each was to have access to this book. I advised them to keep track of progress by reviewing and updating it frequently. This proved to be a valuable tool as time went on. Since we took care to not note any information about specific missions, the secrecy of the possible polar crossing was not jeopardized.

I held a second meeting, this one with all the ship's officers. We met in the wardroom after regular work hours. I repeated my briefing, again emphasizing the secrecy aspect. Like the senior officers, the group was enthusiastic about the possible mission and just as eager to begin getting ready.

I knew I had to get a head start in case the White House authorized a transpolar trip. I put in a formal request letter to the Pentagon, suggesting that *Nautilus* should make a second—but undefined—polar probe in late summer of 1958. If the White House discussion resulted in a firm go-ahead, we would need additional navigation and sonar equipment. If my bosses at the Pentagon gave even tentative approval for another polar probe, then I had an excuse to begin locating and installing the improved under-ice gear.

The world was changing rapidly, giving some urgency to any plans we may have had for a spectacular voyage for *Nautilus*. The international Cold War was smoldering ominously. Sputnik's success and our own dismal space-launch failures had been demoralizing. The voices of those who were convinced the United States had already lost the technological race grew louder and louder.

If the president of the United States had a keen interest in having *Nautilus* do something compelling, then my crew and I would do all we could to make it a reality. I also knew there were a thousand and one things to do to get ready should such a mission be authorized. We would have to accomplish it all while maintaining absolute secrecy, even as we kept the day-to-day schedule and commitments of the most famous and visible vessel in the world.

That was our job by Thanksgiving 1957.

17

THE PRESIDENT AND THE ADMIRAL

E ven though I could not see clearly how every piece or
phase would come together, we were working on a proposed under-ice, ocean-to-ocean voyage across the top
of the world, and in the process we intended to go by way of
the North Pole. *Nautilus* would be the first ship of any kind to
reach the Pole. We would cover two thousand miles of mostly
uncharted waters, including four hundred miles in the Pacific-
side approaches with its shallow depths and ice of unknown
thickness.

Would there be a "squeeze" problem? Most likely. A high-
latitude navigation problem? Definitely. Was it even possible
for a submarine to make it through? Only one way to find out.

The interaction between the White House and the
Pentagon around that time is an intensely dramatic part of
this story. In almost every instance, my knowledge of the
details of what went on in Washington was assembled after
the fact and in some instances many years later. Two very large
stars had to come into alignment, and they were both heroes
of World War II: Dwight D. Eisenhower, president of the

United States, and Admiral Arleigh "31 Knot" Burke, Ike's chief of naval operations.

But there were other players in this scenario. Jim Hagerty was an early proponent of using *Nautilus* to exhibit some kind of technological demonstration to counter the media blitz over Sputnik. He was the longest-serving presidential press secretary in history and keenly aware of his job to make the administration look good. It was clear that he immediately saw our ship and its remarkable abilities as an asset to be used to take the focus off the Russians and their spectacular feat.

There was still consideration of doing the around-the-world submerged cruise too, a feat that would be successfully accomplished by Commander Edward Beach and USS *Triton* (SSRN-586) in 1960. Captain Aurand later said the reason for pursuing the North Pole transit first was because of the feeling that a submerged circumnavigation of the globe would certainly be a remarkable endurance run. But having *Nautilus* go from the Pacific to the Atlantic by way of the North Pole would hold high drama in addition to the great military value it would signify. That was the press secretary's angle. The polar trip would be more likely to get worldwide attention while improving the image of the United States in light of Sputnik.

President Eisenhower was enthusiastic about a transpolar mission from the beginning. Captain Aurand commented later, "The president bit on it like a fresh piece of fish!" But the commander in chief also wanted to hedge his bets. Aurand further reported, "I told the president about [the polar transit]. He thought it would be a great thing to do. He asked me to see if Admiral Burke thought it was all right. So I went over and saw him."

The admiral was receptive. Not everyone else was on board, though.

Aurand later said, "When he first learned about the proposal, Admiral Hyman Rickover was against it, and understandably so. Many submarine people thought it would risk *Nautilus*, which was unquestionably true."

Others in the chain of command felt that we simply were not ready to attempt such a thing. It would have been difficult for me to argue with them on that point! Fortunately I was in no position to have to do so. The ultimate decision rested with President Eisenhower and Admiral Burke.

Burke decided the trip was worth attempting. He gave the succinct three-word order, "Set it up!"

It was typical of the man. A native of Colorado, born far from the sea, he became a true hero during World War II when as commander of Destroyer Squadron 23 he often pushed his ships while pursuing targets to all the speed their boilers could manage, which earned him the nickname "31 Knot" Burke. He eventually served an unprecedented three terms as chief of naval operations.

After setting the mission in motion from the navy's perspective, Burke called on Captain Frank Walker, head of the Pro-Submarine Section, to provide him with an outstanding submarine officer of his choice, someone to work directly, exclusively, and in absolute secrecy with CNO on "a project of great national importance." Walker chose one of his own staff members, Commander Marmaduke G. "Duke" Bayne, for the job. In my opinion he could not have picked anyone better suited for the duty. Duke was an officer and a gentleman who possessed great ability, skill, and judgment, and he retired as a vice admiral.

At that point we had approval for a crucial and spectacular mission from the highest levels of both government and the military. We had a mandate to keep it secret. We had a point man within the Pentagon with whom we would work to get the job done.

We would soon have a name of my choosing for the mission: Operation Sunshine.

But the captain and crew who had to pull it off were back at home

Rear Admiral Arleigh Burke tours *Nautilus* in May 1955. The admiral later played a big role in the historic North Pole transit by *Nautilus*.

in Groton, still left almost completely in the dark, unaware of the intricate, thickening scenario that was playing out back in Washington.

DECEMBER 6, 1957

At 10:45 in the morning local time, at Cape Canaveral, Florida, the countdown reached "zero" for the launch of Vanguard TV–3. In the rocket's nose was a small satellite designed to study the space environment. Network television cameras carried the launch attempt live to the nation and much of the world.

The booster ignited right on schedule, sending down a plume of smoke and flame. But as the rocket began to rise, it seemed to freeze in midair, only four feet off its base. As the country—and the world—watched, the missile lost thrust and settled back down to the launch pad. Its fuel tanks ruptured and exploded spectacularly, destroying the rocket and severely damaging its launch pad.

The satellite was thrown clear by the explosion, landing a short distance away. Though damaged, its transmitter still gamely sent out a beacon signal on 108 megahertz.

The next week's issue of *Time* magazine carried the headline: "Sputnik prompts a frenzied failure."

On the same page, the publication reported on the ten thousand federalized Arkansas National Guardsmen still in place at Little Rock's Central High School.

LATE DECEMBER 1957

Six weeks passed with no word except for a brief telephone call from Captain Aurand after my second visit to the White House. He told me simply, "Things are generating." It was a concise but encouraging message, one that added to my confidence to aggressively move ahead in making preparations. Handling the secrecy, as directed by Aurand and, as I learned later, by President Eisenhower himself, was not an easy matter. Perhaps my most difficult challenge was not being able to tell my own superiors what was going on.

Nor was it easy not sharing the details of our proposed mission with the crew. I felt a strong sense of guilt in withholding details of what lay in store for them. I felt strongly that only volunteers should undertake the hazardous venture we were planning. To take at least a step in that direction, I arranged for my officers to survey their men quietly, one by one, pointing out to them that another under-ice mission of some sort might occur during the upcoming summer. They were to ask specifically if the crew member would prefer to take leave or be transferred to avoid such a mission.

Not a single shipmate so opted.

Duke Bayne, the point man within the Pentagon, and I would become friends as well as colleagues. He later shared with me some of the events that were taking place at the time.

His job was to support *Nautilus* and me as we prepared for what he termed "the momentous polar adventure." He was to provide me with research materials and arrange special surveillance trips, all to help make our transit a success. Duke was informed that he was to work directly with Admiral Burke, not through his chain of command, which was unusual, but necessary to maintain secrecy.

Shortly after receiving the assignment, Duke went with Admiral Burke to President Eisenhower's office to discuss the impending transit. At that meeting in the Oval Office were Duke, Admiral Burke, Captain Aurand, and the president. Duke characterized it as a "go, no go" meeting.

The discussion centered on the readiness of *Nautilus*—and her captain—to undertake the mission as defined. At one point the question of risk came up. Dangers such as the possibility of fire while *Nautilus* was under the ice and unable to surface were discussed briefly. They talked about the thickness of the ice cover and the proximity to the ocean floor, and whether or not it might prevent passage. The risks of severe illness on board the submarine and the serious navigation problems at the top of the world, where all directions were "south," also were mentioned.

They did not dwell on such possibilities and the meeting ended positively. The mission was a tentative "go." Before they left, though, the president did something very unusual and extremely telling.

He pointed a finger directly at each man present—an admiral, a top naval officer, and his own naval aide—and repeated the same words to each: "I want no one—I mean no one—to announce the success or failure of this attempt until I, personally, indicate where and when the announcement will be made."

"It was very dramatic to have the president repeat himself three times as he pointed his finger at each of us, one by one," Duke later told me. "As we left the Oval Office, none of us realized the extreme restraint President Eisenhower's directive of secrecy placed upon the planning for the *Nautilus* transit. We knew one thing, though. He was serious."

Even those normally on the list to be advised on national security matters were excluded. The morning operational briefings for top Pentagon officials did not include any mention of *Nautilus* in respect to the under-ice transit. Normal briefings by the chief of naval operations left out those details as well.

Duke was asked to assist in coming up with a cover story to describe *Nautilus* doing something else while she was actually plying Arctic waters, which involved devising some rational reason for the ship, an Atlantic Fleet vessel, to operate in the Pacific.

Eventually he concocted a cover story. It accounted for the installation of new sonar gear because *Nautilus* was to engage once again in "Arctic operations" along with the new nuclear vessel USS *Skate* (SSN-578) and the conventional submarine USS *Halfbeak* (SS-352) late in the summer of 1958.

Next, to explain why we were in the Pacific in the meantime, the cover story maintained that we were there for special operations unrelated to the Arctic Ocean or the North Pole. We were to leave the Atlantic Fleet, transiting the Panama Canal, and operate up the Pacific Coast. We were supposed to be working with the West Coast SOSUS (Sound Surveillance

System), a network designed to detect the approach of any ship—and especially submarines—to our territorial waters. The West Coast system was relatively new, and it made sense that it needed a test from our nuclear-powered submarine. The plans called for us to make visible stops in Balboa, Panama; San Diego; San Francisco; and Seattle.

We were then supposed to be leaving Seattle on June 7, returning to the East Coast by making a twenty-six-day submerged cruise back down to Panama. There was a reason for creating a long, submerged trip, independent of the earth's atmosphere. Without raising suspicion, *Nautilus* would be able to reject the usual requests for a ride from navy brass. We could simply claim that both space and oxygen were too limited to carry passengers on that prolonged trip.

We had to mollify another group—the many antisubmarine units that usually exercised with us when we were in their part of the ocean. Admiral Burke supplied that excuse. This would be a long trip, studying the problems encountered by the crew members of future long-range submerged cruises. This was quite plausible to anyone hearing it. The Polaris missile submarine program was at the forefront at the time and was a key initiative of Admiral Burke.

Once we were back on the East Coast, we would theoretically make final preparations and depart with *Skate* and *Halfbeak* for the Greenland area in late July or early August. Of course, our actual plan was to successfully complete the ocean-to-ocean transit via the North Pole well before the time when we were supposed to have shown up in New London.

Part of Duke Bayne's job was to keep fictitious track of where *Nautilus* might rationally be each day, then feed that data to Commander Harry Allendorfer, who briefed Pentagon officials each morning. *Nautilus* would be nowhere near the positions Bayne gave Allendorfer. She would hopefully be making her way to the Bering Strait and beyond.

"I suspect as time went on some suspicion developed that *Nautilus* was operating a bit differently than the official briefing indicated," Bayne later said. "However, I never saw any indication of such suspicion."

After the White House announced the results of our trip, Allendorfer realized that he had been deceived by Bayne in regard to what *Nautilus* was really up to. Stung by that realization, the next time he passed Bayne in the hallway, he very pointedly said, "You S.O.B.!"

There were three primary reasons for such a tight cloak of secrecy.

First, in transiting the Bering Strait, *Nautilus* would not pass very close at all to Soviet territorial limits. We would, however, be near her submarine operating areas during much of the voyage. There was always a risk some incident might occur. This is difficult for many to imagine today, but those were very tense times for Russia and the United States.

Second, all those involved felt it was wiser to make the journey first, if possible, and then announce it—after its successful completion. That would help avoid another public-relations fiasco similar to what had been happening with the U.S. rocket failures and the poor timing on the release of the news of our 1957 probe.

Finally, the president himself ordered the ultrasecrecy. He realized that by controlling the revelation of a successful mission of this magnitude, he could assure maximum worldwide attention. On the other hand, if there should be a failure, he alone could minimize the damage and take responsibility.

And that is how our voyage became the most top secret peacetime naval operation in history.

About a month after the dramatic meeting in the Oval Office with President Eisenhower, Admiral Burke decided to formally advise the president of the risks involved in an under-ice cruise. He directed Duke to compose a letter, to come from the CNO, addressed directly to the president. It would detail each of those risks. Duke could not allow someone from the secretarial pool to type the letter. He did that himself.

It pointed out the threat of fire, sickness, material breakdown, navigational difficulty, and the hostile environment of the Arctic. When Duke finished composing and typing the letter, Burke signed it and Duke hand-carried it over to Peter Aurand at the White House.

"Commander Bayne, please wait here," Aurand told him. Then he took the letter personally to President Eisenhower.

A few minutes later, Aurand stepped back into his office with the letter in his hand. He handed it back to Duke.

"The president does not wish to receive this letter," he pointedly reported.

When he got back to the Pentagon, Burke noted Eisenhower's refusal to receive it on the margin of the letter and Duke placed it in the top secret *Nautilus* file in his office.

Months later, when Duke was in the process of winding up the affair, deciding which of the mountain of files to hang on to and which ones to destroy, he asked Admiral Burke if he should keep the letter the president declined to receive.

"Have you any intention of writing a book?" the admiral pointedly asked Duke.

"No, sir."

"Neither have I. Burn the damn thing!" Burke ordered.

And that is exactly what Duke Bayne did.

18

POKER FACE

T he call from the Pentagon was mysterious and unsettling. It concerned an urgent matter "too sensitive to talk about over the telephone."

My orders were to report as soon as possible to the office of Rear Admiral Dan Daspit, head of the Submarine Warfare Branch. As I rode the overnight train down to Washington, I worried about what this sudden summons meant.

When I arrived at the Pentagon, I joined Frank Walker and Duke Bayne and we went straight to Admiral Daspit's office. Daspit had been a top-notch submarine skipper in World War II. He is generally credited with convincing the navy that there were serious problems with the torpedoes he and his fellow skippers were being asked to use against the Japanese. The changes in torpedo design that he helped bring about made a huge difference in the effectiveness of submarines for the balance of the war. Upon our arrival, the admiral asked his chief yeoman to leave the room and then he shut the door. As soon as we all sat down, he gazed directly at me and asked a startling question.

"Anderson, what do you think about taking the *Nautilus* from one ocean to another across the North Pole? Admiral Burke has talked with the president about such a cruise and the president has a keen interest."

Well, this put me in a decidedly awkward position. I struggled to maintain a poker face. Should I tell Admiral Daspit that I helped conceive the idea? If I did, the admiral might conclude that I had deliberately bypassed the usual chain of command. I quickly decided it would be best to continue following Captain Aurand's instructions not to mention I had been to the White House. I hated to deceive an admiral whom I greatly admired, but he was waiting for an answer to his question.

"Yes, it could probably be done," I finally told the admiral, which was the truth. "I'd like to see if Dr. Waldo Lyon concurs before I give you a final answer," I went on.

So Lyon was summoned to Washington. He agreed with my thoughts that the trip should be made from the Pacific to the Atlantic side, attempting from the outset what would be the toughest leg of the trip. If we could get through, we would go all the way. But if at any point we found the ice too dangerous, we would reevaluate our plans on the spot and not subject *Nautilus* and her crew to undue hazards.

Another question had arisen: should we make the trip in winter or summer? During winter the polar ice pack extends well down into and past the narrow, shallow Bering Strait. We would have to stay beneath the ice for a much longer time and for many more miles. In the warmer months, the pack pulls back, receding much closer to the edge of the deep Arctic Basin, so it seemed prudent to attempt our mission in the summer. Spending less time under the ice cover in those shallow waters reduced our risk of serious accident.

The departure date was tentatively set for June 8, 1958.

So why early June, when the argument could be made that later in the summer—mid to late August—would allow more time for the winter ice to melt and retreat northward? That date was not entirely of my choosing, but I did have some influence on the decision. First, the White House wanted to make the trip as soon as possible. From my perspective, I did not want them to lose their enthusiasm. Second, by leaving earlier in the summer, there was the possibility we could avoid the dangerous, deep-draft ice that inevitably piles up along the coast during the winter and then breaks loose and floats out to sea during the summer months.

In the back of my mind was the thought that if we were not able to make the transit on our initial probe, there would still be time for us to return to the Atlantic and make a run to the North Pole and back from that side. At least we would have something to show the president and something for him to show the Russians and the American people.

In many respects the North Pole was merely another point along our intended route across the top of the world. At no time was that axis point our primary objective. But the age-old perception of the North Pole as an almost-magical destination has captured the imaginations of explorers and adventurers for centuries. Now it seemed almost within reach, if not for *Nautilus,* then for one of our sister nuclear ships.

I felt most passionately that *Nautilus* and her crew had earned the right during our 1957 mission to get there first. I fully intended that *Nautilus* be the first.

JANUARY 31, 1958

Belated as it was, history was made when America's first successful satellite launch put *Explorer I* into earth orbit. A different rocket was used this time, one developed by German scientist Dr. Werner von Braun and his mostly German staff at Redstone Arsenal in Huntsville, Alabama.

FEBRUARY 5, 1958

A second try to launch a Vanguard rocket and its payload came after hurried repairs to the launch pad at Cape Canaveral. Following four scrubbed attempts during a period of several weeks, the launch vehicle was finally set loose as TV cameras focused on the rocket. After less than a minute of normal flight and at an altitude of only about 1,500 feet, something went wrong. The rocket broke up and plunged into the cold Atlantic Ocean.

MID-FEBRUARY 1958

We had named our secret mission "Operation Sunshine" with absolutely no sense of irony. I came up with the name based on the story told to me by one of our officers, Lieutenant Ken Carr. Though he was not there, he recalled reports that it was cloudy on the morning of the day *Nautilus* was launched, but just as First Lady Mamie Eisenhower broke the champagne bottle over the bow and *Nautilus* began her slide down the ways, the sun broke out brilliantly. Ken developed the ship's slogan from that event: "The sun always shines on the *Nautilus*." What could be better than naming what could be her most triumphant mission "Operation Sunshine"?

Although our trip was far from certain, I had gained enough information from Washington to believe it would become a reality. By the middle of February, we were ready to put in place serious preparations. The top priority was new equipment. The first piece of gear we requested was a complex device called an "inertial navigator," a sensitive and intricate electronic "brain." Engineers at North American Aviation designed it to guide their sophisticated Navaho missile, storing up information on speed, course, and other forces as it ran toward its target. Properly modified, it seemed to be able to furnish us with a continuous reading on our position, even under the ice at the North Pole. Thankfully the components of the system fit down a submarine hatch. The inertial navigator was installed aboard *Nautilus* in mid-April. When I first saw this intricate array of electronics with its connecting circuits "printed" in gold on circuit boards, I wondered if it could really work, but my skepticism would prove to be unwarranted. After the bugs were out, the inertial navigator—or N6A, as it was called—kept us precisely informed of our position at all times. I thought North American engineers Tom Curtis, chief of the autonavigator test section, and his assistant, George Bristow, working in secrecy under a severe time limit, did a magnificent job of adapting their gear to an unintended use. It was supposed to guide a missile, not a submarine. This apparatus would go on to help revolutionize the ancient art of nautical navigation.

While that work was going on, the Sperry gyroscope engineers installed an additional compass and specially modified the other gyro for high-latitude work. Their chief engineer, Fred Braddon, spent hours with Shepherd Jenks and me, discussing ways to overcome the unique navigational problems that we had experienced on our first trip north.

At about the same time, Waldo Lyon's men arrived with six new sonar instruments, one of which was built exclusively for *Nautilus*. It was more sensitive and efficient than those we used on our 1957 cruise and would enable us to make the first truly detailed scientific analysis of sea ice.

Electric Boat engineers and workmen swarmed about *Nautilus* twenty-four hours a day. We sensed they were curious about all the frenzied activity. If we were going to be coming back to Groton to get ready for another under-ice probe in late July or August, then why all the rushed preparations now? Couldn't we just install the new gear then?

My stock answer was that there would be very little time for such work during that cover-story stopover. We stressed we did not want to rush final preparations for the fictional Greenland ice cruise. We would also have a chance to test at sea in the meantime, gaining experience on the new gear.

It sounded perfectly plausible to me, even if it was a pack of lies.

The rumors persisted anyway. Rear Admiral Frederick "Fearless Freddy" Warder (so named for his World War II demeanor as a submarine skipper) at ComSubLant and I set up a conference with Electric Boat supervisors to talk about the work we would need to get done when we came back through on our fabricated July stopover. Captain A. C. Smith, the U.S. Navy supervisor of shipbuilding at Groton, followed through on my suggestion and published a totally fabricated schedule for Electric Boat employees, showing the arrival date of *Nautilus* in Panama on the return trip home. A great amount of time was spent arranging for the Electric Boat supervisors to fly to Panama to join the ship for the trip back to New London, all so the alleged work items would be expedited.

Admiral Warder even ordered a conference on the planned under-ice operations of *Nautilus*, *Skate*, and *Halfbeak*. Practically every Arctic expert was excited about what the submarine operations might be able to accomplish in the polar region, and they flocked to the conference to learn more about an operation we never planned to conduct.

By this time my officers were completely up-to-date on our true intentions. They helped prepare an imaginary operations schedule for *Nautilus* to enter the ice from east of Greenland. During the conference, we were careful to be exacting and particular about this point or that, hoping to hide even the slightest hint of our true plans. I doubt few fictional missions have had more elaborate preparations. Every one of us turned out to be a pretty good actor.

Some of the *Nautilus* crewmen were far less gullible. As we loaded on-board cold-weather clothing and antifreeze for the fresh-water system of the auxiliary diesel engine, one of the chiefs squinted suspiciously and asked, "Now, if we are headed for a spring trip to the Pacific, why do we need all this on board now? We could pick them up when we come back through."

We repeated our usual answer with as straight a face as we could muster: "Let's do as much as we can now so we don't have to rush in July."

I did not like misleading my shipmates, but in this instance the use of a cover story was almost certainly in their best interests. We continued to attract a great deal of media attention. A mere hint that we were preparing for a special mission would have generated a lot of press speculation. I had a strong feeling that any leak, or even a good guess in some newspaper column, would be all it took for President Eisenhower to call off the whole thing.

One of our real challenges was obtaining charts and publications that would give us what little was known about the area from Alaska through the Arctic Ocean and back into the Atlantic, and on the seas between

Iceland and Portland, England, our eventual destination. We knew it would arouse suspicion in the Hydrographic Office if we put in a routine request for these items. Commander Bayne handled this one. He simply requested, in the CNO's name, charts for the entire Arctic area, suggesting a general interest in the top of the globe.

We discovered in the process that there were still no accurate nautical charts of the Arctic Basin available. There were only aircraft navigation charts that we had used the year before and a published Russian chart showing some soundings, which proved to be highly inaccurate. At our request, Duke asked the Hydrographic Office to prepare a special set.

The HO maintained that they could not possibly be ready by July. Bayne fired back that he needed them "for study" in May and that Admiral Burke wanted them done immediately. These charts—many of which contained soundings we had made on our cruise the previous summer—ultimately caught up with *Nautilus* in San Francisco, just before we left for Seattle, which was to be our final staging point. Shep Jenks kept them locked in a safe. Whenever he wanted to study them, he slipped into my stateroom and bolted the door behind him.

There was no sanctuary at home. Bonny mentioned that I certainly seemed a lot busier lately. Almost every week I was on the train, heading off to Washington. Even when I was home, the telephone got me out of bed in the middle of the night. When I answered, I used an odd double-talk that must have driven Bonny crazy. Truth is, I was gone much more than usual while my ship was in home port. Even when I was home, I spent most of my time in the library, the door shut, charts and books spread everywhere. I was rarely at the dinner table or outside throwing the ball or roughhousing with the boys.

I could sense that Bonny suspected that our next operation was more involved than I was letting on. She did not try to pull it out of me. But she hinted that she knew we were going to do more than the year before. She also let me know that she feared we were about to do something dangerous.

Springtime in Mystic was a wonderful time. Every young person in town seemed to turn his or her attention to getting out on the river and harbor, exploring the many beautiful inlets of Block Island Sound.

I had promised my son Mike that I would get him a boat. We had looked together some, but I had little time away from the preparations for the trip to the West Coast and for our secret mission. We had trouble finding a vessel that was big enough and stable enough for him to operate safely. It also had to fit my limited budget. One dealer was pushing a particular kit, claiming it was sturdy and easy to put together. And the cost was not totally out of reach. I considered myself something of a woodcrafter after my days as a kid at the lumberyard, so the easy-to-assemble boat kit seemed to be an economical answer to Mike's dreams.

Mike was thrilled as we unpacked the parts of the boat and began trying to match them up and put them together. It proved to be a much bigger job than I had anticipated and much more challenging than the dealer had claimed. Somehow I made one critical mistake in the assembly, which made each subsequent step much more difficult. I ended up having to shave and cut and generally redo much of the wood to make it work. That meant many nights working until one or two in the morning after a stressful day at the ship, but I was determined to finish Mike's boat before I had to leave again.

On the night before *Nautilus* was scheduled to depart, I was still trying to make the last of the ill-fitting pieces of the boat go together. Mike finally gave up and went to bed, but I worked on.

Maybe there was some guilt involved. When they were younger, the boys hardly seemed to be bothered by my long absences. I suppose they assumed all dads did the same thing. Many of their friends were the kids of sailors too. Besides, I could identify with his love for the water, for sailing away on his own boat, leaving the entanglements of land behind him.

A few hours before dawn, I finally got Mike's boat together to my satisfaction. After I grabbed an hour or two of sleep, Mike and I hauled the boat down to the water in a borrowed trailer. As the warm sun rose on Mystic, I watched my boy happily pull away from the shore at almost full throttle, wearing his life jacket as we had agreed, looking back, smiling, waving at me.

As Bonny drove me down to *Nautilus* that morning, I hoped the simple, successful launch of a small boat would prove to be a good sign for the historic voyage that my crew and I were about to attempt.

19

LOCATING LEAKS AND FIGHTING FIRES

APRIL AND MAY 1958

As we steamed toward Panama, everything seemed to be going well. After months of secret planning, things had finally come together, and the mission was under way. My spirits were high, and the crew was looking forward to a brief stopover in Panama.

The reactor itself was working perfectly, but then a series of routine checks on the chemical balance of the water in the main condenser indicated something very worrisome was going on. The chloride level in a system of otherwise very pure water was slowly but surely rising. This meant one thing: salt water was leaking into the closed-loop steam system. We began to monitor the situation continuously.

Leaks on submarines are common. Usually they are no bigger than a human hair and are manageable. This situation was different. Salt water was leaking from one or more places in thousands of feet of piping and tubes that were integral to the steam condenser. Salt-water contamination of the pure water in the steam system could cause a breakdown of the propulsion machinery. As salt water blends with the pure water and runs through the stainless-steel steam generator over and over, corrosion and stress cracking surely follow.

I was not worried about that happening immediately. That process would take time, perhaps many months of continuous operation. However, if the leak persisted or got worse, the chloride levels would rise; and if that happened rapidly enough, safe limits of operation as specified in our operating procedures would be exceeded before we could complete our voyage.

Paul Early and Stu Nelson began a systematic inspection, examining every possible leak point they could get to. Unfortunately, many of the thousands of places a leak could occur were impossible to reach for inspection while at sea. I did not want to even contemplate returning to New London for repairs. We would have to resolve the salt-water leak in the next few weeks.

Coincident to the chloride levels rising, unexplained fumes circulating throughout the ship seemed to grow worse. We noted not far out of home port that the air inside *Nautilus* was not as pure as we liked to keep it. At first we thought it might be paint fumes since a great many of the spaces and equipment below decks had been repainted while we were in New London. Paint dries and the fumes diminish, but ours seemed to only get worse and were concentrated in certain compartments. By the time we arrived at Balboa, Panama, the men who stood watch in the engine and maneuvering rooms were experiencing discomfort, their eyes red and watery, and were subject to coughing fits.

I had visions of a tiny leak or a foul odor preventing us from beginning our great adventure. As the solutions to the problems defied us, we adopted the old method of waiting for the troublesome signs to get bad enough that we could finally locate and fix them.

The transit through the Panama Canal, the fourth of my experience and the second as skipper of *Nautilus*, went smoothly. It occurred to me that we might soon show the world another way—and for many a more direct route—from Pacific to Atlantic.

MAY 4, 1958

We left Panama and after a brief run on the surface reached deep water and submerged. Almost instantly the engineers noticed that the smelly fumes had increased considerably. Soon their eyes began to water again. It was clear now that this problem had nothing to do with new paint.

That afternoon Lieutenant Bill Lalor climbed down into the machinery spaces below the main deck to inspect yet another small seawater leak, this one in a propeller shaft. When he started back forward, he saw something that stopped him cold. There was smoke drifting up from the area near the port main turbine.

"It was about as much as you'd expect to see from a man smoking a cigar," Lalor recalled.

Aboard a submarine, crew members fear fire more than flood or an explosion. And where there is smoke—even a relatively small amount—there is fire.

Steve White and Stu Nelson were standing watch at the time in the maneuvering room where the controls for the reactor and the steam system were located. Lalor quickly reported to them that he had seen smoke.

At first they thought it might be oil dripping through a connection on one of the "hot lines" in the steam system. This would have been rather unusual because we ran numerous checks on our equipment and always kept it clean and well maintained. Nevertheless, Nelson passed the word to one of the enlisted engineers to go below, check for that condition, and report back.

Before the engineer could get down the ladder, the situation turned much uglier.

Thick, black smoke suddenly began pouring into the upper level of the engine room. The men on watch there could not see a thing and were struggling to breathe.

Steve White called the control room, reporting, "We've got a lot of smoke back here. People are having trouble seeing."

Word passed throughout *Nautilus*: "Fire in the engine room!"

That urgent message set into motion a quick series of events in which each man performed precisely as he was trained to do. I was racing aft before the announcement was even finished. So were Bill Lalor and Paul Early and several other sailors who had been in the crew's mess.

"I could not believe what I saw," Lalor recalled. "In only the few minutes since I left the compartment, the whole space was clouded with thick, black smoke. The men on watch back there were crying, coughing, and very much concerned."

Well, they should be! By the time I got to the engine room, the smoke made it almost impossible to see or to breathe without coughing. Most of the men in the compartment had covered their mouths and noses with dampened towels and others had pulled on goggles.

The first thing to do was try to locate the source of the smoke. Ernest Holland and Bill McNally pulled on two of the special smoke masks we carried and went down the ladder to the machinery spaces below. There were only two other masks available. The men had to feel their way through the smoke while trying not to touch the dangerously hot lines of the steam propulsion equipment. Several other men followed, carrying CO_2 fire extinguishers.

Meanwhile I ordered the port shaft stopped and its steam turbine cooled down to try to keep the men in the compartment below from being burned. While all this was going on, we brought the ship to snorkel depth and were already trying to vent the smoke out with the snorkel. We were having little success.

It was clearly a serious situation. We had no choice but to take *Nautilus* to the surface, and I so ordered. Once there, we could open the engine room hatch—if seas were not too rough—and let more of the smoke escape.

Fortunately the ocean was calm and no water spilled down the hatch when we popped it open. None of us had time at that moment to ponder what might have happened if we had been under the ice when the smoke filled the engine room—if we had not had the option to surface to a calm sea where we could open the hatch.

Meanwhile, Holland and McNally were working their way, mostly on hands and knees, through the maze of pipes, valves, and machinery below, trying to see where the smoke was coming from. They had to be careful not to grab something hot, but they could hardly see where their hands were gripping in the thick smoke.

Then they found the fire.

The lagging—or insulation—around the port high-pressure turbine had apparently spent years wicking up oil from small leaks. We decided later that the high-speed running we did since leaving Balboa had finally caused the insulation to heat up enough to catch fire. Using knives and pliers, Holland and McNally began pulling the smoldering insulation away from the turbine housing. When the first chunk came loose and air hit the smoking lagging, flames three to four feet high belched outward, right toward the two men. The crewmen behind them quickly doused the flames with liquid foam, carefully avoiding drenching their shipmates with the CO_2. The foam instantly froze anything with which it came into contact. It could have seriously injured Holland and McNally.

"The men were fighting the fire valiantly," Paul Early noted later. "They crawled into holes until all you saw was their feet, ripping at the lagging with the metal rods they had so we could get near the source of the flames."

Most of those fighting the fire were coughing and gagging by then. The four masks were passed from one man to another. No one was able to stay in the compartment for more than a few minutes. Some were nauseated and weak from the heat and smoke. One of the interior electricians, Imon Pilcher, staggered topside and promptly collapsed on the deck. He reported that he had no memory of climbing the ladder or reaching topside.

After several minutes of flailing away through the smoke, two of the men found the controls for the auxiliary diesel engine and started it up. This immediately made a difference in the thickness of the smoke as it drew fresh air in from outside and pumped out the bad air. I told Dutch Larch and Arthur Callahan to stay up on deck and make sure none of the stricken men fell overboard.

Every few minutes or so, more men rushed in to relieve their fellow crew members. The teamwork was perfect considering that it was a miserable and very dangerous job.

Before long the bilges—the areas in the hull where stray seawater accumulates—were stuffed with ugly, charred insulation and messy white foam from the CO_2 extinguishers. About four hours after the source of the smoke was located, the last of the flaming lagging was finally pulled away, doused, and crammed into the bilges.

The fire was out. Disaster had been averted.

Many crewmen performed bravely that day to make sure the fire did not become more serious than it already was. I have named a few of them here and will also mention John Kurrus and Richard Bearden, my two stainless-steel welders responsible for the miracle on the periscope repair during our first Arctic mission.

After things settled down, I reviewed the situation in my mind. I could still smell the foul smoke that seemed to permeate the ship. I faced the facts about what might have happened if the fire had occurred while we were beneath compact ice and unable to surface. *Nautilus* and her crew could have been lost.

I decided that we would have to devote more attention to fire hazards and devise a way to protect the crew from suffocation in case a fire like the one we had just quelled broke out while we were under the pack—or even in open ocean if conditions were so rough we could not open deck hatches to fight the smoke and blazes. We would need some kind of special emergency breathing apparatus and a source of pure air for the crew.

Also, we had to conduct a thorough inspection to make sure there were no other sources of potential fire. We had to replace the affected lagging with something less vulnerable to oil leaks and fire.

Accomplishing these essential things would take time. Time to acquire the equipment and supplies, do the work, and properly test it, but also to wind our way through the bureaucratic maze any such modifications on our vessel inevitably required. Time was not something with which we were abundantly blessed.

As soon as we had submerged again and things were pretty much back to normal, I asked Paul to join me for a cup of coffee. Not only was he the chief engineer of *Nautilus*, but he was the most can-do engineer with whom I have ever worked.

Before we began our chat, he knew instinctively what was on my mind. I would never take *Nautilus* back beneath the ice if we could not take steps to provide an emergency breathing system to sustain the fire-fighting crew in case another fire broke out. He went right to work on the problem and soon came up with an ingenious idea. Without getting too technical, Paul and Lieutenant Donald Fears figured out a way to utilize a reserve air system already in place throughout the ship. They designed a mask with a hose that could easily be connected and disconnected to the reserve air supply. Eventually, enough masks and hoses could be assembled that would allow each person on board to move throughout the ship, if necessary, by disconnecting at one location and reconnecting at the next. They estimated a minimum system could be in place at Mare Island relatively quickly that would immediately provide protection for the watch standers in the reactor compartment, the engine room, and the control room. Hoses up to twenty-five feet in length would be installed in the engine room so that the most critical watch standers could remain on station in a smoke-filled compartment until the ship could find a polynya in the ice cover in which to surface.

I was satisfied. Provided the minimal system was in place, I felt we could proceed under the ice as planned.

In addition to the air-breathing system, we put into action a fire-prevention program that was much more involved than anything ever carried out aboard a submarine. The stringent fire-prevention measures we employed would eventually be incorporated on all nuclear submarines and in the engineering spaces of nuclear-powered surface ships.

Meanwhile, we continued to steam north for the West Coast ports that we were scheduled to visit, our attention focused on San Francisco

Bay, where Mare Island Naval Shipyard was located. Mare Island did a vast amount of submarine work and was highly qualified to make the quick installation we needed on the breathing system, deal with the renewal of lagging in the engine room, and fix that elusive salt-water leak in the port condenser. I drafted a series of messages to Washington and elsewhere to arrange for this work to be done there.

We had scheduled visits to other ports, including San Diego and Long Beach in Southern California; Everett, Washington, in Puget Sound; and finally, the proposed staging area and departure point for our polar trip, Seattle.

There was also unfinished business in that the orders in the safe in my stateroom covered our visit to the West Coast, but so far there was not a written word authorizing and directing our journey to and across the Arctic Ocean. This caused me some apprehension. Maybe opposition had once again arisen. Or worse—perhaps the whole thing had been called off.

Once we docked in San Diego, I got on the telephone with Duke at the Pentagon and asked in guarded words, "Are things still on track?" As Admiral Burke's point man for the mission, he would certainly know.

"I can tell you a relevant operation order is in progress," he said, hedging his words, saying just enough to let me know we were still on. I felt better, but I would not be happy until the orders were in writing and in my possession.

Also, we were supposed to receive our charts of the Arctic Basin region by top secret mail. However, Duke did not want to trust the ultrasecret Operation Sunshine orders to this usually secure means of communication. Not with the president of the United States emphasizing how we must maintain complete secrecy. So Waldo Lyon, who was in Washington on a last-minute trip, carried the orders and charts back with him and hand-delivered them to me in the airport lounge in San Diego.

Back in the privacy of my stateroom, I was able to open at last the package containing the top secret orders. The inner envelope was marked "Eyes Only of Commanding Officer." The operation order itself was labeled "CNO OpOrd 0001-58," indicating it was top secret and the first such order issued directly by the chief of naval operations in the year 1958.

The first words troubled me. They began, "If directed . . ." and then went on to spell out our permission to proceed across the top of the world. I read the rest, but my eyes kept going back to those tentative first two words in the document.

The orders also specifically stated that I was to make contact with Admiral Daspit in Washington on Sunday, June 8. At that time, I would give a report on the material status of *Nautilus* and her state of readiness for the mission. The CNO obviously wanted to hold back on a final go-ahead for the cruise until the Pentagon and the White House confirmed that plans had not changed. They also wanted to get my verification that we were ready to go.

It was quite clear to me that the go-ahead for execution of Operation Sunshine was not a foregone conclusion or certainty on anyone's part. I understood that, particularly given what I had been going through with the leaks and breakout of fire on board. Not to mention the world's political situation being able to change. Like it or not, I would have to take it one day at a time.

As we worked our way up the West Coast, we received confirmation that Mare Island Naval Shipyard was standing ready to help with installation of the new breathing system. Thanks to Paul Early and his engineers, along with the workmen and managers at Mare Island, the emergency breathing equipment was fabricated and installed within our time limitations. In the ordinary course of things, it could take years to get such a system approved and operational. As it happened, by planning and purchasing ahead, Mare Island crews plus *Nautilus* personnel were able to install and get our minimal system working in less than a week, which is amazing. Let me add that this system, as developed and designed by Early and Fears, and with essentially no modifications, is now installed in every nuclear submarine, and in the reactor and engineering compartments of all the nuclear aircraft carriers. To this day, I am impressed and full of gratitude to these two excellent engineers and their wonderful, ingenious system.

Operation Sunshine was staying alive. Our serious problems were being resolved, one by one. Everything, that is, except the tiny, very persistent salt-water leak. It was difficult to imagine that such a minor leak could threaten our entire mission. I was becoming increasingly concerned, not so much because this problem might cause any real danger while we were beneath the ice, but that someone in Washington might consider the risk a valid reason to cancel the trip.

Mare Island engineers reinspected the affected machinery inch by inch. No one could locate the leak. They wanted to keep looking, but I knew the longer we stayed there, the greater the possibility that this issue could be the snag that held us back. I had confidence in the ship. We were still within operating limits. I knew that we could still make it through the Pole and out the other side of the ice, but the leak might give those who were not in favor of our trip an excuse to delay it.

I told the local naval commander that we would be taking *Nautilus* to sea the following morning and steering a course for Puget Sound. Of course, I could not give him even a hint of why it was so necessary that we move on without fixing the leak. When we left the navy yard the next day, several of the yard engineers who had worked so hard to find the leak were perplexed. They showed a great deal of resentment toward Paul Early and me, but there was no way we could tell them not to take it personally, that we had no choice but to sail out beneath the Golden Gate Bridge and head north.

We eased out of San Francisco Bay and set a submerged course for Puget Sound. On the way out, I looked for signs that might predict a successful voyage, but no fair winds blew upon us as we steamed north—still leaking—and with another tragic event yet to come.

"EXECUTE OPERATION SUNSHINE"

We were just entering Puget Sound. John Kurrus was on his way forward to refill his coffee cup when he noticed that one of his shipmates, Torpedoman Theodore "Ski" Szarzynski, a sailor from Chicago, was in obvious distress.

"He was lying down on a bench in the crew's mess," Kurrus related. "He was having trouble catching his breath. Then he just stopped breathing."

It was determined later that Szarzynski had a cerebral hemorrhage and died almost instantly. "'Ski' was like a recruiting poster," Kurrus said. He was a career sailor who boarded *Nautilus* after our '57 ice exploration. His shipmates remember him as a former diver who wanted to learn all he could on board *Nautilus*, sometimes volunteering to stand watch in the sonar room. I remember him as a sharp-looking sailor who always wore his uniform with great pride.

His sudden, unexpected death threw a pall over the entire ship.

We had been scheduled to take a large group to sea for a one-day demonstration cruise the next day. Because of the loss, as well as the physical and emotional exhaustion it brought on, I asked the local naval commander if he would mind canceling the trip. The man seemed offended that I would even ask. I reluctantly agreed to go forward as scheduled. We stopped first at Port Townsend, Washington, to transfer Torpedoman Szarzynski's body to an ambulance sent by the Bremerton Naval Hospital. As it evolved, Joe Degnan, who was from the same hometown of Chicago, accompanied Szarzynski's body.

In fifteen years of service in eight submarines, including eleven combat patrols in World War II, I had never personally experienced a single serious injury or death of a crew member. I was unprepared for the sudden loss of Szarzynski. Thankfully, Frank Adams handled the numerous details, including arranging for Joe to accompany the body back to Illinois and attend the funeral.

The entire crew and I are grateful to Joe for carrying out a difficult assignment for which there is no training.

Still, there was much ahead of us, and I felt the sooner we returned to normal operation and interaction, the better. Even with all that was going on, I still worried about the leak in the condenser system. We had not stopped it yet, though I downplayed the problem in messages sent to Washington. Frankly, I wrote them in as reassuring a manner as honesty permitted.

Then I got an idea. I do not know where the memory came from, but somehow I recalled a casual conversation I had with my father-in-law, Dr. Gastao Etzel. He was a research chemist with DuPont in Delaware, and something he said that day stuck in my mind, only now coming forward. It was a crazy solution, but it might just work, I told myself.

I was not sure how to present an idea to Early that I was not sure of myself, but I called him to my stateroom anyway.

"Paul, when we get to Everett, I want you to send some of your men around town to some gas stations," I told him, ignoring the quizzical look on his face. "Have each man buy several cans of that stuff you pour into automobile radiators to stop leaks."

Early tried to suppress a smile. He could not tell if I was serious or not.

"I'm not kidding, Paul," I told him. "We will do no harm to the steam generator system by pouring radiator block into the seawater pipes. If that type of sealant will work on radiators, it may just work on our condenser system. So, let's accumulate a good supply. It probably comes in pints or quarts, and we'll need a lot of it. Tell your men not to say anything about being from *Nautilus*—or any submarine. No dolphins for sure. They should wear civilian clothes. We have to keep this strictly undercover.

"You know what to do," I continued. "And get enough so we will have some extra for the trip—just in case it works."

Early selected Chief Stuart Nelson to spearhead the acquisition of a product called Bar's Leaks. He and five of his shipmates were off on their odd shopping spree and eventually returned with dozens of containers of the stuff.

Think about it. Here was a multimillion-dollar nuclear-powered submarine, the most advanced ship in the history of the world, and we were using $1.80 cans of automobile radiator leak block to fix it. Looking back, it seems humorous, but at that time it was serious business. Incredibly, it seemed to do the trick. The leak—wherever it was—stopped. The problem would never arise again.

When we arrived in Seattle, I decided to begin a plan I had been mulling over for the entire trip from New London. I wanted to take a last-minute look at the ice near the Bering Strait and along the coast of Alaska on into the Chukchi Sea. We would have to do such a flight undercover. Only minutes after tying off our lines at Seattle, and while wearing civilian clothes, I slipped past the welcoming committee and made my way over the gangway. Waldo was already waiting for me at the airport. We had reservations on a commercial airliner scheduled to leave only minutes later, bound for Alaska.

I was now "Charles A. Henderson," a civilian technician working with Dr. Lyon's department down in San Diego. I had fake identification papers to prove it. It was not unusual for Waldo to be in Alaska, looking at the ice conditions, so he used his real name.

"I thought things like this only happened in thriller novels," Waldo told me as we climbed the steps up to the plane's doorway. But we had orders from the commander in chief, President Eisenhower, who made it clear that we would do whatever it took to keep our mission a secret.

We left the ground in Seattle and quickly soared out over the rugged coastline of British Columbia, headed for Fairbanks. After an overnight stop there, we flew on to Nome where we blended in with a group of tourists, seeing the city from a bus, eating reindeer steak. Later we flew farther northward to a tiny village called Kotzebue. Lyon had arranged for a charter plane, a single-engine Cessna 180, flown by a colorful bush pilot named Ernie Cairns. He was under the impression that we were simply two scientists gathering data for a scientific presentation.

I was a bit concerned when my first glimpse of Cairns was of him waist-deep in the engine compartment of his plane.

"She's fine," he assured us. "I checked her out a few minutes ago. I just need to work on this thing here a little bit before we take off."

There was no doubt that aircraft was in need of work, and not just in the engine area. Waldo and I paced back and forth, trying not to show our concern, but soon we were winging our way toward the Bering Strait, the sixty-mile-wide passageway between the Russian mainland in Asia and Cape Prince of Wales, Alaska. It is the western tip of North America. At that time Alaska was six months shy of becoming our forty-ninth state.

We zoomed disconcertingly low over this bleak region, the plane's engine hiccupping occasionally. At times we were fifty miles from land. I tried to concentrate on collecting information. We noted many stretches of open water along our prospective route once we cleared the Bering Strait and entered the Chukchi Sea, which was an encouraging sign. We also noted, though, some hillocks amid the floe where patches of ice had collided, driving up sharp-featured obstructions. We knew that those spikes of ice likely extended downward as well. Waldo and I agreed that conditions were not necessarily ideal, but it was probably worth trying the cruise.

As we were nearing the end of the flight, Cairns casually mentioned that we would soon run short of fuel if we did not put the airplane down and locate some more. He turned the nose of his airplane toward where he was convinced there was a small Inuit village. He said he seemed to remember that there was a cache of gasoline left there by bush pilots, just in case somebody might need it. The sputtering of the engine and the bouncing of the needle against its peg on the instrument panel confirmed that we needed it now.

He managed to set us down on a sandy beach without flipping us over nose first. By the time we jolted to a stop, a group of Indians appeared out of the thick woods. Cairns spoke with them, and they quickly fetched several five-gallon cans of fuel, enough to get us back to where we had taken off. As Cairns revved the engines and tried to get the plane back to what passed for a runway, the aircraft would not budge. The fuel had made us heavy enough that we sank axle-deep in the wet, muddy sand. Our pilot prevailed on the friendly villagers to give us a push, which they kindly did. We finally got rolling. As we made it airborne, we managed to clear a tree trunk at the end of the runway by what had to be only inches.

Years later I received a letter from another Alaskan bush pilot.

"You probably took some risks on that trip under the North Pole," he wrote. "But those were nothing like the risks you took flying with Ernie Cairns, I am sorry to say." He added that many of his bush-pilot friends predicted that Cairns would one day take his final, fatal risk; and sadly, he did. He died in a crash.

Luckily, we made it back, landing on a rough airstrip at Point Barrow. There we said our good-byes to Ernie Cairns, paid his bill in cash, and took the "airport limousine" (a covered truck that could easily have been in service during World War I) to the hotel, a Quonset-hut-type structure, at one o'clock in the morning. I registered as Charles Henderson and went straight to my room to get some rest. Restful sleep never came. I had too many things on my mind. The fact that it was still bright daylight outside did not help.

Frank Adams met me as I came aboard *Nautilus*. He told me that Admiral Rickover would be making a surprise visit to the ship in about an hour. I got along with Rickover as well as anybody did. Since leaving NRB, Rickover occasionally stayed with Bonny and me at our home in Mystic when he made a trip to the New London sub base or Electric Boat. But I also knew how he felt about risking *Nautilus* to explore under the Arctic ice. I did not relish a surprise visit, especially today.

A quick tour of the engineering spaces with Paul Early confirmed that Chief Stu Nelson had already cleared away any evidence of the radiator leak treatment. There was no point in complicating Admiral Rickover's visit by telling him about our practical solution to the salt-water leak.

Midafternoon the admiral crossed the gangway in his usual quick-stepping manner. He proceeded to do a two-hour inspection of the nuclear propulsion plant. He was friendly but all business, as was his nature. Along the way he fired rapid questions at Paul Early and his engineers, preferring such direct give-and-take with the men who did the work rather than asking me as the skipper to get the answers for him.

Eventually he came forward and joined me in my stateroom. I did not know what to expect. I had not discussed our proposed operation with him. I assumed, however, that the Pentagon, the White House, or both had made him aware of the details by then. The polar trip did not come up at all in our cordial conversation.

Then just before he rose to leave, he did a most unusual thing. Without comment, Rickover handed me a small scrap of paper he retrieved from his suit pocket. He had written on it the simple phrase: "If necessary to reduce primary system leakage, it is satisfactory to the Bureau of Ships to reduce the pressure from 1,600 p.s.i. [pounds per square inch] to 1,400 p.s.i." He signed it "H. G. Rickover."

At first I was puzzled, but then once he was gone, it dawned on me what he was doing. This was the admiral's way of contributing a final option in support of the success and safety of our mission north. His note meant that if a problem developed in the reactor main coolant loop, such as a water leak, it was all right to bring about a limited drop in operating pressure. It confirmed there was adequate leeway in the system design to permit a safe reduction. Rather than coming right out and saying, "You have my blessing, Anderson," or wishing me good luck beneath the ice, he did the same thing in his own inimitable way.

I found that action on Rickover's part very inspiring, and to this day I deeply appreciate it.

Shortly afterward, I learned about another unexpected passenger who had come aboard *Nautilus*. This one could complicate things too. He was navy psychiatrist Captain Jack Kinsey, attached to the Washington group that was preparing the Fleet Ballistic Missile (FBM) program. Since the FBM submarines were expected to spend very long periods at sea, and most of it submerged, there was great interest in how their crews would react to such deployments. Kinsey happened to be qualified in submarines, and our cover mission—the long, submerged endurance run to the south— had attracted him. Of course, we were not headed that direction or on that mission at all, but we could not tell Kinsey that when he boarded.

We had no option but to smile and welcome him aboard, whatever our destination. Once we were under way and I could tell the psychiatrist where we were actually headed, I would have a real quandary. What if he decided he wanted no part of it? Did I insist he remain aboard for the entire transit for security reasons, or did I return to the dock and send him ashore?

I admit I was irritated at the navy bureaucracy for sending him to us without even checking to see if we had a spare bunk for him. If they had, I would have told them to wait for another opportunity, though that might also have raised the curiosity of those back in fleet headquarters, wondering what mission *Nautilus* was on that was so sensitive that it would preclude having the doctor aboard.

We had had several other well-meaning psychiatrists aboard *Nautilus* in the past. *Nautilus* sailors found great humor in the fact that these psychiatrists came aboard to study "stress." In the crew's opinion, ours was the most comfortable submarine yet built, the world's best way to travel. A ride aboard was, to their way of thinking, typically as stressful as lying in a hammock on a sunny summer day!

So with a good supply of automobile radiator leak treatment stashed away and with Captain Kinsey watching our every move, looking for signs of stress, we were almost ready to get under way for our assault on the Arctic.

Then came the time that I was to call Admiral Daspit at his home. I had to report on the state of our ship and get the final approval, as it would come down from Admiral Burke to proceed with Operation Sunshine or not. The butterflies in my stomach were not flying in formation. This call would remove the final uncertainty about the execution of our mission.

To make sure I would not be disturbed, I bolted the door before I dialed the telephone—the one connected to outside lines—from my desk. To my great relief, Daspit answered on the third ring. I could hear his strong, friendly voice loud and clear. I wasted no time.

"Admiral, we are ready to go," I told him confidently.

"Execute Operation Sunshine," he responded immediately.

"Thank you, sir. Thank you very much."

His terse command charged me like a bolt of electricity. When I hung up, I was no longer tired at all. After months of uncertainty, we received a definite order. I quickly ran the list once again in my mind of what we had to do next.

The first concerned the crew. They were still unaware that we were going north, not south. Should I go ahead, finally, and tell them?

I decided to wait until we were under way. With occasional visitors coming to the dock or on board, I did not want to risk someone overhearing a clue as to our intentions. I did not want to have to take away the opportunity for the crew to make a final call home before we sailed. If they knew our destination, something might slip out.

I took it as a personal responsibility to tell Dr. Kinsey once we got under way that we were headed on a top secret mission across the Arctic, not south to the equator. I would tell him that if he preferred to not go, I could arrange for him to return to the dock from which we had sailed and he could go back to his regular duties. When I actually gave him the news, he seemed a bit stunned, but recovered quickly. He told me that he would like to go along with us and was actually quite enthusiastic about the trip.

We had one more minor problem with our main turbine system that delayed us leaving until about midnight. After the repairs were completed, we were ready to begin our momentous journey.

0024, JUNE 9, 1958

"Ready to get under way," Paul Early reported.

Mooring lines were singled up.

"Take in all lines," I ordered after a final look around the ship from the high vantage point of the bridge. "Right full rudder. All back two-thirds."

21

EN ROUTE TO ENGLAND— VIA THE POLE

MONDAY, JUNE 9, 1958
"0026: UNDERWAY EN ROUTE PORTLAND, ENGLAND VIA THE
NORTH POLE."

As *Nautilus* moved slowly through the inky midnight blackness of Puget Sound, I sent word to Lieutenant Bob Kelsey, a Coloradoan who had watch on the main deck, to paint over our identifying numerals on the bow, stern, and sail. Our orders were explicit: remain undetected, and if someone did spot us, we were to conceal our identity. There would be little doubt who we were if someone spied the big "571." Even civilians knew it. We had been in the papers and on television regularly during the past few years, including the last few days in Seattle.

By the time we exited Puget Sound, the paint would be dry and would not wash away when we went deep.

Finally, the time had come for me to inform the crew that we were not headed for Panama. Instead, we were bound for England, not by way of the Panama Canal, but the "short route" across the top of the world, and we intended to go by way of the North Pole.

This brought to an end several months of double-talk and sometimes not-so-nimble tap dancing. As soon as practical, I made my way to our 1MC announcing system to brief the crew. Some of them had spotted Waldo Lyon by that time and put two and two together. They knew his presence meant the equator was not in our immediate future.

"All hands, this is the captain speaking," I spoke into the microphone. "Our destination for this trip is Portland, England . . . by way of the North Pole."

The reaction of the crew was electric—very positive—just as I knew it would be. I did not see any evidence of apprehension among the crew. Nor did they seem to resent being kept in the dark. Instead, there was an air of professionalism, sharpness, and competence that filled me with the deepest sense of admiration. Their reaction confirmed for me once again that my opinion of these men was correct. No better crew had ever taken a ship to sea.

John Krawczyk immediately went to work with his camera, documenting the journey. He had already earned the nickname "One More, One More John" because of his continual snapping of photos.

We steamed at moderate speed to keep from washing off the fresh paint that covered our hull numbers. Off Marrowstone Point we went to full speed. The bow of our ship dug in, shoving a massive wall of water before us. This vessel was designed to run best while submerged. That was her element. When we reached a certain speed on the surface, we wasted power as we pushed the bow wave ahead of us. There was no such occurrence when we were submerged, and we could make better speed.

As the sun rose, the officer of the deck steered elaborate courses to keep *Nautilus* away from merchant ships and small craft that dotted the vast expanse of the sound. We were flying no colors and showing no identifying numbers. That fact alone was enough to get someone's curiosity aroused.

"0840: CLEAR OF THE STRAITS OF JUAN DE FUCA."

Once we were a few miles past Swiftsure Lightship, I told the officer of the day (OOD) to take us down. With two growling blasts of the dive klaxon, we slid beneath the surface of the Pacific Ocean and were soon running at twenty-three knots at our cruising level of 350 feet.

The most challenging and dangerous part of the mission ahead of us— or so we assumed—was to make our way through the ice-choked, narrow, and shallow Bering Strait, one of the most hazardous bodies of water in the world for any kind of ship, but especially a submarine trying to remain undetected. There were two ways through. One was to the west, on the Siberian side of

Captain Anderson (center) gives instructions to the crew, flanked on the left by Dr. Waldo Lyon, a scientist specializing in submarine operations beneath the polar ice pack, and on the right by LCDR Frank Adams, executive officer of *Nautilus*.

St. Lawrence Island, a chunk of land that straddled the south end of the Strait like some warning beacon. The other was on the Alaskan side of the island.

I had decided to try the western approach for several reasons. On our great circle route, the Pole was closer that way. The water was also deeper, if only by a small degree. In addition, I had read in an old pilot book that the dangerous shore ice on that side tended to recede earlier in the year than it did on the Alaskan side. The eastern route was much shallower in places. At times we would have to run so shallow that the sail or even the upper part of the hull would be above water, which would make it much more likely that we would be detected. It also meant that we would have to dodge ice effectively while we were on the surface since we would be unable to dive beneath it.

As we made our way closer to the spinelike Aleutian Islands, the ship was unusually quiet. With our recent busy schedule, many of the officers and crew had not had sleep in more than twenty-four hours. Still, with a group of men whose average age was just over twenty-six years old, their recovery time would be quick. I was not so certain of their soon-to-be-thirty-seven-years-old skipper. I did my best to keep up with them.

"1555: LT. JENKS AND DR. LYON BRIEFED THE CREW."

Frank Adams hosted the first of several under-ice familiarization lectures for the crew. We wanted everyone to perform as a smooth-running team when we reached the ice and went beneath it. Special watches were trained, detailed instructions were issued, and a data-collection team was formed. They would fulfill the section in our orders that directed us to collect extensive scientific data, an important part of what we were going up there to do.

"1840: SHIP PASSED DOWN PORT SIDE."

Late in the afternoon the sonar team detected a lone freighter about five hundred yards away, directly on our track ahead. As we sped along beneath this ship, we quickly gained enough information that we could have accurately delivered a lethal torpedo attack had we been on a combat mission. The truth was, we were always ready to attack should such action be necessary. No matter where we were going or what our mission, we could never forget that ours was a dangerous planet, and especially at that time in history. *Nautilus* was—first and foremost—a warship.

"1940: SECURED SNORKEL VENTILATION."

We only ascended from our cruising depth to raise above the surface our periscopes, radio antennas, and snorkel air supply and exhaust tubes. We also took a look at the stars to confirm our underwater navigation. Once we had sent and received radio messages and refreshed our air with the snorkel, we returned to the depths. We were fully capable of operating without outside air for weeks at a time, but I wanted to conserve our oxygen supply banks for the long submerged cruise across the Arctic Basin.

Somewhere in the back of my mind, too, there was the ever-present thought of being prepared for anything catastrophic. I hoped we would never need all that oxygen, but we had it if we did.

TUESDAY, JUNE 10, 1958

Reading and watching movies were the primary recreation on board while we were on a trip. We usually carried one film for every day we expected to be at sea. Each movie was shown twice, typically once in the afternoon and then again after the evening meal, so every watch-stander had a chance to see it.

Some got more frequent screenings. *Gunfight at the O.K. Corral* was a crew favorite.

"We showed that movie so many times, we'd turn down the sound and the crew would take the parts of the actors," John Kurrus recalled.

We had loaded aboard thirty different movies on this trip. One of the first to be shown after we left Seattle was the Cold War submarine adventure *Hell and High Water*, starring Richard Widmark. The crew laughed out loud each time they heard a particular line of dialogue in the film—a statement that was not supposed to be funny. Widmark's character asked, "Who would have thought six months ago I would be on a submarine headed for the Arctic?"

The men never grew tired of that line!

On long cruises and cut off from the regular rotations of the sun, we always tried to establish familiar routines while under way in the dark depths. After leaving Seattle, we set our clocks—which had been on Eastern Standard Time—ahead four hours, to Greenwich Mean (or Zulu) Time, and planned to keep them on the international standard all the way. Our intent was to live by the same time for our entire voyage. And in the latitudes where we were headed, a slight course correction could take us quickly across several time zones. Trying to stay on local time was almost impossible.

As usual, crew watches were four hours on, eight hours off, with two officers on each watch. I wanted to be extra cautious, though, so I increased the number of officers to three—a diving officer in the control room, a conning officer at the periscope station, and an engineering officer in the maneuvering room.

As we steamed northward, Dr. Lyon and his technical assistant, Rex Rowray, checked out their sensitive new ice-detection equipment. They soon found a problem. The water pressure at the depths at which we were running had punctured one of the topside ice detectors. We had several others in reserve, so none of us saw this as a serious setback.

WEDNESDAY, JUNE 11, 1958

We got word by radio that a severe storm was passing directly ahead of us, moving to the north. It would have no effect on *Nautilus*. Without radio reports or surface observations, we would probably have never known it was there. We were very concerned, though, about what it might do to the ice in the Bering Strait and beyond. The high winds and crashing waves could cause the floes to pile up and become thicker than usual.

That afternoon as I was passing through the ship's passageway, I over-heard one of the cooks, Richard Murphy, who had come aboard *Nautilus* since our '57 under-ice probe, talking with Electrician's Mate James Morley.

"You know, Morley," he was saying, his face and tone as serious as could be, "last year I was a nobody. Today I am on my way to the North Pole!"

THURSDAY, JUNE 12, 1958

The temperature of the seawater had been gradually falling as we moved away from the warming influence of the Japanese current. At cruising depth, the control room bathythermograph read thirty-eight degrees Fahrenheit. It had been awhile since *Nautilus* had operated in water this cold.

During the morning we descended to test depth—a highly classified 713 feet—in order to check for leaks. Fittings that were fine in warm water could begin to leak in a colder environment. Control room electrician Imon Pilcher, an interior communications electrician from Kansas, checked in with each compartment by telephone, collecting any reports of problems.

"All compartments report no leaks," Pilcher told Diving Officer Bob Kelsey.

Nautilus was holding tight.

"0830: CAME TO PERISCOPE DEPTH. NO RADIO TRAFFIC."

One of the factors of life at sea on a nuclear submarine, and probably the biggest drawback, was the lack of news from the outside—or topside—world. The nuclear submarines copy radio periodically, but only for brief periods to receive important and official messages. Their aim is to remain undetected, and the longer they hover near the surface, the more likely someone will see them.

Press broadcasts can be received in most places on the globe, but schedules rarely permit slowing down to project an antenna for anything except official navy traffic. With today's digital capability, it is possible to get more updates for the crew, including personal news from home—called "family-grams." In those days, and in this respect, we were more isolated than people would be on space flights.

"1009: CROSSING ALEUTIAN TRENCH."

We approached the Aleutian Chain and the Bering Sea in the afternoon, which meant we could no longer run at our preferred depth. We would now have to navigate carefully, keeping a sharp eye on the fathometer as it kept track of the depth of the water beneath us.

"2206: LAND IN SIGHT. COMMENCED MANEUVERING THROUGH UNIMAK PASS."

We went to periscope depth late that evening and could see the rugged islands of the Aleutian Chain. We were about 1,700 miles from the mouth of Puget Sound. We confirmed our position using the snow-capped peaks that were visible in the periscope optics. Finally, when we were lined up for the center of a narrow channel between two clumps of land, Unimak Island and one of the Krenitzin Islands, we increased depth and speed for a dead-reckoning submerged shot through the pass. By midnight we had successfully threaded the needle and brought our ship to yet another new body of water for *Nautilus*, the Bering Sea.

FRIDAY, JUNE 13, 1958
"0900: EVENING TWILIGHT."

Our routine continued uninterrupted during our transit of the Bering Sea. As long as we were at sea twenty-four hours a day, scheduled work or relaxation periods remained unaltered. On the surface, the sun set just after 0900 Greenwich Mean Time and rose at 1400 in the afternoon. Tomorrow, though, it would barely go down before it rose again as we moved farther north. We paid little attention to the rising and setting of the sun, however, in our isolated world.

Up and down the length of the ship, men did their jobs quietly and efficiently. It seemed like business as usual, not a voyage of historic proportions, but I knew every man was aware of the import of our mission, as well as the potential problems that lay ahead of us.

We left the Pribilof Islands astern as we rode along barely a hundred feet above the featureless bottom of the Bering Sea. I could feel interest in the mission rise even higher among all hands. There seemed to be more curiosity than usual in Shep Jenks's chart. Richard Bearden and Engineman Norman A. Vitale became "engine room navigators." They hung a large chart near the reactor plant controls and kept an up-to-date plot of the ship's progress toward the Pole.

"1715: FOG. VISIBILITY REDUCED TO 100 YARDS."

On the way to the ice fields, we held exercises to prepare for emergencies we quietly prayed would never happen. There were fire and collision drills, simulated flooding, the sudden detection of dangerous ice, or anything else that might block our path. We practiced vertical ascents to periscope depth, rehearsing near vertical surfacing in a polynya or lead.

I was apprehensive about the hundreds of miles of ice-laden shallow water that lay ahead of us. Fortunately I could be relatively confident of water depth in this region. Enough soundings had been taken through the years to provide some certainty. A big factor was the flatness of these shallow waters in the Bering and Chukchi Seas. This was due to the silting process through eons of time from the summer melting of ice that had floated out from the coasts carrying a cargo of sand and dirt.

Ice thickness was another matter entirely. It varied from year to year and from season to season—sometimes from day to day. With wind and current, it was usually in motion too.

In Waldo Lyon we had the world's foremost authority on sea ice, but he was unwilling to speculate about the depth of ice shafts we might encounter. My own estimate, based on what we saw in our mission the previous year, was that forty-foot drafts were unlikely unless we ventured very near shore. I had no plans to do that.

As we would soon learn, my guess about the depth of the ice proved to be dangerously inaccurate.

22

CLOSE ENCOUNTER

"0300: SONAR CONTACT, DIESEL DRIVEN."

E arly in the morning we made a routine trip to periscope depth to copy radio traffic and check our position. While we were close to the surface, Chief Sonarman Jim Norris stood watch on our "big ears." He reported a distant ship, probably more than twenty miles to the west. We gained all the information we could from that distance, but our schedule did not permit a more thorough investigation. We guessed it to be a diesel-driven merchantman rather than a Soviet submarine operating in this lightly traveled area.

"0721: BOTTOM CONTOURS FLAT AS A PANCAKE."

We skimmed along at moderate speed, still barely one hundred feet above the smooth ocean floor. The almost featureless bottom of the Bering Sea—as well as the Chukchi, its sister sea lying to the north through the strait—constitutes about the flattest known section of sea floor on the globe. In places, the water depth changed little more than a foot in ten miles.

Lyon completed the check of his equipment and pronounced it ready for the ice fields ahead. This was his twelfth trip to the Arctic. Simply having Waldo and his assistant aboard gave us all more confidence as we traveled on to a new frontier.

"1045: SLOWED. CAME TO PERISCOPE DEPTH."

Once again we came up to fix our position and compare it to the dead-reckoning plot (estimating where a vessel will be by advancing a known position, using course, speed, time, and distance to be traveled). We also ventilated the ship. In all, we were at periscope depth for an hour, snorkeling to make sure we had good fresh air throughout *Nautilus*. From this point forward, I planned to use our normal air-revitalization procedures.

Commander Richard Dobbins, our physician, and his two assistants, Chief Hospitalman John Aberle and Hospitalman First Class Robert Jarvis, routinely checked instruments that told us how close to normal our air was.

It was evening—though our clocks read noon—when we completed our snorkeling operation. The sea had been cooperative, very calm with no wind. Thankfully the storm that preceded us had moved away, but it left in its wake a dense, heavy fog. We slipped back deeper and commenced a quick check of our magnetic compasses. If the gyrocompasses failed again, as they had on our '57 probe, we might have to rely on the magnetic one for steering and dead reckoning to find our way from beneath the ice.

They appeared to be working fine so far, though. They would become more temperamental as we got closer to the magnetic pole.

"1822: SIGHTED ST. LAWRENCE ISLAND AND THE SIBERIAN COASTLINE."

When we next came to periscope depth for a quick navigational fix, we could clearly see the snow-capped mountains along the bleak Siberian coast and the rugged rocks of St. Lawrence Island. By then the sky had become a beautiful, cloudless blue and the sea was flat calm. We could not stay around to admire the scenery, though, and went back down, heading for the slightly deeper passage between Siberia and St. Lawrence Island—our western "door" to the Bering Strait.

We were now entering an area where charted water-depth soundings were scarce. If the Russians had more accurate charts, they certainly were not going to share them with us. We would have to rely on our own equipment if we wanted to stay out of trouble.

"2130: PICKING UP ICE IN SMALL CHUNKS, WIDELY SCATTERED."

We picked up our first electronic signs of ice overhead late that night. Soon all our topside equipment had detected chunks of ice as well. We could also see its shadows through the periscope, the larger pieces deflecting what was left of the sunlight. It was not very thick, nor were there many chunks of it yet, but we slowed down in case some piece that was deeper than the rest should project downward to where we ran.

The word spread throughout the ship that we had spotted our first ice. A number of the crew gathered around to watch the ice indications. For some of the crew members, this was their first experience with the floe. They seemed impressed. The others—the ones who were aboard for the previous year's under-ice trips—just remarked, "Brash and block again," or "Just like last time."

There was one major difference, though. We were now vastly more restricted in the shallow Bering Sea than we had been in the deep Atlantic off Greenland. Hemmed in between the ice above and the ocean floor below, we would have to take the utmost care to avoid striking one or the other.

Our margin for error was growing more and more narrow.

SUNDAY, JUNE 15, 1958

The new watch came on at midnight, the first of the voyage to relieve with ice overhead. We regularly passed beneath floes, some of which were forty yards across with a draft of about twenty feet. The coverage was around six-tenths of the sea's surface area. It was very cluttered. I had not expected that much ice at a latitude this low, but there was no denying what we were seeing.

At the time, about forty-five feet of water was all that separated us from the silt bottom of the Bering Sea. Moreover, there was only about twenty to twenty-five feet of clearance to the ice overhead. We were also following a course that would take us east of the International Boundary Line that separated the territories of Russia and the United States, keeping us out of Soviet waters. It was like driving your car down a building's hallway with your eyes closed, relying on someone else to tell you which way to steer. And doing it at thirty or thirty-five miles per hour.

At twenty minutes past midnight, we passed underneath an especially big block of ice, probably broken off from the Siberian coast. It projected downward thirty feet below the surface. Had we not had enough water beneath us to go deeper and sneak under it, we would have had to take horizontal evasive action. There was precious little room for ship control.

I glanced over at Waldo. There was a look of surprise on his face. I am certain that it mirrored my own.

"0020: REVERSED COURSE TO 222 DEGREES TRUE."

The thickness of ice floes that form in the open sea is relatively predictable. The depth of floes that break away from a shoreline is not. I thought about the even shallower stretch of sea that lay directly ahead of us around the west side of St. Lawrence Island and mentally envisioned a piece of what had only recently been shore-fast ice, one that was maybe only ten feet deeper than the last one we had seen.

It was a disturbing possibility. I quietly mentioned to Waldo that I did not like the looks of the ice picture we were seeing. He agreed. We had just squeezed beneath a massive chunk of deep ice and there was likely more in our path.

I walked over to Ken Carr, the conning officer, and ordered him to reverse course.

The Arctic and its treacherous shore ice had, in effect, slammed the western door in our faces. *We never expected this to be easy*, I reminded myself.

Perhaps only Lyon and I were aware of the reasons for the sudden change in direction at that moment. Our operation order was clear. The safety of the ship and men was paramount. I did not have enough information on ice conditions off the Siberian coast to chance proceeding farther without undue risk. It was likely the ice we found had broken free from the Siberian landmass and drifted toward St. Lawrence Island. I did not know the characteristics of the Russian land ice or how much more shallow the water would become. I did know that our own northern Alaskan coast sent forty-five-foot-draft chunks floating out to sea in unpredictable configurations. My decision to turn around was an easy one. Disappointing but easy.

In hindsight, I realized it would have been better to probe where conditions were most familiar—on the Alaskan side of the strait—instead of trying the deeper but lesser-known route to the west. Lyon was much better informed on the conditions, currents, and waters between St. Lawrence Island and the Alaskan coast. It was there that both he and I thought we might have a better chance of an ice-free passage as far as the Bering Strait, even if the water was shallower and the running would be necessarily slower. We would need to carefully pick our way in spots.

My intentions now were to go around the southern side of St. Lawrence and make a run toward the strait from the eastern side of the island. We set such a course back toward the southeast at moderate speed while still keeping watch for deep-thrusting ice. Meanwhile, both Frank Adams and Shep Jenks, who had been awake it seemed almost since we left Seattle, could finally go get a few hours of sleep.

The rest of the crew seemed unaware of or not concerned with our turnaround. In the galley, Jack Baird, our leading commissaryman (nicknamed "Mother" by his shipmates), baked a cake and decorated it to say "Happy Dad's Day." After all, it was Father's Day. John Krawczyk came by and added "Arctic Ocean 1958." He snapped a picture of his handiwork even though he was not yet geographically correct.

At 0600, after clearing the area where we spotted the daunting ice, we made a stationary ascent to periscope depth and obtained a fix on St. Lawrence Island. We also decided that our new ice-measuring sonar was working well, once we had learned how to interpret the data it presented.

The weather remained clear, sunny, and windless, with a calm sea and no ice in sight. We did have an indication showing up on our equipment of some small chunks off the bow. Looking through the periscope on that bearing, I saw instead two Alaskan seagulls swimming along. Though we had missed the diagnosis, it was still reassuring to know that ice that small could be picked up on our gear. Later, sonar picked up and tracked a diving cormorant, a seabird native to the area.

"1100: SLOWED AND CAME TO PERISCOPE DEPTH."

When we came up for a fresh look, the weather had grown very foggy again with only about a thousand yards of visibility. We took a LORAN fix, ventilated, and continued on our way. At 1300, I passed the word about our intentions to the crew. They were disappointed about the little detour in our trip. I let them know that there was the possibility of our going into water so shallow that we would be forced to run on the surface. The comments from the crew in general were, "I hope it's not on my watch!" or something similar.

Then I received the report that the master gyrocompass was once again giving us trouble. Ray McCoole, the chief interior communication technician, worked with it constantly. Roland Cave, another interior communication tech, prodded him good-naturedly. McCoole was slated to leave

Nautilus for officer duty at a nuclear power billet ashore when we returned from this mission. Cave was urging him to get the compass fixed before he left us. Ray McCoole narrowly missed a tragic end later in his career. His wife was injured in an accident and hospitalized just before he was scheduled to sail with the submarine on which he served at the time. His commanding officer (another former *Nautilus* officer, Wes Harvey) told him to remain behind with her while the submarine left for only a three-day post-overhaul cruise. That submarine was USS *Thresher* (SSN-593), which suffered a mechanical problem on that short trip and went down. All aboard perished. Ray McCoole was spared because of his wife's accident.

The water was shoaling on the eastward side of St. Lawrence. We were running at an eighty-five-foot keel depth with only about forty-five feet of water under us. Then, during the 2000-to-0000 watch, the master gyrocompass quit altogether.

In the ship's newspaper—this day cleverly titled *The Panama-Arctic Shuffle* (the paper's name changed daily)—there was a blurb that gave all of us something to smile about, despite our frustration with the ice and the faulty compass.

"Classified: Lieutenant Harvey wants to know if it is Russian or American ice that has been giving us trouble."

MONDAY, JUNE 16, 1958
"0000: NO CONTACTS EXCEPT BIRDS AND WATER. VISIBILITY GOOD."

Our transit around the southern side of St. Lawrence Island completed, we turned north again toward the Bering Strait. With one door locked, we would try the other. The sea continued to be disconcertingly shallow—so shallow that we were running with the top of the sail just barely underwater. Paul Early, as conning officer, kept a continuous watch through the periscope. The water was not deep enough to duck under any floating obstacle, so we had to steer around occasional chunks of ice, and we proceeded at frustratingly slow speeds.

Captain Anderson surveys the first chunks of the polar ice pack from the bridge of *Nautilus*.

At 0511, a mast was sighted almost dead ahead on the horizon. I was called immediately. My first impression when I saw the distant object was that we had ourselves a snorkeling submarine, possibly Soviet.

What in the hell is he doing way up here? I thought. *Could he be a Russian?*

These were relatively deserted waters, so a sighting like this one was of special interest. I was also concerned because by this time, a portion of our sail was above the surface. I knew if we could see their periscopes or snorkel, they could almost certainly see us.

As we drew closer, though, we could see it was only a drifting log with a couple of protruding roots, making it look a lot like a submarine with its periscopes or snorkel extended. We were near the mouth of the Yukon River, so we soon saw such logs drifting all about. At 0807, an almost completely submerged log lay directly in our path. Before we had time to retract the periscope, it struck the log a glancing blow. Fortunately there was no damage.

Early in the afternoon of June 16, we passed our previous high-latitude mark for this cruise. The weather remained clear, the sea temperature was well above freezing, and there were no signs of ice. Bird life was abundant. News that we were proceeding northward under far more favorable conditions electrified the crew.

"1849: SIGHTED KING ISLAND."

Through the crosshairs of our periscope, we spotted the rugged features of King Island just south of the Bering Strait. We turned west to deeper water in order to squeeze through the strait, hopefully below periscope depth. Bill Lalor, the conning officer on watch, spotted a few chunks of ice ahead at about 2130. Shortly thereafter we turned due north, skirting the ice that lay to the west. One floe was sighted two or three feet out of the water. It appeared to be about a mile across.

We had now reached our next key milestone—the entrance to the Bering Strait, the gateway to the Chukchi Sea and to the forbidding Arctic beyond.

23

REVERSE COURSE

E arly the morning of the seventeenth, through a periscope we saw geographic features showing we had arrived at the entrance to the Bering Strait. Near Fairway Rock, we spotted the Diomede Islands, the Russian-owned Big Diomede and the U.S.-owned Little Diomede—populated only by a very small native village. Soon, too, the vast Siberian and Alaskan coasts broke through the thick haze.

We remained at periscope depth in these shallow, restricted waters. Thankfully there was no sign of ice except in the distance, over near the Siberian side. The seas were running about four feet high with numerous whitecaps but not too rough for us. These were near ideal conditions for us to get through the strait without being detected by radar—either from the Russian side or from our own.

It was vital that we remain undetected by both American and Russian interests. In the political climate of those times, our presence there could have caused all sorts of problems. Even if our own forces learned that we were not some Soviet ship nosing around, our mission and its secrecy would have been compromised. Either way, the trip would almost certainly have been canceled.

"0530: PASSED THROUGH BERING STRAIT."

Our entry into the Chukchi Sea was almost anticlimactic. After pointing for this milestone for so long, and after the turnaround west of St. Lawrence Island, the trip through the Bering Strait was a breeze.

Like the Bering Sea south of the strait, the Chukchi was another flat and shallow body of water. We had some 420 miles of this sea to cross before we entered the much deeper Arctic basin. The question in our minds was whether we would again encounter heavy ice such as what we ran into near St. Lawrence Island. If we did, we would not be in a very good position with only 100 to 170 feet of water depth available in most parts.

"0745: ICE SIGHTED."

We ran northward, trying to keep at least 135 feet of water below us. Soon we sighted our first piece of Chukchi Sea ice about five miles ahead. It was a single mini-island, about 50 feet by 30 feet. We measured its upward projection to be about 10 feet above the sea surface. This meant a draft beneath it of perhaps 30 to 40 feet, maybe more. Its irregular shape reminded us of a sailing ship.

We did not stay around to get a closer look. We changed course to avoid the floe. As we passed it, I could see the sunlight shining through, setting off a prismatic display of light greens and blues. It was quite beautiful—beautiful but dangerous in such shallow waters. We knew the ice had roughly the same consistency as a poor grade of setup concrete, and that was nothing with which we would want to collide.

"0925: ICE WAS PLENTIFUL."

We continued to zig and zag, avoiding the patches of ice. It reminded me of the maneuvering that surface ships did back in World War II to prevent submarines from lining up for easy torpedo shots. Soon the ice covered the surface almost completely, and I gave the order to submerge, to go to 110-feet keel depth and slow to eight knots.

"1108: CROSSED THE ARCTIC CIRCLE."

While we continued to cruise toward the North Pole at moderate speed, passing under occasional floes and chunks, we crossed the Arctic Circle at longitude 168 degrees, 39 minutes west. All hands instantly became official members of the "Order of Bluenoses," the "fraternity" of those who have crossed the Circle. It was difficult, though, to appreciate cold weather while riding along in the comfort of our controlled environment aboard *Nautilus*.

The spirits of the crew were at a high now. If we continued to make such excellent progress without having to squeeze beneath deep ice keels, we should make it to the Arctic Ocean. Then, as best we knew, there was clear sailing to the Pole and beyond.

I did not want to declare victory over the ice just yet, but I was beginning to feel confident that our first assault on the North Pole and beyond would be successful.

"1203: COMMENCED VERTICAL ASCENT."

About midday we crossed an uncharted shallow spot where the water began to shoal to 120 feet. Since we had not detected any ice on the sonar for the past fifteen minutes, I decided to come up and check the situation. Just to be sure, we carefully watched all sonar indications, and finding no ice, I ordered that we raise our "ice pick"—one of our radio antennas that we used like a curb-feeler. Then I watched it through the periscope as we came up

On the bridge of *Nautilus* approaching the polar ice pack. Visible are LT William Cole (back of his head), QMC Lyle (Doggie) Rayl (in light shirt), LCDR Frank Adams, the executive officer aboard *Nautilus*, and Captain William R. Anderson.

to confirm that sonar was correct in reporting no ice overhead.

We came up slowly and found clear water all around. Since we were now far from land in one of the most desolate spots on the planet, I ordered the boat surfaced. We could make much better speed on the surface than submerged in waters as shallow as these, and we could see approaching ice much better. We had lost so much time on our aborted Siberia-side approach to the Bering Strait that I was anxious to push on as quickly as we could.

It was a beautiful day near the top of the world. We ran north at fifteen knots, making small course changes from time to time where necessary to avoid islands of ice. We made good progress for the next seven hours. We had to be vigilant, though. We could not afford to attempt to imitate an icebreaker and plow through pack ice. Our rudder, diving planes, screws, and much of the sound equipment were exposed and could be damaged.

"1720: SIGHTED ICE FIELDS AHEAD AND TO PORT."

At about seven o'clock in the evening, at latitude sixty-eight, thirty north, we entered the true polar ice pack. We had no choice but to submerge again and commence the long run through the ice-filled ocean ahead. We continued our course northward.

Ice covered about 5 percent of the surface, and our overhead sonar appeared to be picking it up regularly. The biggest pieces we saw projected twenty feet below the surface or fifty feet above the highest point of our ship. The sea bottom was forty feet below us. We felt it safe to cruise at eight knots, but we watched the situation with special care.

After an hour or so of observing the recording pen for the topside sonar as it graphed the underside contours of the ice, I decided that we were finally clear of the dangerous masses that had broken off from the shore. We appeared to be under the more predictable polar pack. We had traveled some 1,383 miles beneath this very same type of ice on our 1957 cruise. We felt that we knew what to expect from it.

Chief Stu Nelson wandered by.

"Captain, what about a couple of 'going home turns'?" he said with a grin.

I authorized the conning officer to add on a couple of knots of speed—the "going home turns" Chief Nelson requested—and then I strolled down to the crew's mess to watch a few minutes of the movie that was playing there. I also wanted to gauge the spirit of the off-watch crew. The movie was *Hot Blood*, with Jane Russell and Cornel Wilde. The men seemed to be enjoying themselves.

I quickly gave up on the movie and went to my cabin for some rest. On the way I paused briefly at the ice recorders. Waldo was there as usual, intently watching the pen dance.

Everything appeared okay. I went to my cabin, lay down, and closed my eyes.

"2250: PASSED UNDER A 47-FOOT-DRAFT PIECE OF ICE."

At about eleven o'clock in the evening, my nap was suddenly interrupted by a voice from the speaker in my stateroom. It was Lieutenant Bill Lalor, on watch as conning officer.

"Captain, will you come in, please?"

Even though his voice was far from frantic, I knew such a summons meant trouble. No crew member awakens a sleeping skipper without reason. I hustled down to where Lalor waited near the ice recorders.

"We just passed under ice that projected forty-seven feet deep," he reported. I could easily see the sweeping pen of the recorder receding only slightly after drawing a line that marked a point a mere twenty-one feet above us.

"Left full rudder, and take us down to 140 feet," I ordered, which was twenty feet deeper and a meager twenty feet above the sea floor. I cautioned the control room crew to use only a slight down angle for the maneuver to assure we did not accidentally plow the bow into the bottom.

We were in our first tight-squeeze situation. There was no room for error.

Then in a calm, precise tone, Sonarman Al Charette gave a chilling report. Two massive ridges of ice lay directly ahead, and we were almost under the first one.

I ordered our speed cut to dead slow. We appeared to be under a gigantic mass of ice that was more than a mile wide, and there appeared to be no easy way to get out from beneath it.

I confess a chill ran up my back.

There was only one thing to do: reverse course as efficiently as possible. I ordered the rudder kept at full left as we did so, hopefully taking us in a sharp turn away from the wall of ice. But who knew what other upside-down peaks of ice lay in our path out from underneath this tight spot?

The recording pen moved downward once more. I stared at it intently. So did Rex Rowray, who was now running the equipment, and Bill Lalor, who was also coordinating and checking on *Nautilus's* course, speed, depth, and reports from sonar. I prayed the trace would stop, go back the other direction.

As we passed underneath the next downward-pointing ridge, the pen finally receded. We all exhaled. We had cleared that one by a mere twenty-five feet.

The more formidable barrier still lay ahead, according to the equipment. I again stared in disbelief at the picture of it on the upward-beaming sonar. None of the books and scientific reports I had read said anything about ice such as this.

I would not have been surprised to feel a shudder and jolt, to hear the grinding of steel against solid, rock-hard ice, to feel the deck pitch beneath our feet as we collided with the immovable ridge, to feel the sudden inrush of ice-cold seawater.

Unbelievably, the recording pen was now so close to the reference line that corresponded to the top of our sail that they were almost one merged stroke on the moving paper. It traced along that way for what seemed to be an eternity.

We prayed.

Then, thankfully, the pen began to recede upward. The space between *Nautilus* and the deadly ice was once again widening. We had cleared.

I will never forget the calm demeanor of the watchstanders that night. Lalor at the conn, Charette on sonar, Lieutenant Bill Cole on the dive, Rowray on the ice recorder, Clarence Price on the bow planes, Ray Kropp on the stern planes, Chief Frank Skewes as the chief of the watch, and Bob Scott at the helm. Better than anyone else, they well understood that we were in a tough situation, but there was no panic.

Al Charette later recalled just how close to disaster we were during those tense few minutes. "For a brief time we were sandwiched between very thick ice above us and the sea floor below us. Not only did we not like this sandwich effect, but we did not want to be trapped behind a wall of ice either."

Al pointed out that there are no icebergs, as such, in the Bering or Chukchi Seas. The pieces of ice that *Nautilus* was dodging were known as "ice keels." Sea ice (salt water) and icebergs (fresh water) come from different sources and form in different ways.

Sea ice is created when the air temperatures get so cold that the ocean surface freezes into solid sheets. When these floes bump into one another, or if they are forced against a landmass or into constricted passages, the floes either "raft" up on top of one another or are broken up. Excess ice is pushed upward or downward. The upward projections are called ice "ridges." The downward projectiles are termed ice "keels." The keels then move around with the floes of which they are a part, propelled by wind and sea currents. The deepest ice keel ever seen by a submarine was 189 feet, spotted by USS *Lapon* (SSN-661) in the Lincoln Sea, between the northern reaches of Canada and Greenland.

By comparison, icebergs are pieces of fresh-water glaciers that break off—or "calve," as oceanographers describe it—as the glacier meets the sea.

Unlike ice floes, icebergs can melt unevenly and turn on end. They can be larger and much more hazardous than sea ice keels. Some icebergs extend to greater than 2,700 feet—half a mile—below the surface of the sea!

We did not expect these keels to be as frequent and as deep as what we encountered. Al Charette pointed to another complicating factor: "It is important to remember that *Nautilus* is 320 feet in length and it would not take too much of an angle in those close quarters to put us in serious trouble. Buoyancy control and depth and angle control become increasingly important as the sandwich effect gets worse. Radical changes were out of the question."

Imagine trying to turn around your minivan inside your garage while constantly maintaining forward speed!

"When we encountered the second keel, we had an additional nine feet of clearance above the sail, but that was because the captain had just taken us down twenty feet. That meant we had given up twenty feet below the keel. We were getting squeezed even tighter, and it was about to get worse."

Charette related that he was shocked by what he saw on his sonar display: "I reported to the captain that the next ice keel ahead of us looked wider than the one we had just passed under. The sonar display—on the one thousand-yard scale—indicated the ice keel to be at least sixteen hundred yards wide. That was almost a mile! I also reported that it would be deeper and denser, according to the echo quality. All three keels were oriented east-west. As we passed under the third ice keel, we determined it was hanging down an amazing eighty feet below the surface."

How close to disaster were we? Charette—with his perfect view at his sonar scan—can tell you: "Everyone in sonar and the attack center, and especially those watching the upward-beaming scanners, was hunching down, applying body English, somehow trying to assist *Nautilus* as she ducked beneath this mass of ice. I am still convinced that we ran through slush at the bottom of the ice keel!"

Every man on watch was aware of the danger in which we had found ourselves. Charette said, "One can only imagine the tension at the diving station in the control room as the diving officer, helmsman, stern planesman, and bow planesman anticipated impact with the keel. What would the proper reaction be if the front edge of the sail struck the ice?"

Al's best estimate was that our sail cleared the underside of the ice keel by eight feet. A man of average height standing on our sail could have reached up and touched the solid, treacherous ice as we crept beneath it.

Al also pointed out that if we assumed anything less than a perfect angle, we could have easily collided with the ice or stuck our nose hard into the muddy sea bottom.

As I stood there that night, hearing my crew members once again begin to breathe, it took only a moment's reflection to realize that this phase of Operation Sunshine had already failed. I had expected to find ice no deeper than forty feet. We had narrowly survived somewhere between eighty and eighty-three feet, and we had no idea if that was the deepest keel we might encounter. Had the sea floor been another one or two hundred feet deep, there would be no problem. It was not. To the north, along our projected course, the sea was even shallower and the ice could easily be even deeper as we steered closer to the Arctic Ocean.

There was only one prudent option: head back south.

Waldo, I learned, thought we should have pressed on. But I had the responsibility of a ship and 115 men. We had underestimated the ice, and retreat was in order.

The hardest part was announcing this to the crew. Then we had to go look for a safe place to surface so we could make our report to Admiral Burke and ask for instructions.

I spent a long time drafting my message of failure to CNO. How could I tell him that the most important peacetime submarine mission in history had come up short? I decided to do it in precisely those words, make the report to the point, and add that the operation would probably be feasible later on in the summer, after the ice had melted some more and its boundary had receded into deeper water.

I had no reason to expect that I would be the skipper on that future mission. If we got back to port, it could take too long to get permission and to prepare *Nautilus* for a third attempt, our second during the summer of 1958. If commanding officer rotations ran true to form, I could be at my next assignment before a late-summer-1959 attempt would be made.

As disappointed as I was, I had every reason to thank God for pulling us through and out of danger. I paid special thanks for the alertness and ability of sonar supervisor Al Charette. Al eventually retired at the rank of commander and as of this writing makes many speeches about his experiences aboard *Nautilus* and does a tremendous amount of work with the *Historic Ship Nautilus* and the Submarine Force Library and Museum in Groton. He also hosts tours of the ship and is a very entertaining and informative docent.

I said a prayer of thanks that evening for the conning officer, Bill Lalor. He did not waste time wondering if the reports from sonar were authentic enough to disturb me. He had called without hesitation.

And I thanked the Almighty for enabling me to size up the situation quickly and take the proper evasive action. I seem to recall a certain pressure on my right shoulder telling me to go deeper, an inner voice that said, "Twenty feet," even though it placed us dangerously near the sea floor. It turned out to be the absolute best choice I could have made. Had it been only ten feet, we would have collided with that final ice keel. I have always been pretty good at sizing up operational crises and acting quickly, but I believe I had divine guidance in this situation.

Toward midnight, I found Rex Rowray having a cup of coffee in the wardroom. I joined him and we talked about our close encounter.

"You know," he said, "I feel as if I aged at least a year while I was watching that needle dip down on the recorder."

"I feel as if I aged at least a year today too," I said with a grin.

And it was true. Doubly true.

It was June 17.

It was my thirty-seventh birthday.

24

RETREAT TO PEARL

made certain to take a positive tone in my message to Admiral Burke. I attempted to convey the confidence I felt that another attempt to transit through the North Pole to the Atlantic could be successful if attempted later in the summer. By then melting would have caused the pack's boundaries to retreat farther northward, and we would be much more likely to find a way through to the deeper Arctic Ocean. I also suggested that we proceed to and prepare for another attempt from Pearl Harbor, Hawaii.

I was quite anxious about the response from Washington. There was a real chance that the Pentagon and White House would simply conclude either that what we had tried was premature or that it was simply too risky and they would call the whole thing off. I was concerned once again that we may have delayed under-ice exploration because of what happened to *Nautilus*. An Atlantic-side run to the Pole by *Skate* might be authorized to make immediate headlines. The round-the-world-while-submerged voyage might take the place of our North Pole transit.

Then there was the supersecrecy factor. Could the concealment be maintained during a period of one to two months with all hands in *Nautilus* now fully aware of our goals? I feared that the White House might be so pessimistic about the possibility of someone leaking the truth about our mission and the resulting dramatic reduction in the impact of Operation Sunshine, even if the transit was successful, that they would nix another trip.

I later learned that the president's press secretary, Jim Hagerty, had made a rather interesting wager. On hearing that many of our crew would be granted leave during our stay at Pearl Harbor, he bet Captain Pete Aurand a dollar that a leak would occur. Aurand was really happy that he won that bet, as was I. Hagerty later acknowledged this was one bet he was delighted to have to pay off on.

No one knew exactly what would happen if the news of our attempt and ultimate failure to make it across the Arctic Ocean had leaked out. My fears of the consequences of such a breach of secrecy were such that I immediately started drafting a special set of orders to be put into the hands of every person on board—U.S. Navy and civilian alike.

Those orders very specifically instructed everyone not only to forget where we had been but also to be ready to make up a cover story. It was crucial that they understand how deeply the president of the United States and the top naval brass in the Pentagon wanted our mission to remain a complete secret.

"I cannot impress on you too strongly the grave responsibility that rests on each of you individually to carry out this order," my order stated. "Not only is it necessary for each of you to 'forget' entirely everything that has happened or been divulged to you regarding this operation, but you must each also actively participate in maintaining a plausible cover story for what we have been or will be doing. I cannot imagine a situation requiring greater discretion, common sense, alertness, and loyalty."

I went on to say, "Neither rank or rate, nor the lack of it; nor time on board; nor years of service; nor any other factor change the degree to which you are personally responsible."

The last half of the document gave details of our cover mission.

Paragraph four summed it up nicely: "You may come in contact with those who conjecture that *Nautilus* has done this or that or plans to do this or that. Do not let conjectures on the part of others cause you to lower your guard."

Even a lucky guess by someone had to be greeted with the most non-committal of poker faces.

I still have not heard one word about a crew member leaking information about our mission to anyone during that time, not even to close family members.

"0002: CHANGED COURSE TO DODGE ICE CHUNK."

As we made our painful retreat back toward the Bering Strait, the ice cover began to thin out once again. At times our sonar detected chunks of twenty-to-thirty feet draft, but we saw nothing like the monsters that had turned us around way short of our goal.

At 0740 on June 18, all sonars reported clear water overhead, and we made a vertical ascent to periscope depth. I raised number two periscope.

"All clear. No close ice in sight. Control conn, raise the port whip. Radio, transmit the message to CNO."

Surprisingly quickly, a navy radio operator at Pearl Harbor flashed back the abbreviated signal that meant they were hearing us loud and clear. Radio propagation is notoriously spotty from these high latitudes. Radioman Harry Thomas touched his transmitting key and sent out a stream of *dits* and *dahs*. In moments, the word of our aborted mission would be in the Pentagon. I had no real idea what kind of reception it would receive or how they might react to its contents.

We found good visibility at the surface with a breeze and a four-foot, choppy sea. I decided to run at periscope depth as long as the water remained free of ice in the hopes of getting a quick reply back from Admiral Burke. But soon we saw more ice on the horizon, and we had to duck below to ride beneath it. In normal circumstances, we would much prefer running submerged. It was smoother and faster. But in water this shallow, we had to inch our way along painfully slowly, dodging the heavier floes. After months of submerged cruising at high speed, I had become used to making such quick progress while submerged. It seemed especially tedious now to have to proceed so slowly.

"1859: ICE FIELDS ON BOTH SIDES."

Late in the afternoon we approached a particularly shallow reach, extending some forty miles along our return track. When we came up this way, this section had been ice free so we had covered it rapidly, both on the surface and at periscope depth. Going back south was clearly going to be more interesting than I first thought.

Obviously the fresh southwesterly breeze had carried the big islands of ice eastward across our course. Much of it appeared to be of coastal origin, likely broken off the Siberian coast. Some was quite chunky and had deep drafts, making it advisable to stay on the surface or at periscope depth and dodging them rather than pulling the plug and running underneath, chancing colliding with a sudden keel. Once again we were impressed with the unpredictable nature of the ice. We knew better than to take it for granted.

Just before 7:30 that evening, I surfaced to look around. What I saw gave me pause. We were boxed in on three sides by large patches of thick ice, and there was always the chance it could completely encircle us if we remained there. It might be days before conditions allowed us to run on the surface again. We had no choice but to go under the floe.

I told Paul Early, who was officer of the deck on that watch, to turn the ship around to a northerly heading—toward clear water—and to prepare for diving. After we had eased back down to cruising depth, we once again came around to a southerly heading, now beneath the ice. And once again, we quickly found ourselves in a tight squeeze in some spots. Sonar identified the heavier masses, and Lieutenants Lalor and Carr, the conning officers, directed the ship around and past the keels that were too deep for us to pass beneath them. Reports from the fathometer came constantly and were followed closely. Our track on the chart was a jagged, zigzagging line, as if a drunk driver were at the helm of the mighty *Nautilus*. But this was classic submarine maneuvering. So long as we could find enough room to fit through, we could make slow progress through the maze of ice.

We were all relieved when the water depth finally began to increase gradually. Once we had passed the 120-foot curve—which was not usually considered deep for us—Shep Jenks joked, "Captain, we've just crossed into Jenks's Deep!" I agreed we should ask the Navy Hydrographic Office to name this "extremely deep" region after our navigator.

THURSDAY, JUNE 19, 1958
"0314: RECEIVED CNO MESSAGES MODIFYING OPERATION ORDER."

When we eased into an open stretch of water that morning, we ascended vertically to check for an answer to our message to CNO. I had mixed feelings when I saw "top secret reply" on the schedule being broadcast back to us. I was glad that Admiral Burke had responded quickly and hoped that was a positive omen. If so, it would be the first I had observed in some time.

I went to my stateroom, sat at my tiny desk, unfolded the decoded message, and began to read.

"I concur entirely with your prudent action in withdrawing from the ice pack. It is obvious that you have made a maximum effort. I tentatively concur with your recommendation to lay over at Pearl until conditions improve. Set course and stand by for further instructions. Remain undetected."

It was signed, "Arleigh Burke."

I do not think there could have been a more thoughtful message from a boss or a more understanding approach to our dilemma. Although Admiral Burke had not endorsed another try for the Arctic transit that summer, he did not say no either.

The short message gave a great boost to my morale. When I briefed the crew, their response was the same as mine. The tone aboard *Nautilus* changed instantly from a sense of defeat to one of determined optimism.

We continued south through the Chukchi, skirting a hundred miles of drifting pack ice, back through the Bering Strait and within miles of the Soviet Union, and into the shallow Bering Sea. Destination: Pearl Harbor, Waikiki, the Pali, the Hawaiian Village, and Diamond Head. Though we had hoped our next landfall would be England, Hawaii was the best we could have hoped for at that point.

So far as we knew, the chance of our making a run to England via the North Pole in 1958 still existed.

FRIDAY, JUNE 20, 1958, TO SATURDAY, JUNE 28, 1958

Our trip from the Bering Sea to Hawaii was a routine submerged voyage, filled with drills, field days, training, and paperwork. One factor made the transit something other than routine, though—the top secret nature of Operation Sunshine. As we left the Aleutians behind, I issued the first top secret instruction of my career, the one previously mentioned.

No facet of the operation was to be discussed with any person—on board or ashore—either verbally or in writing. Private conversations on board were authorized, but only with the commanding officer—yours truly—or executive officer. All hands were to make a diligent search through their personal things and seal up anything that might give a clue of where we might have been or where we wanted to return, which included letters, papers, and notes of any kind. They were to be sealed in envelopes labeled "Top Secret" and locked up under rigid custody. So were the ship's logs, charts, records, and reports. Three combination safes aboard *Nautilus* were crammed full of such material.

One of the crew had stenciled a couple of white undershirts with a North Pole insignia. They had to be locked up.

Steve White noted, "This is the first time in history that anybody owned a top secret skivvy shirt!"

We made sure to hide our cold-weather clothing and special Arctic gear. We had to repaint our topside hull numbers too. Someone noted that beards might be associated with cold-weather work, not an exercise near Panama, so everyone shaved. One crew member actually asked Dutch Larch if he could be allowed to keep his beard by sealing it in a top secret envelope. I have no record of Dutch's response. Bill McNally and John Kurrus had prepared North Pole cachet stamp parts so they could "cancel" stamps on mail from the Pole. They were locked away.

Meanwhile I had to write some fiction. I needed to create a report of a southern voyage by *Nautilus* and share it with all hands. We should all be able to tell the same fabricated story.

Our cover story concluded, "It was a routine cruise—material problems were few and atmosphere control was the best experienced to date. Elaborate plans were made for the first equator crossing by a nuclear-powered ship. However, on June 20, still considerably north of the equator, the ship received the change in operation orders diverting us to Pearl."

It was, after all, not a total lie.

25

PREPARING FOR "PANAMA"

E arly on Saturday morning, June 28, we eased along in the tropical depths near Oahu, the hub island of the Hawaiian group. Our course took us on beyond Diamond Head to the southwest. There we merged with our imaginary position, as if we were returning from just north of the equator. I wanted the shore-based listening devices to hear a submarine approaching from the south.

At 0600 we swung to the north and lined up for the entrance to Pearl Harbor. By then the large information chart that detailed our Arctic travels had been removed from the crew's mess and replaced with a South Pacific chart. On it were lines showing our imaginary travels from Seattle southward and then back to Hawaii.

In the early dawning light and precisely on time, we ascended to periscope depth to see sparkling, breathtakingly beautiful Oahu clearly visible through number one periscope. It was especially striking in contrast to the landscapes we had most recently scanned. I gave the order, and in seconds *Nautilus* rose silently to the surface.

As I climbed to the bridge, I took a quick look around. Our super-structure was in surprisingly good shape despite more than six thousand miles of high-speed submerged running. A deck party under the direction of Dutch Larch quickly painted and restored our identifying side numbers and names, so we looked the same as we would have had we actually been on the southern voyage.

As we entered the harbor, a small boat eased alongside, allowing Admiral H. G. Hopwood and Rear Admiral E. W. Grenfell to step aboard *Nautilus*. It was quite a surprise to be met at the harbor entrance at that early hour and warmly welcomed by Admiral Grenfell, the top Pacific sub-marine boss, but also by Admiral Hopwood, the commander of the entire Pacific Fleet. It was an impressive welcome for skipper and all hands.

As we moved into the harbor, a huge flower lei, thirty feet long, was draped across our bow. Helicopters hovered overheard, dropping a deluge of multicolored orchids onto our decks and the water around us. Vessels resting in the harbor let loose a chorus of blasts from their whistles. An impressive cadre of fireboats and tugs sent water high into the air, the mist catching myriad rainbows. Hundreds stood on the sea walls and piers to view and greet us. Once we arrived at our assigned berth at the sub base, hundreds stood by while a navy band played "Anchors Aweigh" and lovely island girls danced the hula.

We managed to keep Waldo and Rex hidden until we could sneak them ashore.

Most of the welcome was simply for a distinguished first-time visitor. This was the initial trip to Hawaii for *Nautilus*. I knew that the admirals—though not anyone else who welcomed us—were aware of our failed mis-sion. By arranging this spectacular reception they were graciously lifting our spirits. I was filled with emotion and gratitude to both of them and to the service branch they represented. It is truly wonderful to belong to an organization such as this.

That is how our three-and-a-half-week stay in warm Hawaii began, waiting for the Arctic ice to melt and recede. We encountered continued goodwill and assistance from everyone, and the record shows we recipro-cated by conducting more than three thousand military and civilian personnel through the ship on guided orientation tours. We also took more than two hundred people to sea during trials that we conducted toward the end of the stay.

The usual shuffle at dockside occurred, including old hands leaving for new duty stations while new faces showing up to replace them. Lieutenant Tom Tonseth, who had made both Arctic voyages with *Nautilus*, left to go to Nuclear Power School at New London. Lieutenant Don Fears went to duty aboard a new nuclear submarine, USS *Triton* (SSRN-586). Chief Ray McCoole was commissioned an ensign, a new officer, and headed for the indoctrination course at Newport, Rhode Island. Chief Yeoman Howard James went to work with the first skipper of *Nautilus*, Captain Wilkinson, who had since become a division commander in New London.

Nautilus receives a glorious welcome to Pearl Harbor after the unsuccessful attempt at a Pacific-to-Atlantic North Pole transit in early summer 1958. The welcome and the assistance of the naval staff at Pearl raised the spirits of the *Nautilus* crew and helped them get under way on the successful mission later in the summer.

Like Lieutenant Tonseth, all three of those men had been aboard for both our trips north.

Lieutenant David Boyd, a plankowner who left *Nautilus* to become the *Skate* navigator before I took command, once again went from *Nautilus* to *Skate*. He had been back on board *Nautilus* for TAD (or temporary additional duty) to gain under-ice navigation experience on *Nautilus*'s inertial navigation system, at that time the only one operational in the navy.

Lieutenants Donald Hall and Robert Kassel, each a recent graduate of the nuclear training program, reported aboard for duty. So did Seamen Billy Fowlkes and Roger Hall and Fireman Richard King. Yeoman Second Class Clemente Ortega from Comfort, Texas, reported aboard from the sub school in New London to replace Howard James.

Captain Kinsey, the navy psychiatrist, happily stuck with us, as did George Bristow and Thomas Curtis, our resident North American Aviation engineers. Joe Degnan, who accompanied home the body of crewman Szarzynski, rejoined us as well.

Lyon was back aboard after a brief visit home to San Diego. His assistant, Rex Rowray, reported to *Skate*. Archer Walker, Lyon's assistant on our 1957 cruise, returned for his second under-ice adventure.

The first closed-circuit television for a submarine was installed to help us to better judge ice conditions overhead, giving us a far better view than we could get through a periscope. It would be most helpful in locating leads or polynyas in the ice.

I would not be there to see all this activity. A mere four hours after we docked at our berth at the sub base, I was already in an airplane, headed for Washington, D.C., to confer with Vice Admiral Thomas S. Combs, deputy chief of naval operations for operational research and development, and Rear Admiral Daspit. After that I was scheduled to brief key members of the White House staff and then go to New London to confer with Rear Admiral F. B. Warder, ComSubLant. Admiral Hopwood had made his personal navy transport plane available for the trip. He had also agreed to my request that I be allowed to take along for short leaves back home as many of the crew as the plane could accommodate—about twenty-five men.

One subject I wanted to discuss in Washington was more aerial reconnaissance flights, a series of them on a regular basis during the time of our next voyage. After our close encounter, accurate and up-to-date surveys of the ice-choked, shallow-water portions of our route would prove invaluable. The visual information would help us determine if and when conditions had opened up to the extent necessary so we could depart Pearl for a second try. If we got the okay to make a second attempt, we had to make it count.

Typically it would have been no problem for the chief of naval operations to set up such flights. Security was the complicating factor in this case. Any personnel involved in such reconnaissance flights would have to be unaware of their real purpose.

When we landed in Washington, I headed straight for the Pentagon to speak with Duke Bayne about the best way to get the flights done without blowing our cover. We considered several options and came up with the ideal solution. Why not send a *Nautilus* officer incognito to Alaska? Admiral Combs and Admiral Daspit concurred with the plan.

From Washington, I headed directly to Connecticut. For several *Nautilus* personnel—myself included—the trip to New London presented the welcome opportunity to see our families. William was growing as fast as the weeds in Bonny's vegetable garden. Mike reported a problem with his boat's steering cable. He felt we had been "gypped."

Taking time to help a young man fix his boat sure puts things in perspective. As hectic as things were and with as many things I had to keep track of, the act of helping my son fix his boat was very good for me. It brought home, literally, what it was all about. I finally got some emotional and mental rest, albeit for a day or two. The North Pole temporarily reverted to the place where Santa and his elves hide away and make Christmas toys and goodies.

Still, I had to consider the details of the flights over the Chukchi Sea ice. It was neither needed nor practical that I take on this job. I thought the logical person to go was our navigator, Shep Jenks. No question he could handle the assignment.

Luckily he was on leave in New London at the same time that I was, so it would be easy to get things rolling. I grabbed the telephone and dialed his home number, hoping I could catch him there. Thankfully, he answered.

"Shep, let me apologize to Barbara for interrupting your time at home, but there has been a change of plans," I told him. "I can't tell you why, but I need you to stay home and not fly back to Pearl just yet. I'll see you tomorrow night at my place, okay?"

I could tell from the slight pause that Jenks had questions, but he simply told me fine, that he would see me the next evening. At least he had some additional time with his family.

There in my backyard in Mystic, with a warm summer breeze coming

Captain Anderson and LT Shepherd Jenks, the navigator for both attempts to reach the North Pole in 1958. Jenks, who later entered the ministry, delivered the eulogy at Captain Anderson's funeral at Arlington National Cemetery in 2007.

up the river and the fireflies twinkling in the tree branches, I told Shep about what we wanted to do and why it was so important that it be handled properly. He immediately grasped the situation.

During the following few weeks, he would be posing as a special representative of OP-33, a branch of the office of the chief of naval operations that had absolutely nothing to do with submarines. Its job was to plan, among other things, Arctic and Antarctic operations. Through Rear Admiral Warder in New London, he received a set of orders that made no mention of *Nautilus* or anything close to a submarine organization. They gave Jenks an open ticket to go wherever necessary to complete any unspecified job required.

The plan was for Shep to fly to Alaska as a representative of the mysterious OP-33. There he would arrange for a particular program of aerial ice reconnaissance flights over the Chukchi Sea and the southern reaches of the Arctic Ocean. He would go on enough of these flights to ensure he had a good firsthand knowledge of conditions, arrange for the flights to continue until after *Nautilus* passed through the shallow Chukchi Sea, and work up a system of getting the required information on the ice conditions to us as we made the transit.

Less than two days and about four thousand miles later, Jenks was in Kodiak, Alaska. He was authorized to reveal his true mission to Rear Admiral A. W. McKechnie, commander Alaskan Sea Frontier. His dolphins, his *Nautilus* cigarette lighter, and his *Nautilus* tie clasp were in his bureau drawer back in Connecticut. His wallet contained no ID cards that might reveal his connection to *Nautilus* or submarines.

By Thursday, July 10, Jenks was at Eielson Air Force Base in Fairbanks, and early the next morning was in a P2V, airborne on the first of the so-called "triangle" flights over the proposed future track of *Nautilus* on her run to the Pole and beyond. "Triangle" refers to the flight paths chosen, which were triangular in shape in order to cover a greater area than a mere in-and-out along a straight line.

On his first trip, Jenks got a good look at the ice pack in the Chukchi

Sea. It was formidable, heavily ridged at the boundaries. He had seen plenty of the stuff on his first two ice trips aboard *Nautilus* but never from this perspective. He noticed that the lead that formed along the northwestern coast of Alaska during the summer months was wide and relatively ice free.

Jenks drafted a message for me with the help of the navy ice observers and sent it to CincPacFlt in Pearl Harbor. From there, it was hand-delivered to Rear Admiral Grenfell at ComSubPac and then to me at *Nautilus*.

Shep made many flights over the ice and made certain they would continue. The ice observations, containing the exact information we would need, would continue to be sent as requested. Jenks was then ordered to return to *Nautilus*. On the way back he bought an Eskimo doll for his daughter. The first thing we made Shep do when he got back to the ship was to put his daughter's doll in the three-combination safe classified top secret.

Meanwhile, thanks to Admirals Hopwood and Grenfell, a second group of *Nautilus* crew members flew home for a short leave. And Bonny took advantage of my few remaining days in Pearl by following me by commercial airline. In the evenings after I finished my work, we sometimes relaxed with old friends, reviving memories of our days in Pearl that had been so special for us and where our youngest son, William Jr., had been born. With all the work that I had to do at the ship, however, we did not get as much time together as I had hoped.

I was heartened each day to look at Admiral McKechnie's ice reports. Conditions were becoming more and more favorable with each report for a second attempt to get through the Chukchi Sea and into the Arctic Basin. Response in Washington to our plan for another trip north was positive. The mission was a "go." We confidently set our departure date for July 25.

We needed to develop another cover operation plan to justify our being out of touch during this voyage. Admiral Grenfell announced that *Nautilus* was about to make a submerged endurance run from Pearl Harbor to Panama. Along the way we were to be conducting underwater sound tests. The Panama alibi had worked once before, so we simply recycled it.

For the entire stay in Hawaii, our crew and the men from the sub base repair shop worked practically around the clock on the Mark 19 gyrocompass that had failed us near the Bering Strait. For a bit we were convinced that we had fixed it. Then on our operations in and out of Pearl Harbor, we noticed that the compass was becoming more and more erratic. This was not a good development. It had to be in perfect operating condition before we could even think about leaving on another polar visit.

The submarine staff officers at Pearl Harbor were quite put out with all the fuss over one simple erratic compass. After all, we had three other compasses that worked perfectly well at most points on the globe, and certainly between Oahu and Panama. All I could do was look them in the eye and say, "Well, that's right. But on *Nautilus*, we never get under way unless everything . . . and I mean everything . . . is working properly."

I held my ground. The ice reports remained encouraging. As anxious as we were to get under way, we still had plenty of time to make sure the compass was good to go before we started north on July 25.

Then I received a startling report about activities at the sub base in New London.

26

THE RACE IS ON

The news came about a week before our planned departure from Pearl for Operation Sunshine II. I was in my stateroom doing some paperwork when someone knocked on the door. It was one of the crew asking if he could meet with me for a few minutes on a confidential matter.

"Absolutely," I told him and closed the door behind him to afford us some privacy.

The crewman (I will call him "Smith") explained that he was one of those lucky enough to go back to New London during our Hawaiian interlude. While there, he went down to where the brand-new nuclear submarine *Skate* was located to visit a buddy who had duty aboard the ship. Smith was waiting for his friend to get off duty when he accidentally overheard an interesting bit of information.

A *Skate* officer, at morning quarters, was delivering something of a pep talk to the crew, urging them to push ahead on their preparations for their upcoming departure. Their departure for the Arctic!

As the pep talk progressed, it became clear to Smith that the goal of *Skate*'s voyage was to "beat *Nautilus* to the North Pole."

Smith went to great lengths to assure me that he was not snooping but that he could not help overhearing the *Skate* officer's talk. I assured him that I believed him and that he was doing the right thing in telling me about this development. I also promised I would protect his identity, and I always have. I also told him how important this information was and that it might result in some significant changes in our approach to Sunshine II.

The paperwork on my desk was now forgotten.

I stared at the ship's clock on the wall as it ticked off precious time. The news about *Skate* was disturbing, to say the least. So far as I was aware her skipper, Jim Calvert, knew nothing about our true intentions for *Nautilus* in respect to Operation Sunshine. I was confident no member of the crew had let anything slip. Officially, Calvert was supposed to know only of the announced cover plan that would send *Nautilus*, *Skate*, and *Halfbeak* together on an Atlantic-side penetration toward the end of the summer.

Why would the crew of *Skate* be asked to accelerate their ship's readiness for sea in order to beat *Nautilus* to the North Pole? What gave them the idea that we were headed that way?

I could only conclude that Commander Calvert had somehow learned about the ultimate goal of Operation Sunshine. Apparently *Skate* now had orders that appeared to give her opportunity for an Atlantic-side dash to the Pole should *Nautilus* fail again or be delayed in our run from the Pacific side.

Something about that scenario worried me greatly. Poised in case we failed again or were delayed? Maybe that was the rationale, but it left too much room for failure to communicate or for simple misunderstanding. *Skate* might simply ply ahead with the hope of an assured victory over *Nautilus*. From what my crew member overheard, it certainly appeared she was on the verge of actually making such a run.

Jim Calvert was an old acquaintance. We were classmates at the Naval Academy and sub school. Each made war patrols in the Pacific. We were

PCOs at Admiral Rickover's NRB. We studied the reactor prototype at Arco, Idaho, at the same time.

I recall that when the Korean conflict began, I was on shore duty as an NROTC instructor in naval weapons at the University of Idaho, but was anxious to return to sea duty. I conferred with Jim, who was then detail officer at submarine headquarters, and told him of my desire. He seemed surprised.

"Andy, I have a note on your card that you and your wife are expecting a baby," he told me. "I assumed you wanted to stay home for the time being."

That response confirmed two things. First, I had not been forgotten; I was still in line to work my way up to my own command. Second, Calvert had a big heart for an old friend. I explained to Jim that his information was at one time correct but sadly Bonny had recently miscarried. I made it clear I preferred sea duty to NROTC. He read to me a list of ships that were being put back in commission. *Trutta* was one of them. Since I had helped put her into mothballs when she was first decommissioned after World War II, I knew she was a good ship. I told Jim a spot on *Trutta* would be great. He obviously came through. That is how, in February 1951, I came to rejoin the *Trutta* crew as executive officer.

Jim Calvert was an exceptionally able submariner and a tall, dashing, handsome fellow. He eventually served as superintendent of the Naval Academy and retired a vice admiral. To his credit, he was also smart, aggressive, highly competitive, and politically astute.

He understandably had ambitions on being the first to take a submarine to the North Pole and had encouraged, if not actually put out, the claim that "*Nautilus* had her chance [to get to the Pole in 1957]. Now it's *Skate*'s turn."

As I sat in my stateroom and stared at the Arctic charts on my little desk, I could only assume that *Skate* was not planning to politely bow to *Nautilus*. I assumed these two ships were now in an undeclared race for the Pole, and, if so, *Nautilus* needed to be at sea and headed north at the earliest possible minute if we stood a chance of getting there first.

The truth of the matter was that *Nautilus*—except for having a lot of Arctic experience compared to *Skate*, which had none—was severely handicapped in such a mad dash. For *Skate* to get to the Pole, she would only need to travel 630 miles under ice from the Atlantic/Greenland side, and would be in good, deep water all the way, most of which was charted by *Nautilus* in 1957.

For *Nautilus,* coming from the Pacific side, there would be double that distance under the ice, almost all of which was uncharted. The first three hundred miles were known to be shallow waters laden with much deep ice. We had proved that fact, too, with near disastrous results, only a month before.

As I have stated, the act of getting to the Pole is an accepted historic measure of success in exploring the Arctic and not a small challenge any way you approach it. But President Eisenhower's goal for *Nautilus* was finding a militarily strategic, ocean-to-ocean, under-the-ice path. The North Pole—though quite alluring on its own—became an almost incidental point on the route across.

I understood why Calvert, his crew, and probably others in the navy felt that "*Nautilus* had her chance." However, with the many lessons we had learned in *Nautilus*—some the hard way—and all to the benefit of subsequent explorations, I felt I owed it to my crew to give them the opportunity not only to be the first all the way across the top but also to be the first to the Pole in the process. There was no time to waste but race or not, I would not risk my ship and crew to gain advantage until I knew we were ready.

We were waiting on three things: better ice conditions along our proposed route, a fully functional emergency breathing system, and a working gyrocompass. Shep Jenks and the men flying the triangle routes over the Arctic were reporting that ice conditions had improved dramatically. Installation on the final phase of the emergency breathing system was complete and being tested. A gyro expert was on his way from the mainland to fix the compass.

I immediately went to see Admiral Grenfell and explain my situation.

I asked if *Nautilus* could advance its departure from July 25 to as soon as the Mark 19 gyrocompass was repaired—hopefully the twenty-first or twenty-second. I was aware that this would cause the admiral some sticky problems. He would have to cancel—without explanation—quite a few VIP visits to the ship if we left early. He graciously took me off the hook. He agreed that we should depart as soon as I felt that everything was ready, and I am still grateful for that stirring vote of confidence.

When I got back to the ship, I called Frank Adams and the other senior officers together and told them of my meeting with Admiral Grenfell. We set a new target departure for late Tuesday afternoon, July 22. That date would give us a three-day head start over our previous plans. Paul Early assured us that when the gyro expert got there, an around-the-clock effort would be made to get the aggravating thing fixed.

Thankfully, the chief engineer from Sperry Corporation, Fred Braddon, turned out to be an expert indeed. It took him only a short while to find the source of trouble in the Mark 19, and he soon had it corrected. He was so good, I wanted him to come along on our trip, but he could not.

When news spread that the compass was now in working order, the atmosphere up and down the length of *Nautilus* was once again electric. We were finally ready to head north for our second try from the Pacific side.

Bonny left for Mystic. I could not tell her when I would see her again or even when we would next talk on the phone.

I also said good-bye to Admiral Grenfell. He and his organization at Pearl Harbor had given us tremendous support and understanding for which I am eternally grateful. I told the admiral that I would long remember his inspiring leadership.

So there we were, 116 men all scurrying about *Nautilus*, readying ourselves to start two races: the Cold War race with the Soviets to demonstrate superior technological capability and the undeclared race for the North Pole with *Skate*, our own sister nuclear submarine.

PART IV
OPERATION SUNSHINE II

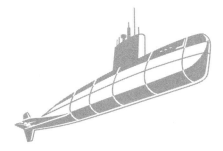

"Captain, you might even say we pierced the Pole."

—Tom Curtis, navigation system technician aboard *Nautilus* on the polar trip

27

"THE PANAMA-ARCTIC-PEARL SHUTTLE"

TUESDAY, JULY 22, 1958

"1958: ENROUTE, HAWAII TO EUROPE, VIA GEOGRAPHICAL NORTH POLE."

Darkness had fallen. *Nautilus* slipped quietly—almost silently—through the calm Pacific waters off Pearl Harbor. As soon as we were well clear of the shore and sea traffic, I ordered our deck crew to paint over our side numbers and names once again, erasing the "571" and *Nautilus.* We were on our way for our third polar voyage.

We set the clocks ahead, this time to Seattle time, again with the intention of keeping to the same zone to avoid the distraction of the quick changes we would experience at high latitudes and converging time zones. I did not want to jinx us this time by setting the clocks to British time.

"2321: SUBMERGED."

As we cleared the entrance channel, I called for full speed and felt the same familiar thrill I always did when the ship surged forward at my command. I was also aware that the mood on *Nautilus* was markedly different this time—different from the throbbing excitement of our departure from Seattle back in June. It was replaced by calm determination and an almost palpable sense of confidence. Twice we had experienced the same chastisement that others who challenged the Arctic before us had received. Now, I felt we were wiser, more experienced, better equipped, and much better in tune with the icy challenges that lay ahead of us.

I was pleased to receive the reports that all our navigational equipment seemed to be working well. Porpoises had been reported playing alongside our bow as we left Oahu behind. A good omen for a submarine sailor.

Just after 11:00 p.m., we submerged and went deep in the waters to check for any leaks. At three minutes past midnight, we ascended from seven hundred feet and leveled off at cruising depth. At over twenty knots, we sped through the Kauai Channel and set a course for Yunaska Pass in the Aleutian Islands. This was to be a fast, submerged transit. Our powerful reactor would put out near maximum-rated energy almost around the clock until we arrived in the shallower waters of the Bering Sea. We only planned to slow long enough to pick up radio traffic. The automatic steering system kept us dead on course as we ran northward.

At 8:22 a.m. *Nautilus* reached yet another milestone. She passed her 40,000th league (120,000th nautical mile) on nuclear power. There was no celebration to mark the event. It slipped by unobserved as all hands aboard were more focused on their jobs and the mission ahead.

We were only twenty-four hours out of Pearl when we received our first ice summary message, compiled from the continuing reconnaissance flights that Shep Jenks had set up. It was good news. Conditions were becoming more favorable all the time. Even the quicker and more direct western door around St. Lawrence Island appeared to be wide open for us this trip.

THURSDAY, JULY 24, 1958

The miles slipped by quickly. Our voyage to the Bering Strait was another record run for *Nautilus*.

Despite our smooth ride north, we were not idle. Tom Curtis and George Bristow continually fine-tuned the N6A inertial navigation system with the help of *Nautilus* electronics technicians Robert Rockefeller and Barry Lerich. Lyon and Archie Walker continued an intense check and double-check of their latest under-ice equipment. All over the ship men were busy looking for fire hazards, peaking up equipment, checking to make sure spares were stowed and readily available, and doing the other one thousand and one things necessary to be ready—no matter what. Others worked and studied, getting ready for qualification exams, hoping to earn their dolphin pins at the North Pole.

As I passed through the ship and neared the crew's mess, I could hear the jukebox playing songs that reminded us of Hawaii. Card games and cribbage tournaments were organized. The first edition of our daily newspaper was published, this time titled *The Panama—Arctic—Pearl Shuttle Boat News*.

We slowed about 11:00 p.m. to copy radio traffic. There was only one message for us this time, but it had special meaning for Engineman First Class Harry Hedin from Grand Forks, North Dakota. He received the news that he was a father for the third time, an eight-pound baby girl named Clara. Both mom and baby were doing fine.

FRIDAY, JULY 25, 1958

We were ahead of schedule due to melting, retreating ice. The area near the Aleutians had been transformed into an entirely different world than the one we had visited only a month earlier. The ship was practically on automatic. Sophisticated electronic instruments steered and guided her through the ocean depths while crew members kept a close eye on gauges and dials and other instruments that reported the condition of all systems aboard our ship. That powerful, mysterious—and so often misunderstood—force that propelled us did precisely what it was supposed to do—now and in the dreams of visionaries like Hyman Rickover and others.

SATURDAY, JULY 26, 1958
"1959: RADAR FIX OFF YUNASKA AND HERBERT ISLANDS."

We intended for this Saturday to be our last day in the Pacific for a while. We were approximately twenty miles from land, so we established our precise position with merely a momentary exposure of our radar mast above the sea's surface. It was a very foggy and overcast day, but the conning officer, using number one periscope, briefly sighted Yunaska Island. When we plotted that bearing with our radar ranges and bearings, we had proof of our position. We quickly left the bleak, dreary world above and increased depth to take advantage of the deep water remaining before we reached the much shallower continental shelf.

Soon we were once again in the Bering Sea. I gave the order to descend to three hundred feet and increase speed to twenty-two knots. Midway through the Bering, we popped up again to periscope depth and once more used radar to establish our position. It is necessary near land that navigation be a very precise art.

We were all struck by how much the water had changed since we were in the mid-Pacific. As seen through the periscope, the color had gradually shifted from the clear, warm blue of the tropics to a cold and cloudy green. There were no longer crisp whitecaps riding on deep, blue swells. Now they were whitish-gray, and they tumbled at the crest of steep waves. Bird life in this area was far more abundant than I would have expected. Orange-billed puffins waited until our periscope was almost to them and then, panicked, tried to take off with little success. They flapped their wings frantically and seemed to try to run across the water fast enough to get their chubby bodies airborne, but all they could manage was to bounce along the surface for twenty yards or so until they were clear of our periscope.

"2300: COPIED PEARL HARBOR FOX BROADCAST."

On one of our trips to just below the surface to copy radio messages, I received a brief personal communication from Admiral Grenfell. It took my breath away when I first read it. I scanned it again to make sure I had not misunderstood it.

The admiral informed me, without comment or elaboration, that *Skate* had damaged a propeller and had entered dry dock at New London for repairs.

While the news eased my fears that *Skate* would somehow beat us to the Pole, given the advantage of coming from the deeper Atlantic side, I had to assume that the pressure was still on. We had a lot of shallow water before us, and even with the increasingly favorable ice reports we were receiving, we still did not know what we might find on the other side of the Bering Strait. No one did. We would be exploring virgin territory.

When her propeller was fixed, *Skate* could still get under way and make good time heading north. We later learned that Jim Calvert's ship was damaged in a collision with the submarine tender USS *Fulton* (AS-11), but no one was hurt.

I read the cryptic radio message several more times before I folded it and put it away in my safe. I did not advise the crew of the content or the nature of Admiral Grenfell's message. It contained no details, so I had no idea of the extent of the damage to *Skate*. Dry-docking and propeller replacement might only cause *Skate* a day's delay. The primary reason I did not share the information, though, was because I did not want to seem to be even mildly gloating over the misfortune of our sister submarine. Besides, the news would not alter our plans, and I did not want to disturb the inspired focus the crew was now demonstrating.

SUNDAY, JULY 27, 1958

This Sunday found us still in relatively deep water, rushing almost due north. In the western part of the Bering Sea, the deeper water extends for some three hundred miles north of the Aleutian chain, so we laid our course to take advantage of it.

During the morning, we worked some more on our sound equipment, adjusting to get the best possible performance in the tough, ice-laden miles ahead. Sonarmen Chiefs John Michaud, Jim Norris, and Al Charette, and Sonarman Second Class Bill Gaines (who eventually rose to the rank of captain and held two submarine commands) all hovered around their equipment with electronic test gear until they finally announced that they were satisfied.

"1322: DUE WEST OF THE PRIBILOFF ISLANDS."

Shortly after midday we were west of the Pribiloff Islands, and we finally changed course to miss St. Matthew Island. As we crossed the one-hundred-fathom curve, we dropped our speed to eighteen knots and brought *Nautilus* up to 150 feet. We silently said good-bye to deep water beneath our keel. We would not have that luxury again until we were well into the Arctic Ocean.

As I felt the engines slow and sensed the slight change in vibration, I could not help but reflect once more on what an amazing vessel we had. We still had more than five thousand miles to go before we reached our next port, but we had no worries at all about running out of fuel. Many years later in 2004 at the fiftieth anniversary of the *Nautilus* commissioning, I was startled to hear the director of the Naval Reactors Branch, Admiral Frank Lee Bowman, report that U.S. nuclear submarines being built now would never have to be refueled—not in their entire lifetime of approximately thirty-three years!

During the evening, we drew abeam of St. Matthew Island and changed course slightly to head for St. Lawrence Island and the Bering Strait beyond.

We were continuously taking soundings. As the water depth changed even slightly, we adjusted our speed, depth, or both, accordingly. This part of the Bering Sea is not nearly as flat-bottomed and predictable as the northern and eastern sections. Waldo told me that was because not as much ice melted in these waters, thus depositing its load of fine silt it had picked up from the coast. Scientists now speculate that the Bering—and the Chukchi to the north—will become shallower with time as a result of the soil brought out from the shore.

That night a special committee met behind closed doors to plan our North Pole celebration. I had no idea what they were working on but trusted that whatever they came up with would be appropriate. Appropriate but

Meeting aboard *Nautilus* during her first attempt across the top of the world in June 1958. Standing left to right: LT John Harvey, LT Dave Boyd, North American Aviation engineer Tom Curtis, LT Robert Kelsey, LT William Lalor, LT Steve White, LCDR Frank Adams, COB Lynus "Dutch" Larch, Joseph Marchand, Charles Black, and John Draper.

decidedly original. Ours was a creative group. Bill McNally, one of the heroes of the fire off Panama and the unofficial cartoonist for the ship's newspaper, was the committee's chairman, so I knew it would be spectacular.

There was a lot of interest in the contests for designing the flag to fly to signify our voyage and for coming up with the best honorary designation for submerged North Pole visitors. Since we would be pioneering such a distinction, we needed something to correspond to Bluenoses. The appeal of the contests was heightened by the fact that the prizes were seventy-two-hour liberties that Frank Adams had authorized once we were in Europe.

MONDAY, JULY 28, 1958

At midnight the ventilation was lined up and a battery charge was started. I wanted the battery almost fully charged at all times so we would have an adequate source of emergency power while underneath the ice. The battery was charged only until it commenced evolving hydrogen gas. After that we stopped to prevent any buildup of the explosive gas in our sealed atmosphere. Submarines and their crew members had been lost to fire and explosion from hydrogen released by a battery charge.

We had our first glitch of the voyage just after one o'clock in the morning. The stern diving planes—the devices that helped to control the angle of diving and surfacing and to maintain a constant depth—began to act erratically in normal power. We quickly found the trouble in the electrical control system. The stern planes had been one of our most reliable systems. We put them on emergency power, repaired them, and returned to normal operation four hours later.

We were now passing through cold Siberian currents, and the water temperature was dropping. As we crossed the twenty-five-fathom curve (the sea was about 150 feet deep), we slowed to ten knots. Through the periscope, we could see St. Lawrence Island. Shep Jenks obtained a visual fix. We could also see Siberia—the Soviet Union—off the port beam. The sea was a flat calm. So far we had not seen any ice to speak of.

At about 5:45 p.m. we came to periscope depth to look for floes. We were in almost the exact spot where we had encountered the heavy ridged ice back in June, the ice that was so thick and menacing that it caused us to turn around and seek the eastern door north to the Bering Strait. There was no ice in sight.

As we made twelve knots northward, our long-range sonar picked up a ship contact several miles to our southeast. I slowed and came to periscope depth for a quick look. A two-second observation confirmed exactly what the sonar had told us. We lowered the periscope and eased back down to cruising depth. I did not want to take even the slightest risk of the contact spotting our periscope. Besides, he was not going to bother us, and we certainly were not going to bother him.

TUESDAY, JULY 29, 1958

At one in the morning, with Lalor at the conn, *Nautilus* came to periscope depth to find the sea glassy calm and visibility limited to about three miles by a light, cold fog. We got a fix on Fairway Rock and the pair of Diomede Islands, confirming we were near the entrance to the Bering Strait. Shortly afterward, we altered course to enter the narrow passageway between two continents. I ordered full speed ahead.

I turned to Shep Jenks and asked him to give me distance, time, and average speed from Pearl. He had the numbers in front of him, already calculated: 2,901 miles in six days, four hours, and nine minutes, and an average speed—including our departure through Pearl Harbor and through 483 miles of shallow water—of 19.6 knots. Even I was impressed!

Once we cleared the strait, we were set to try the next squeeze we had been anticipating—the very shallow reach of the Chukchi Sea, the place where we found such trying and near fatal ice conditions during our previous trip. Today our passage seemed a calm waltz compared to the discordant zigs and zags required back in June. We were able to maintain speed at fifteen knots in completely ice-free water. The wait at Pearl Harbor for better ice conditions was paying off. But for how long?

About five that afternoon, Lieutenant Steve White, the engineering officer on watch, reported a ground fault on the ship's electrical bus. The crew immediately went to work to try to locate the malfunction. Such an electrical problem could cause a fire should it arc, or it could injure someone who came into contact with certain affected equipment. We had to find it and fix it immediately.

After two intense hours, the electricians found the problem. Condensation had caused cold water to drip from a circulating water line, and that led to a short-circuit between two cables feeding power to a small portable heater. Moisture buildup and condensation inside the hull of a conventional submarine are quite often the cause of electrical problems, not to mention discomfort and all sorts of other nagging issues. But the excellent air-conditioning system of *Nautilus* usually kept it at a minimum, even in cold waters like those we were then plying.

At no time did we feel that the problem with the stern planes or the electrical breakdown threatened the mission. Still, we breathed easier once the repairs were made and I tried not to see them as bad omens.

"2324: SIGHTED ICE BEARING BETWEEN 278 AND 355 DEGREES TRUE, RANGE ABOUT FIVE MILES."

We reached latitude seventy degrees, five minutes north. Someone noted that we were then about sixty miles north of the point where the treacherous ice had forced us to turn back during Operation Sunshine I four weeks before. Though we had already spotted ice—and some of it rugged—we were able to skirt it by making small course corrections. As we slipped past, only a few hundred yards from the edge, I peered intently at the ice for the better part of an hour.

To tell you the truth, it was mean looking—dirty, ragged, marked by high ridges and hummocks or knolls. It looked threatening, challenging, and nothing at all like the pure white and relatively level floes we had seen on the Atlantic side during the 1957 cruise.

When I spotted through the periscope a sharp-edged ridge of ice projecting about the height of a man above the sea surface, I thought of the ratio of ice below the surface to that above it—about nine to one. This meant the top of our sail would have to be more than fifty feet below the surface to clear that relatively innocent-looking spike of solid ice. From what we knew of the sea depth in this area, that would leave precious little water beneath us.

Would our quest be ended once again by the lack of water and the surprising depth of the ice keels?

We would soon have our answer.

28

WHERE NO MAN HAS GONE BEFORE

WEDNESDAY, JULY 30, 1958

At midnight we were submerged, cruising at twelve knots, scanning all the while for ice through the periscope and with our sonar gear. We were at seventy degrees, forty-five minutes north at about one o'clock in the morning. That location put us 1,115 nautical miles from the North Pole. Things were looking up now that we had left behind the point of our previous involuntary turnaround and were still making encouraging progress northward.

Then suddenly fog closed in and we were forced to slow. Soon we found ourselves in the midst of what Bill Lalor called "ice cubes." These were only a few feet across and lay very low in the water. I worried most about our periscope getting damaged if struck by a big enough block, as had happened to us the previous year. We had no choice. We came up to the surface.

In the process we caught a chunk of ice on the deck. That looked like a nice souvenir to me, so I ordered a deck party to retrieve it and put it in our freezer.

We quickly saw that we were in the middle of considerable ice. There was no way to know if we had reached the edge of the mostly solid pack or not, but we were almost certainly near it. We slowly twisted back around to a southerly heading to move out of this brash and block.

"0306: CLEAR OF ALL ICE."

Since we were on the surface in a truly isolated area and adequately shielded by the dense fog from any aircraft that might fly over, I decided to work on some of our topside equipment. Several of our ice-detecting sonars had flooded out again. We had also lost one radio antenna. In a couple of hours, the flooded topside fathometers and the antenna were back in full commission. The air in the boat was fresher, and most of the crew took advantage of the opportunity to visit the bridge and view this seldom-seen part of the outside world.

The ice we had spotted was off our port as we moved north, so I decided to steer about ten miles to the east, and from there begin to probe north for deeper water. I was still concerned that the water was too shallow to allow us to make much progress while submerged, so we needed to work our way to deeper water. We ran on the surface, making anywhere from five to fifteen knots as the eerie fog drifted in and out. By early afternoon, we were at seventy-two degrees, twenty-four minutes north, frustratingly close to seventy-three degrees north where we hoped to encounter an area of deeper water. But before we saw any sign of it, we again steered into ice and dense fog. We had to head south and then east again before once more turning back north.

This time we only got to seventy-two degrees, fifteen minutes north, so we zigged yet again. At a little before midnight, we were fifteen miles farther east, moving at fifteen knots, and the visibility was much better. The horizon to the west was covered with ice, but the north and east appeared to be clear so far.

Maybe this time we would find a way through.

Nautilus crew members on watch: left to right, unidentified crewman, LT Shepherd Jenks, Daniel Brigman, William Brown, and Clarence Price.

"2340: SIGHTED MAJOR ICE. HEAVILY HUMMOCKED."

Despite the midnight sunlight, some of the ice appeared to be almost black. Evidently it was ice that either formed near land or was pushed there, and it had picked up a load of dirt. It was very irregular in appearance, and some of it was thirty-five to forty feet high, which meant as much as 120 feet of ice jutted downward below the surface. *Nautilus* simply would not fit between those black keels and the muddy bottom.

All the time we were on the surface, our radio operators were trying to grab the latest ice message. When we finally got the word, though, we learned that the flights had encountered the same low fog as we had. There was no update.

We would have to do our own looking if we hoped to find a path through.

THURSDAY, JULY 31, 1958

Before we left Hawaii, I had calculated that by the last day of July, we would be in the Atlantic Ocean. So much for optimism! There we were, in the middle of the Chukchi Sea, still searching for water deep enough or seas that were ice free enough to allow us passage. Maybe Operation Sunshine was not meant to succeed.

None of the radio traffic mentioned *Skate*. I had no way of knowing if she had been repaired and Calvert and his crew were on their way to the North Pole. But common sense told me she could be. I knew Jim Calvert well enough not to underestimate him.

We probed along, pinging downward in hopes of detecting deepening water. The pack was all along our port side, lurking like an unbreakable barrier, with scattered pieces floating around us. The pesky fog continued to come and go. To avoid the heavier ice, we changed course six times in four hours, creating a mark on our charts that resembled a jagged scar.

Years later, John Youtcheff, a distinguished space scientist, naval officer, and good friend, happened to get a look at a copy of the chart of our erratic route. He jokingly suggested that either the skipper or the navigator had been dipping into the medicinal brandy. I assured him no such thing occurred, but it did look like the path had been drawn by someone stumbling around.

Just before two o'clock in the morning, we ran into another ice cul-de-sac. The water was still too shallow to dive and squeeze beneath the ice. The floe ahead of us seemed impenetrable. I reluctantly decided to change course yet again and head southeast to look for the Barrow Sea Valley. I had really hoped to find a deeper route through the Chukchi, but time was getting away from us. And it was not just *Skate*. I pictured President Eisenhower and Pete Aurand in the White House, awaiting word that we had made it through. Duke Bayne and Admiral Burke back at the Pentagon too. And the others who had risked their reputations and careers on getting *Nautilus* to the North Pole and beyond.

We simply had to find a way, and we needed to do so very, very soon.

"0500: RAIN FALLING STEADILY."

I had instructed that the passive electronic search equipment be manned so that we could keep watch on the radar frequencies. We certainly did not want a chance encounter with a Russian vessel or aircraft. But Shep Jenks reminded me that our own reconnaissance planes were scheduled to fly this day, and we did not want them to spot an unidentified submarine meandering along on the surface either. Talk about having no friends!

When our officers of the deck, Lieutenants Ken Carr and Bob Kassel, came down from the bridge to go off watch, they were dripping wet. They reported that it was raining hard, almost like a tropical shower back in Hawaii. Waldo told us that they had witnessed an extremely rare occurrence in the Arctic—because it almost never rained there. He added with a grin that the two officers should feel honored. They were probably among only a few people in history who had been rained on in the Arctic.

They shivered and climbed out of their foul-weather gear and then dashed off to warm up with mugs of hot coffee. I am not sure either man felt special at the moment. It also occurred to me as I continued my search for omens that this unusual weather might not portend our successful completion of this mission. I hated to think that the sun might not always shine on *Nautilus* just because we said it did.

Just after noon we picked up aircraft radar and assumed it was our own ice-reconnaissance plane. We slipped below the surface to make sure they did not see us. Shortly after submerging, sonar reported odd sounds. It took only a moment to determine that a school of walruses had surrounded us, lazing on a medium-sized ice floe and probably trying to figure out what kind of huge walrus we were. Just listening to their happy barking helped our dispositions.

As we proceeded south and east at periscope depth, we had to wend our way around thick fingers of deep ice, which had apparently been blown away from the pack by the north wind. On one occasion we were temporarily trapped between two of the ice peninsulas. We had to make a time-consuming detour to find a way out.

Even then it was a tedious, nerve-wracking experience, one that kept the entire crew on its toes. At periscope depth we could not see far enough to follow along ice-free stretches to the southeast. We had to dodge one

Wardroom meeting aboard *Nautilus* during the second 1958 attempt. Gathered around Captain Anderson (seated, center) are LT John Harvey, LT Kenneth Carr, LT William Lalor, navy psychiatrist Captain Jack Kinsey, civilian scientist Dr. Waldo Lyon, and LT William Cole.

bobbing ice block after another. With fog closing in about 10:00 p.m., it was clear that our situation was deteriorating. I am sure most aboard *Nautilus* would not have been surprised had I ordered us to head back south and abandon the effort.

I was not prepared to do that yet. We still had a chance, but we had to surface. I ordered us up so we would not risk damaging the periscope on the "B & B."

"2116: SURFACED FOR BETTER ICE DODGING AND TO REPAIR GARBAGE EJECTOR."

If I was looking for bad omens, the next was a particularly messy one.

The garbage disposal unit on *Nautilus* was a vertical ten-inch-diameter tube that extended from the scullery through the bottom of the ship to the sea. When the outer door was shut, our mess cooks could open the inner door and fill the ejector with bagged and weighted trash and garbage. Then with the inner door shut and the outer one opened, we could discharge the bags by pumping water into the top of the tube and flushing them out. Interlocks kept both doors from being open at the same time, which could flood the ship and lead to a very ignominious and possibly disastrous situation.

Our outer door had become jammed. While still submerged, we flushed, back flushed, and applied air pressure to it, but nothing worked. This could be a serious problem. With crew and guests, we carried 116 men. Each man had three meals a day, which created an abundance of garbage. While under the ice—or submerged for any reason—we had no way to dispose of all that refuse.

In order to free the outer door, Lieutenant Steve White, the damage-control officer, went to work with his repair gang. They isolated the area of the ship to make it watertight, then pressurized the entire compartment, which included the crew's mess, chief petty officers' quarters (called the "goat locker" by most), the galley, and the officers' quarters and wardroom. The air pressure was just high enough to prevent any entry of seawater if the inner door to the disposal unit was opened.

The interlocks were defeated and the inner garbage ejector door was opened. Chief Engineman Frank Skewes and Engineman First Class John McGovern, our two leading auxiliarymen, removed some bags that were trapped in the outer door.

That fixed it.

FRIDAY, AUGUST 1, 1958

We continued to feel our way back southeast toward Point Barrow, the northernmost part of Alaska, still skirting the boundary of the ice pack. Hopefully we would soon run across the deeper water we sought that would allow us to speed northward once again. The sea remained calm, but intermittent patches of dense fog visited us, making visibility very poor.

Sometimes we maintained just enough speed to be able to steer the submarine safely. When the fog allowed, we could easily see the pack boundary to our left. Medium-sized blocks of ice were adrift from the floes, and we had to avoid those at all costs. That sometimes took us farther south than we really wanted to go.

It was interesting to note that some of our systems had taken a great leap forward in development—nuclear power, for example. Other systems had lagged, and they would have to be further developed before comfortable penetration of the ice pack in shallow water would be feasible. I made notes and hoped that, even if we failed, the things we learned in our attempt could be applied to future missions to the Arctic.

Then just north of Point Franklin, Alaska, we found what we had been looking for—deep water.

We first established our position by very short radar sweeps. Then we headed northeastward. We had rounded the corner of the pack and were now headed directly toward the Barrow Sea Valley and what we hoped was the true deepwater gateway to the western Arctic basin. No one knew for sure, of course. We were still relying on soundings and reports that were suspect at best. But right now that was our best and only hope to proceed beneath the solid sea of ice that lay between the North Pole and us.

Finally, I heard the sweetest song I had ever heard.

"Captain, the water is getting deeper," the fathometer operator calmly reported. "It's now 180 feet and still going down. Two hundred feet. Three hundred feet. Four hundred feet. Still getting deeper!"

I quietly thanked the Almighty and allowed myself a deep sigh of relief. The men on watch cheered, so loudly I am surprised they did not hear us all the way to Barrow.

"0425: COMMENCED HIGH SPEED VENTILATION FOR A LONG DIVE."

With ice in sight on our port side and dead ahead of us, we were at long last in water deep enough that we could slide beneath the most impressive keels. We had managed to locate the very head of the Barrow Sea Valley. Lieutenant Bob Kassel, who had just joined us in Hawaii before this cruise, dived the boat for the first time and leveled off at two hundred feet.

Just before water covered the top of the periscope, I caught a glimpse of the sky. It was a beautiful, clear morning with a full moon, the sun rising, and a soft but certainly chilly southerly breeze blowing.

I ordered a course to follow the sea valley northeastward until we found even deeper water. The conning officer, Ken Carr, had all sonars manned to keep a careful watch to avoid deeper drafts of ice. Doggie Rayl and Shep Jenks had gotten one last fix through a moon sight and the one LORAN line that was available at our remote location.

I watched the fathometer closely. It confirmed for me that the ocean floor was gradually deepening. I told the diving officer to take *Nautilus* even farther down to avoid any possible ice. As the valley deepened and widened, we increased speed accordingly.

We had just pulled from a crowded surface street onto the expressway, and we intended to make up for lost time.

"0715: CROSSED 100-FATHOM CURVE."

At long last we were in the Arctic Ocean. *Nautilus* was at cruising depth, and I ordered speed increased to eighteen knots. Stu Nelson again came by the periscope station and requested "going home turns," so I obliged and authorized twenty knots. Soon we were in plenty deep water. I ordered the ship to 713 feet to test for leaks before we got too far beneath the pack. As ever, *Nautilus* was tight.

It was almost as if you could hear the ship hum, happy to once again be in her natural element—deep water. All equipment seemed to finally be working perfectly. At last I was able to issue the order I had been waiting for throughout our maddeningly erratic meanderings along the edge of the ice pack: "Come left to 000," I told helmsman David Greenhill, a torpedoman from San Francisco. We were soon pointed true north. I noted it was

8:52 a.m. and we were on the 155th meridian. The North Pole was dead ahead of us, a mere 1,094 miles away.

Frank Adams and I were now on "watch and watch." One of us was up and about at all times. Frank was in every sense a "co-skipper." Whenever he took over, I could turn in and rest without worry, knowing the ship was in the best of hands. I had served with Frank when we were both officers on USS *Tang*. Even though his wife, Novie, was pregnant at the time of our 1958 cruises to the Arctic, I never saw Frank's attention waver from the job at hand.

We still observed menacing shafts of ice above us on sonar, but now it was more a curiosity than a threat. We were traveling at a safe depth, well below any possible ice formation.

Hospitalman Robert Jarvis from Centralia, Illinois, was taking a break from his job of keeping track of the quality of our atmosphere inside *Nautilus*. He eased back, a pipe in one hand and a fresh cup of hot coffee in the other, and smiled contentedly.

"Here we are, pinging up and down and all around, running along at twenty knots, fresh air all day long, a warm boat, and good hot food," he observed, raising the steaming cup of coffee. "We sure have the situation in hand." Then he nodded his head slightly. "I'm just glad we don't have to walk all the way across that ice up there to the Pole, the way Admiral Peary did it."

No one disagreed with Doc.

29

POINT OF NO RETURN

SATURDAY, AUGUST 2, 1958

A s I watched Lyon's gear trace the bottom of the ice above us and observed the steady work of the watch standers all around me, I began to wonder about the mythical "point of no return." That was the spot where, if we had trouble, it would be better to continue on northward than to try to return to Point Barrow behind us.

I had calculated that such a point would be at the "Pole of Inaccessibility," the geographic center of the ice pack, the point that was the most difficult to get to from any direction. From where we were at that time, it was about four hundred miles our side of the geographic Pole.

With 116 people aboard, *Nautilus* ran at six hundred feet below the surface at eighteen to twenty knots, following a course of 000 degrees true, just about forty-four hours away from reaching our first objective. With our television monitor, we could watch the ice scudding past overhead like wind-blown summer clouds. We worked in our shirtsleeves in the air-conditioned comfort of our remarkable vessel. Reaching the North Pole would be the culmination of one of the most thrilling and fantastic adventures upon which any sailor had ever embarked. I think I know how the crew of Christopher Columbus's ships felt—and those who sailed with Magellan and Captain Cook. The sense of being in a place where no man had ever been before, of fulfilling the dream of so many who had attempted it before and failed, was not lost on us.

We also were more than aware that we could not cruise with total abandon. Comfortable and confident as we were, we still had to be as alert as we would have been had we been at battle stations attacking an enemy.

Overhead was incredibly rough, almost solid ice with upside-down pinnacles that already projected downward as much as eighty feet or more from the surface. That jagged ceiling averaged at least eight to ten feet thick. We knew we had to remain vigilant while standing watch, even if the deeper water now gave us some room to duck if need be.

Admiral Robert Peary poetically described the polar ice pack near the North Pole as a "trackless, colorless chaos of broken and heaved-up ice."

Sir John Ross left for those of us who followed him a cogent reminder: "Let them remember that sea ice is stone, a floating rock in the stream, a promontory or an island when aground, not less solid than if it were a land of granite."

Waldo continued to monitor his equipment hour after hour, watching the recording pens dance hypnotically as they traced the underside contour of the ice above us. We were having a wonderful look, a scientifically and tactically invaluable examination of something no man had ever enjoyed before. Lyon's upward-beamed fathometers were greatly improved over what we had used for our previous two cruises.

Waldo was elated at what he was seeing. It would take months to analyze his now-priceless recordings. It was original data, like a first close-up and accurate look at the surface of a strange, distant planet. During each hour he collected more data than had been gathered about the ice in this region in all of history.

Then he made a tentative, disconcerting finding: "The estimate for ice in the Arctic basin may have to be increased by a considerable factor." He was by then seeing ice keels jutting downward more than one hundred feet.

Of course, we had to continue scanning ahead of our bow and looking downward toward the sea floor as well. There were no charts in existence of the ocean floor over which we now traveled. Would a peak abruptly rise up in front of us, ominously echoing our sonar pings? What if the ocean floor suddenly began to rise beneath us and to squeeze us toward the sharp-toothed ice pack above?

What a disappointment—and what a mammoth navigation problem—that would be! There was still so much for man to learn before undertaking routine transpolar voyages. We would discover much of that firsthand during the next few amazing hours. That is what exploration is all about. I could only hope we would gather that knowledge more by trial than by error!

"0100: SOUNDINGS, WHICH HAD BEEN RUNNING ALONG AT 2,100 FATHOMS, JUMPED UP SUDDENLY."

We were at seventy-six degrees, twenty-two minutes north—about one-third of the way between Point Barrow on the northern Alaskan coast and the geographic North Pole. Almost before we could catch our breaths, our readings rapidly decreased to a depth of about five hundred fathoms—about three thousand feet. That was certainly no problem yet, but how much more shallow would it go?

I camped alongside the fathometer for several hours and watched as the surprisingly rugged terrain unfolded beneath us. I saw fantastically steep cliffs rise thousands of feet above the basic ocean floor. Two or three times I ordered speed slackened as a promontory seemed to be rising right up to meet us, then resumed as it topped out safely below us and we left it behind. The shape of these spectacular undersea mountains appeared phenomenally rugged, equal to, if not more acute than, the peaks of the Rocky

Mountains or the Himalayas. We later learned that we were cruising along over the Alpha-Mendeleev, an underwater mountain range with a surface area estimated to be greater than that of the Alps, and only recently discovered by an American ice station.

There were times when this undersea range kept coming up so relentlessly on the fathometer trace that I feared it might rise to the point of blocking our way or force us to probe slowly for a way around it. Fortunately, the roughly nine-thousand-foot heights they reached left us with a clearance of several hundred feet, but each peak gave us reason for concern.

I remember taking a brief turn around the ship to see how everyone was doing. Jack "Mother" Baird, the chief cook, was busy making doughnuts for breakfast.

"Care to try one, Captain?" he asked.

"I don't mind if I do," I answered. I could not resist. I have a sweet tooth. That may have been the best doughnut I have ever put in my mouth.

In the torpedo room I saw torpedo batteries on charge to keep them at maximum readiness. We knew there was little chance of encountering any kind of hostile vessel way up there, but Richard Jackman, torpedoman first class from Massachusetts, could prepare the tubes for firing on an instant's notice if a target appeared or for blasting holes in the ice if we should suddenly need to surface. Also on watch in the compartment was Torpedoman First Class James H. Prater, a Kentuckian who, like Jackman, was making his third Arctic cruise aboard *Nautilus*. He maintained the oxygen bleed from the storage tanks into the ship's atmosphere, making sure the air we breathed had the right amount of oxygen for healthful breathing.

"Prater, how's everything up forward?" I asked him.

"Just fine, Captain," he replied. "Seems like the closer we get to the Pole, the better *Nautilus* runs."

It was true. If a submarine could purr, our ship was certainly doing so.

Next I walked aft to the periscope station. Shep Jenks was poring over his track chart, plotting our position.

"Are we still on track, Shep?" I inquired, knowing the answer already.

"Yes, sir, Captain!" he said with a big smile. "We're not off even by a gnat's eyelash."

He told me that the new high-latitude compass and the inertial navigator were making navigation much easier than it had been on the previous year's trip.

As I toured the ship, someone mentioned the possible reaction of the scientific personnel working on one of the ice islands overhead if we suddenly zoomed underneath at close to twenty knots. It was an interesting thing to ponder.

I ran into Chief Hospitalman John Aberle with the latest atmosphere

LT Shepherd Jenks and Lyle (Doggie) Rayl give full attention to the course plot as *Nautilus* navigates beneath the treacherous polar ice pack en route to Europe by way of the Arctic Ocean.

readings. Our air revitalization components were working efficiently enough to maintain us in the recommended atmospheric conditions. Our air was likely as clean or cleaner than that at the surface.

Other men kept a sharp eye on the ice, charting every one of the infrequent leads and polynyas they saw, just in case we needed to make a sudden dash for the surface. In an emergency we might have to spin around and attempt to thread one of those needles in a hurry. We could have surfaced in one of them and reported our position, but I did not want to take the time or the risk unless we had to.

A lot of interest had developed on the contest to design a cachet or postal mark for envelopes that were to be mailed at the North Pole. I had reasoned that we could assume and later get confirmation of authority to act as an official post office at the North Pole, which meant that the stamps on the envelopes could be canceled with the ship's name and date and our very interesting location at the time of their mailing. There were two superb entries in the competition. One was done by Bill McNally, a very talented artist, and John Kurrus, who was almost as good a cachet designer as he was a periscope welder. The other entry was developed by John Krawczyk and was a bit more adaptable to the face of an envelope. I thought both were worthy of winning the seventy-two hours of liberty in England. I told the judging committee to award all three men the prize.

As the date of our arrival at the Pole became more and more certain, Frank Holland carved the cancellation stamp out of a piece of gasket material. We were ready to cancel stamps mailed at the "North Pole Post Office."

"2000: PASSED THE 'ICE POLE.' "

At 83.5 degrees north, we passed abeam the "Ice Pole," or "Pole of Inaccessibility." It was so named because this is the geographical center of the Arctic ice pack, the most remote point in the Arctic Ocean. Someone mentioned that "Pole of Inaccessibility" was no longer such an apt name, thanks to a nuclear submarine named *Nautilus*.

The day went by with no problems. No faults to rectify, no casualties to overcome. The ice was continually monitored, and it showed almost complete coverage, broken only by occasional cracks between the giant floes. Even with the thick canopy over us, there was still some light filtering through. When I looked through the periscopes, I could see something surprising: phosphorescent streaks in the water. This was something we saw in tropical waters all the time, but I was amazed to see the phenomenon here. It was so cold that the outside of some of our engine-room seawater pipes was caked with thick layers of rime ice.

During the night we passed underneath some prime surfacing opportunities, but we left them behind after noting them on our charts. Time was a factor. We still did not know if *Skate* was ahead of us, coming our way. And everyone in Washington who knew about Operation Sunshine would assume now that we were under the ice, plying toward the Pole. They most wanted to hear from us when we had successfully accomplished our mission, not necessarily when we were still hours away.

We made plans to place our auxiliary gyrocompass in a directional gyro mode, which meant that instead of seeking north, the instrument would tend to seek the line that we were following already. That line was on a great circle course up the Western Hemisphere, across the North Pole, and then due south again; but then we would be in the Eastern Hemisphere. If our master gyrocompass lost its north-seeking ability, as we fully expected it to do as we drew nearer the northernmost point on the planet, then we would shift to the auxiliary compass and have something by which we could reliably steer in the darkness below the ice pack.

We had two other navigational aids that would provide further checks. Our North American inertial navigator and the Sperry gyro-syn, which was also in gyro mode, would let us know if we veered off our intended heading. We were lucky that Tom Curtis and George Bristow were traveling with us, continually monitoring the N6A inertial navigation system better. We still made extremely slow course and depth changes in order to ensure that all of the gyrocompasses remained properly oriented.

Someone suggested that when we reached the North Pole, we put the rudder hard over and make twenty-five tight circles, like some kind of nuclear-propelled carousel. That would make *Nautilus* the first ship to circle the earth twenty-five times. It was a dizzying thought!

Tempted as I might have been to authorize it, I knew it was out of the question. This was no time for stunts. I did not want to delay the completion of our true mission, the full transit from the Pacific to the Atlantic through the no-longer-mythical Northwest Passage. Man had waited centuries for such a feat. I did not want to take any longer than was necessary to get it accomplished.

The North Pole. Latitude: ninety degrees north. Longitude: you name it! Anything from zero degrees to 180 degrees, east or west.

Down through the centuries, writers and explorers have painted it as the point of ultimate difficulty and mystery. Actually it is a point of ultimate truth. For example, as an axis point of the earth's rotation, does it stay fixed in location, always pointing to the same point in space, or does it wander like the magnetic pole does? The answer appears to be that it wanders. The amazing thing is that it deviates so little. By some estimates, its meandering draws an irregular circle less than twenty-five feet across.

If the Pole were to move appreciably, the earth's tilt would reflect that movement, which would certainly result in significant weather and climatic changes.

Let us be thankful the earth's wobbles are so small and that the constancy of the North Pole is immutable.

30

NAUTILUS 90 NORTH

SUNDAY, AUGUST 3, 1958
"1007: CROSSED LATITUDE 87 NORTH."

om Curtis's N6A confirmed that *Nautilus* had just broken our own record of highest northern latitude attained.
With every mile we were proceeding farther north than
any other ship in history had ventured under its own power.

As we grew nearer to the Pole, the navigation party scru-
tinized their data almost continually, recommending small
course changes to send us directly across that specific point on
the globe. After so many weeks of frustration and so many
miles of steaming, I am not sure any of us could have handled
finding out later that we missed the Pole—even by a mile or
two. We watched our instruments very closely. Shep told me
years later that he did every calculation twice to make sure no
mistakes were made.

Frank Adams and I spent our time either at the conning station in the attack center or at the base of the grand staircase in
the control room. That was where the navigator and quarter-

masters did their work and the ship control party maintained course, speed, depth, and angle on the boat. From these spots, Frank and I were able to keep an eye on the two nerve centers of the ship and remain within arm's reach of Lyon's overhead sounders located at the top of the grand staircase.

I was primarily interested in navigational accuracy, something so difficult to attain and maintain in the high-latitude regions where everything is "south." Like Shep Jenks and his team, I wanted to be very precise in reporting our exact arrival at the North Pole. I knew that the disputes still raged regarding the claims of others to be the first to reach the Pole across the ice or to fly over it in an airplane. There was no room for controversy over which ship got there first.

If Shep Jenks took time off to sleep during our transit, I was not aware of it. His attention to detail and meticulous planning were a true inspiration to the members of his navigating team, as well as to me. Later Shep observed, "Our Nav team, by the grace of God, had individual personalities and gifts that perfectly fit the challenge we had on each of the voyages north."

Doggie Rayl was a perfectionist, and a man lucky to be alive to make the trip to the North Pole. Rayl was a signalman aboard the battleship USS *Arizona* (BB-39) at Pearl Harbor on December 7, 1941. He was sleeping topside to escape the heat below when the Japanese attacked. The explosions blew him overboard, and he managed to scramble to another ship. That is how he survived the *Arizona*'s sinking.

The other quartermaster, Ronald Kloch, not only was good at navigation but also had a sense of humor that could defuse the most tense situation. He liked to pop out a false front tooth and let it hang like a fang. That never failed to crack up Jenks and the team.

Richard Williamson was the steady hand, the one who never got excited, and was the best liked of them all. Williamson would go on to serve as chief of the boat on USS *Jack* (SSN-605).

This diversity and perfect mix of talents and personalities was typical of the crew with which I served on *Nautilus*. Everyone was absolutely different and a great man in his own right.

"2315 EASTERN DAYLIGHT TIME (1915 SHIPBOARD TIME): PASSED UNDER GEOGRAPHICAL NORTH POLE."

I made my way deliberately to the ship's microphone. I intended to announce our crossing as we received exact distances to the Pole, called off to me by Jenks. I could not help but think of Peary, Cook, Byrd, Amundsen, and all the others who had braved this inhospitable frontier. I wondered what they would have thought if they could have experienced our seventy-two-degree comfort, with very little immediate danger, and witnessed this magnificent crew and our superb, tried-and-true ship. At this historic moment I wanted to recognize those brave, far-thinking men, but first, I had another thank-you to offer.

"All hands, this is the captain," I said. "We are about to achieve a goal long sought by men who have sailed the seas—the attainment by ship of the geographic North Pole. As we approach the Pole, I suggest we observe a moment of silence dedicated, first, to Him who has guided us so truly."

The ship was completely silent except for the constant pinging of the sonars, probing for ice or other obstacles in our path. I could feel the emotion of the men who stood around me in the control room. I know there were many prayers of thanks offered up at that quiet moment.

"Let us pause also in tribute to those who have preceded us, whether to victory or failure," I spoke into the microphone, "and in our earnest hope for world peace." I glanced at Jenks and took a deep breath. "Now stand by. Ten, nine, eight, seven, six, five, four, three, two, one. Mark! 2315 Eastern Daylight Savings Time, August 3, 1958. For the U.S.A. and the U.S. Navy—the North Pole!"

Just that quickly, the first ship in history to be "under way on nuclear power" became the first ship in history to reach and cross the North Pole. And just that swiftly, we were no longer headed north.

The bow of USS *Nautilus* was now heading away from the Pole, pointed due south.

31

"A VOYAGE OF IMPORTANCE"

As cheers rang out up and down the length of *Nautilus*, especially in the attack center and the crew's mess where many of the men had gathered, I decided for my own satisfaction to make certain we had crossed the absolute top of the world. I turned to Tom Curtis, the keeper of the inertial navigation system.

"Tom, are you certain we passed exactly over the North Pole?"

He grinned.

"Captain, you might even say we pierced the Pole."

I cannot think of a better way to summarize that historic day in 1958 than in the words of one of our youngest crew members, Seaman (Quartermaster Striker) John Yuill:

I remember standing my watches with an ever-increasing degree of anticipation, but without really knowing what to expect when the moment came. As we got closer and closer to the Pole, the tension throughout the boat increased. We were at four hundred feet making over twenty knots.

The crew's mess was crowded with just about everyone who was off watch at the time.

Then, suddenly, it was all over, just like Christmas to a child—all that waiting and anticipation—gone, but unlike Christmas, this would never come again. A feeling of post-celebration "blues" settled over me, but it didn't last long. There were watches to stand, equipment to monitor and maintain, and a long way to go before we were safe again in open water.

A sounding taken with our precision depth finder just as we crossed the Pole indicated the water depth there to be 13,410 feet. In 1909, Peary reported the Arctic Ocean to have a depth of "greater than 9,000 feet" at the Pole. The Russian explorer Ivan Papanin, who landed an airplane on the ice at the Pole in 1937, reported it to be 11,483 feet. We were confident our precise navigation and electronic measurement devices had finally given the correct answer.

The ice near the Pole was compact and running up to about thirty-five feet draft, though as noted, we had seen keels extending downward greater than one hundred feet. In most spots the ice depth averaged generally from five to eighty-five feet thick. The seawater temperature was 32.4 degrees.

As we left the point of the Pole behind, I admit that I considered stopping long enough to find a place to surface, to announce to the world that *Nautilus* and her crew had accomplished the first objective of her mission. That thought quickly faded. It would take us awhile to try to find a hole in the ice, and even if we did, such meandering could confuse our navigational accuracy. We had come too far to get ourselves lost beneath the ice now!

The crew was quick to announce the polar "firsts." There were all manner of claims to be the first at the North Pole to do such things as take a shower, wash clothes, and the like.

The most noteworthy declaration was from one of the youngest seamen aboard who said, "Well, that's fine, but where do you think I was when

One of the envelopes bearing the North Pole transit cachet and postmarked from the "North Pole" post office. One of these envelopes is in the National Postal Museum, a part of the Smithsonian Institution, in Washington, D.C.

the skipper gave the mark? I was up between the torpedo tubes, as far forward as anyone could get. That means I was the first guy to get there!"

I went from the control room forward to the crew's mess to join the festivities planned by the North Pole committee. They had done a great job. The master of ceremonies was Chief Hospitalman John Aberle. Doc had started the program just before we crossed the Pole. When I joined the celebration, I had the privilege of signing a letter to President Eisenhower telling him of the voyage that he, personally, had made possible by his initiative, approval, support, and backing. It began, "I hope, sir, that you will accept this letter as a memento of a voyage of importance to the United States." I also signed a letter to First Lady Mamie Eisenhower, acknowledging her christening of *Nautilus* at the 1954 launching.

Next, with a good number of the crew looking on, I administered the oath of allegiance to Electrician's Mate First Class James R. Sordelet, who became the first man to reenlist in the navy at the North Pole. And I had the honor of congratulating eleven members of the crew who had just completed their "qualification in nuclear submarines" through their diligent work and study.

Santa Claus—who bore a remarkable resemblance to *Nautilus* crewman Bill McNally—welcomes the submarine to his "neighborhood," the North Pole. The suit was made from medical cotton and red flag bunting.

We also announced the winner of the competition to name the equivalent name to Bluenoses to designate Pole travelers. We would all, from that day on, call ourselves "PANOPOs," the acronym of "Pacific to Atlantic via the North Pole."

As the celebration continued, a distinguished world citizen who had somehow found his way aboard crashed the party. Santa Claus, in complete regalia, joined the group in the crew's mess. Although he bore an uncanny resemblance to Bill McNally, there was no doubt that this was the real Santa. After all, we had just cruised through his neighborhood! Mr. Claus was quick to let us know he was not totally pleased. He berated us for invading his private domain during his vacation season. He also admonished us for our failure to observe his restrictions on the use of garbage disposal units by submerged transiting submarines.

In the spirit of cooperation, I pleaded ignorance of such a restriction and promised on behalf of all the ship's company's children to abide by all his rules, henceforth. That seemed to appease the jolly old man, and he promised that the coming Christmas season would be a merry one for all our families.

If that actually was McNally inside the Santa outfit, I could not imagine where he came up with the idea of making the suit from medical cotton and red flag bunting.

Chef Jack Baird had prepared the North Pole cake, iced to show a polar projection chart and track. It was cut and distributed. I can report it was especially delicious, both for its quality and its symbolism of the fulfillment of goals for which we had worked so long.

The celebration over, we turned to the challenge of finding our way into the Atlantic through the Greenland-Svalbard portal. We had to work to concentrate now with this first major accomplishment completed. The long, hard leg of our journey was behind us. Open water lay only a day and a half's passage to the south. We knew almost certainly—from our Atlantic-side penetration a year earlier to a point 180 miles from the Pole—we would have deep water from that point on.

But we were not out of the woods yet.

Executive Officer Frank Adams slices the cake during the onboard celebration of *Nautilus* reaching the North Pole.

Without a course change, we were pointing *Nautilus* due south. The master compass was secured, turned around, and then permitted to begin the slow process of settling on the new meridian. It was somewhat disconcerting to look at the auxiliary gyro. It still indicated our course to be north. It had been set as a directional gyro so it was simply pointing out into space, rotating at the same rate as the earth. The helmsmen laughed about steering south by a compass that was clearly pointing north!

In the back of my mind, I could not help but think about Calvert and *Skate*. Was it still possible that they had beaten us to the Pole and were already on their way back to open water to tell the world? Would it be like

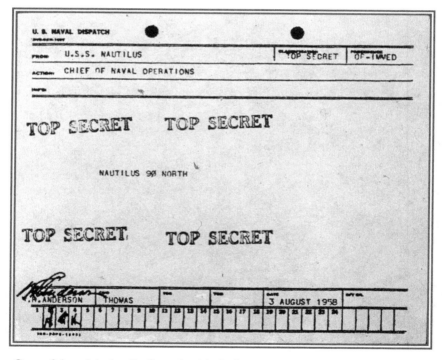

Copy of the original radio dispatch with the historic message that *Nautilus* had successfully reached the North Pole.

Robert Peary, returning from a failed attempt on the Pole only to hear that his former partner, Frederick Cook, claimed to have been there already, well ahead of him?

I put the thought aside. We could not worry about *Skate*. We still had work to do aboard *Nautilus* to get her home safely.

I had already composed my message to be broadcast relative to our reaching the Pole, just in case we had an opportunity to surface in the vicinity. Our orders from CNO had suggested that we do so if it was possible. We continued to look for good surfacing opportunities so we could transmit, but we did not find any. I kept the encoded message in my pocket.

All it said was, "Nautilus 90 North."

MONDAY, AUGUST 4, 1958

By 7:00 p.m.—240 miles after passing the North Pole—the master gyrocompass settled on the true meridian, and we shifted to steer by it. The N6A inertial navigator continued to check perfectly with the courses we were steering. Maybe the most relieved man aboard was Helmsman Daniel Brigman, a North Carolinian charged with keeping us on track for open water.

Now with the master gyro settled out and operating normally and perfectly, we could afford to change course. I asked the navigator for a course to the Atlantic Ocean via the opening between Spitsbergen and Greenland. That was not quite so simple a request as one might imagine. For accuracy in steering a correct course, the heading would have to be changed one degree for each degree of longitude we crossed along the way. This is called "grid navigation."

After the initial course change from due south to the new track, we would have to make twenty-six changes since we were steering on the twenty-sixth east longitude meridian heading directly for eastern Spitsbergen. I told the conning officer to begin grid navigation. Degrees of longitude were so close together way up there that, once we began, our one-degree course changes were being made at twenty-minute intervals.

By the end of the day, we realized that we were not where we were supposed to be. We were already in waters that we had traversed the previous year, but the soundings were not matching at all. The N6A showed we were actually northwest of our dead-reckoning position.

Polar navigation! It is without a doubt the most difficult combination of math and art and educated guesses on earth. I had been following a supercautious plan. I did not want to find we had developed an error large enough that we might run into an ice-covered landmass before we entered the open Greenland Sea. Treacherous piled-up ice awaited us there, and we would be right back in that familiar squeeze as we tried to extricate our way out.

I ordered a slow course change to 170 degrees to run slightly east of south. I knew that would take us toward Spitsbergen, toward open water, and away from Greenland and its shelf ice. Or at least I assumed so.

With good deep water and with navigation appearing to be going well, it was time to start thinking about plans for completion of the transit.

Early on, during discussions with Captain Aurand, he pointed out that if the mission proved successful, the White House would want to make the announcement as soon as possible. He also pointed out that the president wanted our first port to be in Britain, later confirmed to be Portland, England, because of the longstanding friendship between the United States and England.

As planning became more detailed, Aurand informed me face-to-face that they wanted *Nautilus* to proceed to a rendezvous off Iceland. There I was to be picked up by helicopter, taken to a waiting plane, and flown to Washington so I could be present for the press briefing. When I heard this, I started to express some misgivings about such a role. As I spoke, a look came across Aurand's face that told me that the door was closed to any debate about who would be chosen to represent *Nautilus* before the world press. At that time there was no other word regarding details of an announcement except that President Eisenhower would make it.

TUESDAY, AUGUST 5, 1958

At about 4:00 a.m. shipboard time a small patch of open water was detected passing overhead. Shortly after, a giant floe almost twelve miles across unfurled above us.

Not very typical of the edge of the ice pack, I thought as I watched the field of ice go by through number two periscope.

The previous year the outer reaches of the pack were characterized by brash and small blocks, not by floes a dozen miles wide. Then control reported that the sounding was 2,400 fathoms under the keel, much deeper than anything we had seen the year before.

I know I had a telltale frown on my face as I turned from the periscope and stared hard at the chart. The only sounding that deep anywhere on the chart was way back there, just our side of the North Pole. Then, to top it off, I received the report that the water was getting colder, not warmer.

I got a bad feeling. Was it possible that we had been running in circles?

I quickly ruled that out. Too many things checked out. Most likely we had just discovered a new hole in the ocean floor. Nevertheless, I had the nagging thought that we were emerging into some strange body of water, maybe the East Siberian Sea, not the Greenland Sea that we expected.

One thing was for certain: we were not about to strike northern Greenland. We would have been aground already had that been the case. Could we have drifted much farther to the east than we thought and be entering the East Siberian Sea, headed toward rugged, remote Franz Josef Land and the north of Russia?

I still did not think so. I had more confidence in our equipment than that. But the cold water and the unexpected sea-bottom features had me puzzled.

Then, just as I lined up the evidence and was reconsidering our position, I saw something through the periscope as well as on the television monitor that was showing us the bottom of the ice. The light intensity had been varying with the thickness of the floes. Now I noticed a steady intensity of blue-green light. I watched for a minute, then two, then ten.

All detection equipment reported clear water overhead. I ordered speed slackened and that we come to periscope depth—slowly, cautiously, just in case the equipment and the skipper had been fooled by thinner but still potentially damaging ice, as had happened in this very area one year before.

I told the radio room to warm up the transmitter. I knew some folks back in Washington would be interested in hearing from us.

We raised the starboard whip radio antenna to act as our "ice feeler," and I intently watched it as we inched vertically upward. It stayed erect, not bent by ice. Then I saw wave motion.

As the periscope broke the surface, the glare of brilliant sunshine almost blinded me. I know those standing around me saw the flash of light against my face. Ken Carr certainly did.

"Captain, you know the sun always shines on *Nautilus*!" he sang out.

The tension immediately broke. A group of submarine sailors began to breathe again.

"0549: SURFACED IN THE ATLANTIC OCEAN."

I could see several small chunks of ice bobbing in the swells around us, but I decided to not risk damage to the periscope. I ordered us to the surface. I also suspected that in this remote location on the globe, the radio transmitter would need as much elevation as it could get to have its message heard.

I was now confident we knew where we were, and the ice around us did seem to indicate that we were near the edge of the pack. The size of the waves and the swell told me we were in some open sea. It looked very much as the Greenland Sea had appeared when we were last here.

I waited for the navigator to plot our position by the sun, even as we worked our way south around a large, flat island of ice. The floe was brilliant white in contrast to the dirt-laden ice we had seen on the other side of the world. We noticed a small seal lazing in the sun atop a small chunk of ice that had been cast off from the main pack. He did not seem to be at all concerned about us.

Shep Jenks showed up then with the results of his sun lines, and his news confirmed what I consider to be the most remarkable piece of nautical navigation ever accomplished. After almost two thousand nautical miles of computation along the toughest navigation route on the face of the earth, Tom Curtis's inertial navigator's error was equivalent to being one exit off target on the freeway. Just as fantastic were the results of the position Jenks and his quartermasters had obtained using purely conventional means. They were accurate within one mile! That was like having navigational satellite accuracy before the existence of navigation satellites.

I had to brag on them, so I got on the microphone and told the crew the good news. Then I went back to the radio room to see if they were having any luck finding anyone who could hear us well enough to pick up our message for Admiral Burke. Radiomen Terrence Provost and Harry Thomas were fiddling with their knobs and studying their meters, trying to pull the last watt out of the transmitter to the antenna. Provost was on his Morse key, sending the brevity codes that translated: "Any U.S. Navy radio station, this is an unidentified station with two immediate operational messages."

There was no response. It was a frustrating time. There we were with historic news, and we could not find anyone with whom we could share it.

I was considering diving and making a rapid transit farther south to look for better propagation when I noticed one of the radiomen suddenly perk up. Someone was answering his call.

"This is U.S. Navy Radio, Japan. Send a series of 'Vs' so I can tune you in."

In moments the "*Nautilus* 90 North" message was on its way to the Pentagon and Admiral Burke, to Washington by way of Japan. Conditions changed dramatically as Provost began sending the second message, but shortly afterward the navy radio station in—of all places—Honolulu came through the static, responding to our call. Radio Londonderry was in there too.

Soon, with the radio traffic transmitted and receipted for, we were able to submerge and set cruising speed, this time headed for Denmark Strait.

Officially, Operation Sunshine—the highlight of submarine careers for 116 men, the spark the president of the United States needed for a nation stunned by the scientific achievement of its nemesis, the voyage dreamed about by explorers since before the fifteenth century, and an accomplishment that would later be termed one of the greatest water adventures of all time—had been successfully completed.

Sonarman John H. Michaud, writing in the ship's newspaper, summed up the feelings of all of us aboard *Nautilus*:

> We have left our loved ones not unlike the explorers of other times, with prayers to bring us Godspeed and a safe return. We are on that return now with much rejoicing and thoughts of those we left behind. To my fellow shipmates this has been one of the most enjoyable trips that I have ever been on, and without a doubt the most important. May God be with you on all other voyages that you make.

At that point my own reaction was one of relief. Relief and a ton of pride in my crew. I vowed that one day they would receive the credit due them for the excellent job they had done on this momentous trip, as well as those previous cruises that helped pave the way.

But none of us aboard *Nautilus* that day had any idea how the news of our achievement was about to be received by the rest of the world.

PART V
WELCOME HOME, PANOPOS

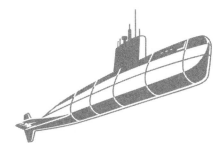

"The skill, professional competence and courage of the officers
and crew of *Nautilus* were in keeping with the highest traditions
of the Armed Forces of the United States and the pioneering spirit
which has always characterized our country."

—From the Presidential Unit Citation

32

"WELL DONE"

THURSDAY, AUGUST 7, 1958
"EN ROUTE RENDEZVOUS FOR HELICOPTER PICKUP."

Operation Sunshine's secret mission would come as a complete surprise to virtually everyone in Washington and the rest of the entire world. Secrecy had been maintained because President Eisenhower wanted "to do the announcing" from the White House at a press conference. Pete Aurand had worked out the plan that would ensure that. My chief objective now was to implement it.

After sending the message to the Pentagon confirming our successful crossing, *Nautilus* was to proceed to a point off Reykjavik, Iceland, and await radio contact for instructions as to exact time and location that a helicopter would rendezvous with us. I was to be picked up and taken to a waiting plane at Reykjavik and whisked off to Washington for the White House announcement. It was a simple enough plan, but if secrecy were to be maintained, enormous planning, coordination, and a good deal of intrigue on the part of Aurand would be required.

Fortunately, I did not have to worry about that part. I focused on the enormous amount of work I needed to accomplish before the rendezvous.

I thought it important to take a complete, official, and highly classified report of Operation Sunshine and deliver it to the hands of my navy bosses in Washington at my first opportunity. I wanted to prepare an unclassified summary of "facts" about *Nautilus* and Operation Sunshine. And I hoped to polish up the unclassified diary I had been ordered to keep. Yeomen Payne and Ortega worked almost around the clock to get everything ready and copies made.

Our "post office" workers gathered the crew's fifteen hundred North Pole letters in a big sack. I packed my personal gear. By the time we made contact with the base at Reykjavik and scheduled the rendezvous, I was ready.

It is worth noting that earlier that day, as we headed for the rendezvous point, *Nautilus* had a distant sonar contact passing to our port. It was the opinion of the sonar crew—and one I share to this day—that the contact was *Skate*, commanded by Jim Calvert and heading toward the North Pole. We would later learn that they arrived there a few days later—on August 12.

Ordinarily, when there is even a remote chance that two U.S. submarines will transit anywhere close to each other with either one or both unaware of the proximity of the other, elaborate precautions are taken to keep them apart. Of course, we could blame it all on the supersecrecy of Operation Sunshine. The people at Atlantic Fleet who managed ship movement were probably unaware that we were even in that hemisphere, let alone near the route *Skate* might be taking to the North Pole.

Once off Reykjavik, *Nautilus* waited in the darkness for the appointed helicopter. It was 11:16 p.m. Eastern Daylight Time but just before dawn on the morning of the eighth off Iceland when the Air Force H-19 helicopter entered the field of our periscope. I put on a life jacket over the coveralls that were concealing my uniform and ordered *Nautilus* to the surface. As soon as the hatch to the bridge was out of the water, Frank Adams assumed command of the ship.

As the helicopter hovered about five feet above our afterdeck, the sea bags that held our outgoing mail and all the other materials, plus my personal gear, were loaded aboard. With the help of another strong arm reaching down to me, I was aboard as well. As my feet left the deck of *Nautilus* and I was entering the hovering aircraft, I could not help but think of the time—only fourteen months before—when a similar helicopter operation had deposited me onto the deck of this same submarine prior to my assuming command. Before I could do much reflecting, I got a real surprise. There, aboard the H-19, was a friendly and familiar face, Captain Peter Aurand. I was both stunned and honored that he had personally made the trip out to fetch me. We gave each other a warm greeting. Then he handed me a note and motioned for me to read it.

> *To the officers and crew of the NAUTILUS*:
> Congratulations on the magnificent achievement—*well done*.
> Dwight D. Eisenhower.

I handed the message down to a crewman on the deck of *Nautilus,* and the helicopter pilot lifted us away and pointed the aircraft toward the coast of Iceland.

I did not know it then, but I had just climbed aboard the most intense whirlwind I could have ever imagined.

33

"THE PRESIDENT IS WAITING"

About fifteen minutes later, we set down directly alongside the navy transport plane that was waiting to take us to Washington. No time was wasted. As soon as we strapped in, the plane sped down the runway and lifted into the air. As we ascended, I imagined my ship, by now at cruising depth, well beneath the rolling wave tops, heading for Portland, England.

Pete and I had so much to tell each other we hardly knew where to start. His excitement began to show as we went over the plans for the upcoming White House announcement and awards ceremony. I showed him my letters to President and Mrs. Eisenhower, the ones I had written when we were in the vicinity of the Pole. I also gave him the press handouts containing facts about the ship and the transit we had made. Finally, for the media, Yeoman Payne had prepared a complete roster of the crew, along with their hometowns. Pete seemed very pleased with our efforts.

He and I began to relax a bit and started sharing personal anecdotes about the adventure. When the subject of secrecy arose, he told me an amazing story about the intrigue surrounding his travel from Washington to pick me up.

He learned about the success of our mission after being summoned to Admiral Burke's office at the Pentagon. After instructing Duke Bayne to make arrangements for a navy transport to fly a certain "Captain E. P. Adams" to Iceland, he returned to the White House and spoke with the president. After noting in his desk calendar that he would be "out of town" for a couple of days, Pete left the White House carrying his valise (appropriately marked with his old, as well as new, initials: "E.P.A.") that contained the congratulatory note from President Eisenhower. By the time he boarded the navy transport at nearby Anacostia Naval Air Station, he had assumed the identity of "Captain E. P. Adams, Sunshine Representative, Iceland."

After arriving in Reykjavik, "Captain Adams" grew impatient with the delay in making renewed radio contact with *Nautilus*. It was very important that we got back to "Casa Blanca" by mid-day on Friday, the eighth of August. Finally, he took over the supervision of the radio watch. He established a prize of one quart of whiskey for the radioman who picked up the first signal from *Nautilus*. He told everyone that "Captain Adams" had been sent by the president to personally hand over a special message to the crew.

Once on the plane, Pete told me it was good to be able to shed his false identity and be Captain Aurand again. I laughed at his sense of humor and admired his wonderful ability to make people around him feel comfortable.

Over the years, I learned Aurand's posing as "Captain Adams" was not his only roundabout method of maintaining secrecy. My brother-in-law, Daniel Mulqueen, provided another example. Under the Freedom of Information Act, Dan obtained a copy of a letter Aurand wrote to an official at the Central Intelligence Agency, thanking him for securing just what he wanted with only the "vague instructions" of providing "a large map of the polar region." Aurand needed a map to show the route of *Nautilus* at the White House conference, and, as it turned out, photographs of that map were distributed around the world. My guess is that he did not ask the navy to provide the map for fear someone there would put two and two—*Nautilus* and the North Pole—together.

I was fascinated with Pete's tales while posing as "Captain Adams," and before settling down for some rest, we spliced the mainbrace with a toast to *Nautilus* and the demise of "Captain E. P. Adams"!

We landed at Anacostia right on time: Friday, August 8, at 10:45 a.m. A car was waiting, and within minutes we were off the plane and rushing to the White House, less than a half hour's drive. At this point, I was more than a little numb.

I sat in Aurand's office, unable to believe where I was and what was about to happen. I tried to stay calm, though there was a swirl of activity around me. I sipped a cup of coffee and secretly hoped some lunch was in the picture before the 1:30 announcement. I was shown a list of the eight or so senior military officers who would be coming in for the event. The names on the list were familiar to me, but I also recognized what I thought was a glaring omission.

Admiral Rickover's name was not there. Had he not been invited?

I was stunned. Without his successful, safe nuclear power plant, an under-ice transit could not have been made. This was an oversight in my opinion, but it was too late to do anything about it.

The surprises were not over. Suddenly Bonny was standing there before me, a broad smile on her face. I could not believe my eyes. As I hugged her, she explained that Admiral Warder had called and requested her presence at a special ceremony in Washington, D.C. Next thing she knew, she and Admiral Warder were aboard a navy plane heading south. She was very surprised to learn the ultimate destination was the White House. She assured me William and Michael were fine with the babysitter back home.

Thankfully, Bonny and I were invited to join Press Secretary Jim Hagerty and Captain Aurand for lunch in a small, private dining room. About the time we finished eating, an aide announced, "The president is waiting, Captain Anderson."

It was all so surreal that I really could not be nervous. Perhaps I truly was numb, because meeting President Eisenhower was not as stressful as I had imagined. He was smiling and cheerful, enormously gracious and pleasant to both Bonny and me. During our brief meeting, I presented him the letters from the North Pole, as well as a special gift for Mrs. Eisenhower from the crew. It was one of the ship's clocks, its hands stopped at the exact moment we crossed the Pole. The president told me he was highly pleased, not only with the achievement by *Nautilus* and her crew but also with the mementos. The clock, I might add, is displayed at the Eisenhower Presidential Library in Abilene, Kansas.

"Without your backing, sir, this voyage would not have been possible," I made sure to tell him, and I meant it most sincerely.

We chatted informally for a minute or two before being led into a nearby conference room. Once again, I was amazed at what awaited us.

There were people, lights, and cameras everywhere. Reporters, photographers, tape recorders, television and movie cameras. I nodded politely to the officers who stood at the front, smiling and watching us as we came into the room.

I learned that Press Secretary Hagerty had announced what he termed a "showcase presentation" for the media and promised them "a very good story . . . with the president participating" if they would show up at 1:30 p.m. on Friday. More than a hundred did. There was only room for seventy-five and chairs for sixty. A reporter wrote later, "The city was alive with speculation, all of it wrong."

The president began with a short statement as the flashbulbs popped and the film cameras whirred. Then, as part of the ceremony, he awarded the Presidential Unit Citation to *Nautilus* and all hands. Secretary of the Navy Thomas Gates later reminded me that this was the first time the award had been given in peacetime. By definition the award is for heroism in action, to a unit that displays remarkable gallantry, determination, and spirit in successfully completing a mission under extremely difficult and hazardous conditions. I lack the words to describe how proud I was to stand there in the White House and accept that award from the president on behalf of *Nautilus* and her crew. Pete Aurand read the citation aloud:

> For outstanding achievement in completing the first voyage in history across the top of the world, by cruising under the Arctic ice cap from the Bering Strait to the Greenland Sea. During the period 22 July 1958 to 5 August 1958, USS *Nautilus* (SSN-571), the world's first atomic powered ship, added to her list of historic achievements by crossing the Arctic Ocean from the Bering Sea to the Greenland Sea, passing submerged beneath the geographic North Pole. This voyage opens the possibility of

President Dwight Eisenhower pins the Legion of Merit on the lapel of William Anderson, captain of *Nautilus*. The award ceremony was part of the hastily arranged press conference to announce the successful transit by *Nautilus* from the Pacific to the Atlantic via the North Pole. The president's naval aide, Captain Peter Aurand, stands in front of the map of the polar-crossing route.

a new commercial seaway, a Northwest Passage, between the major oceans of the world. Nuclear powered cargo submarines may, in the future, use this route to the advantage of world trade.

The skill, professional competence and courage of the officers and crew of *Nautilus* were in keeping with the highest traditions of the Armed Forces of the United States and the pioneering spirit which has always characterized our country.

I will never know how I managed to hold steadfast as the president awarded me the Legion of Merit. As he pinned the decoration on my uniform, the president asked me to convey his personal "well done" to the officers and crew of *Nautilus*. I assured him I would. He and his party immediately left the room, and apparently, I had the helm.

My only prop was the CIA's large map of the polar region with the route of *Nautilus* drawn straight across the Pole. Thus, with my heart in my throat and my eyes half-blinded from all the flashing cameras, I began by admitting right up front that things had been moving very fast lately. "You know I am a little dazed by all this," I told them.

Time magazine, among others, later seized on my admission. "But it was not only Anderson, but the newsmen, the Navy, the nation, the world that was more than a little dazed," they wrote in their August 18, 1958, edition.

Still, I knew it was important that I tell our story as clearly and as forcefully as I could if people were to fully appreciate the impact of what we had done. The excited journalists, fact sheets in hand, interrupted with one question after another, and the barrage went on for a half hour. I detailed for them the route we took, the things we saw along the way, the data we collected.

I was repeatedly asked to provide details about *Nautilus* and the trip that I was not permitted to answer fully. I pointedly avoided talking about the strategic military impact of our transit beneath the ice. But it was obvious that *Nautilus*'s feat had immediately changed things in that regard. *Time* magazine made that point as well.

"In one voyage of one U.S. nuclear submarine . . . the Navy had . . .

Captain Anderson shows the route of *Nautilus* from the Pacific to the Atlantic during the White House press conference at which the feat was announced to the world. This photo and map appeared on newspaper front pages all over the world.

increased the power of the U.S. deterrent by laying bare the Communist empire's northern shores to the future Polaris-missile-toting nuclear submarines," the magazine said.

I was relieved once the press conference was over. When we finally left the White House, I knew exactly where I wanted to go next. The idea had been percolating ever since I saw the list of officers invited to the presidential press conference.

I asked our driver to take Bonny and me to the offices of the Naval Reactor Branch—Admiral Rickover's headquarters.

I found the admiral sitting with staff leaders Bob Panoff, Ted Rockwell, and Dave Leighton. They had been listening to the live radio broadcast about the White House announcement. The admiral appeared to be in a very good mood and was clearly surprised when I popped in.

"My God, Anderson!" he exclaimed. "That was an audacious thing to do!"

"Admiral, Bob, Ted, Dave," I replied, nodding to each of the staff members in turn. "I didn't want to come to Washington and not see you. I hope you understand I can't stay long, but I wanted to pay my respects."

"I'm really quite moved, Anderson," he said sincerely. "That was awfully nice of you. Awfully nice. But you'd better not keep the people waiting. Thanks again. I'll tell my people what you did. It's for them too."

"Yes, Admiral. You are right. It is."

Then we said good-bye and left. We had only stayed a minute or two. It was Admiral Rickover's brainchild—a nuclear power plant that required no oxygen to function—that made our voyage possible, but it was clear to me that he did not want to dwell on the feat. The admiral always looked forward.

A day or so later, a *New York Times* reporter asked the admiral for a comment on the missing invitation to the White House. Rickover brushed it off by saying, "Ah, we haven't got time to worry about things like that." He did not have to worry. Washington was in an uproar for days regarding this perceived "snub."

I learned that there had been a prolonged period of silence in Rickover's office after Bonny and I left.

Bob Panoff finally broke the quiet.

"Wow!" he exclaimed. "How about that?"

34

THE SUN SHINES ON *NAUTILUS*

As I expressed in my North Pole letter to President Eisenhower, ours was "a voyage of importance to the United States." Still, I do not think any of us aboard *Nautilus*, including me, fully anticipated the reaction our adventure would receive.

It hit close to home minutes after the White House announcement. An Associated Press reporter called our house in Mystic. The babysitter told the reporter that young William was taking a nap and Michael was out on his boat fishing. "Sailor's Son Follows Sea" was a headline in the papers the next morning. My parents were contacted that same afternoon at their home in Bakerville, Tennessee, about fifty miles west of Nashville. My mother exclaimed, "This is all news to us—we don't know anything about it. Are you sure it is our son?"

Another reporter was using Yeoman Payne's list to track down wives of crew members for interviews. Upon reaching Marilyn Charette, the young bride of Sonarman Al Charette, the reporter's excited manner so upset her, she burst into tears and exclaimed that she did not care what *Nautilus* had done, she just wanted her husband home!

It would be some time before I would have the opportunity to read extensively what the world press and international leaders were writing about our feat, but from the moment of the announcement at the White House, it was obvious that our voyage had caught the imagination of the world. No detail was too insignificant. People suddenly wanted to know everything about submarines and nuclear power and, yes, the North Pole.

Washington remained abuzz with excitement for weeks. Senator Henry "Scoop" Jackson, who had initially inquired about the possibility of under-ice submarine operations years before, said, "Both the military and peaceful applications of this voyage are enormous. It opens up waters adjacent to all of the landmass of Asia, Europe, and North America." The media agreed with what the senator said. *Time* magazine reported: "Capturing men's imaginations round the world and answering persuasively to Russia's Sputniks, the U.S. Navy's atomic submarine *Nautilus* completed a historic transpolar voyage under the vast Arctic ice pack, fulfilling in a 20th Century way the centuries-old dream of a Northwest Passage.

"Few maritime exploits in history have so startled the world as the silent, secret transpolar voyage of the U.S. Navy's nuclear submarine *Nautilus*, and none since the age of Columbus and Vasco da Gama has opened, in one bold stroke, so vast and forbidding an area of the seas," wrote reporter Paul O'Neil in *Life* magazine.

Though both President Eisenhower and I had been careful not to dwell on the military significance of the feat, the new strategic possibilities brought to light by the journey became a hot topic.

"The real significance of the trail-blazing cruise of the *Nautilus* under the polar icecap is military," wrote John Norris of the *Washington Post*. *New York Times* military correspondent Hanson Baldwin, who had covered Operation Strikeback, said the voyage had "immense strategic implications."

Reaction by European journalists echoed those from America. The Roman publication *Momenta Sera* concluded that our transpolar under-ice crossing confirmed the "technical and scientific supremacy" of the U.S. In London, the *Daily Telegraph* hailed the voyage as "the American answer to the Soviet Sputnik," and went on to say that the transit surpassed Sputnik in terms of human daring.

I was especially interested in what the response from the Soviet Union

Captain Anderson waves from the bridge of *Nautilus* as they approach port after the successful ocean-to-ocean trip via the North Pole. Note the "submerged North Pole transit" flag flying overhead.

would be. Tass, the state-run Soviet press agency, hardly even acknowledged the achievement, other than to denounce the Arctic crossing by *Nautilus* as a "publicity campaign" cooked up to generate more funding for the U.S. Navy.

The Arctic explorer Sir Hubert Wilkins, then seventy, the man who had conceived a plan for taking a converted submarine beneath the ice pack, reacted by saying the voyage was "wonderful." But he also stubbornly maintained that it could have been done long before with a conventional submarine.

In less than forty-eight hours after the White House announcement, and before I could catch my breath, I was once again on an airplane, this time headed back northeastward to rejoin *Nautilus*. The plan was to visit with U.S. Navy officials in London and meet with U.S. Ambassador to England John Hay Whitney. Truly restful, rehabilitating sleep, it seemed, was something other people did. When I landed at Heathrow Airport in London, I once again encountered an excited press. Finally, after my meetings and more interviews, I made it back to my ship, waiting for me a few miles off the port of Portland on the south English coast.

Saying it was great to be back on board sounds trite, but it absolutely was. The crew was as excited as I was tired, but their spirit gave me a second breath. As we pointed the bow of *Nautilus* toward the harbor, we passed the lightship *Shamble*, and the *Nautilus* men on duty topside got their first taste of the world's reaction. The first British cheers from the men performing lonely duty aboard the British lightship-vessel filled us with emotion and more excitement.

Our mission had been so secret that the navy's request to clear our entrance to the port had not been processed completely. *Nautilus* had been docked there once before in connection with the NATO exercises the previous year. Due to that precedent, nobody seemed too worried about our not having the correct paperwork. We finally crossed the breakwater into the harbor about 1:20 p.m., and the welcome that awaited us was staggering. It seemed that every vessel in the harbor was blasting away on its horn or whistle. Thousands gathered on the shore, cheering as we hove into sight. Fireboats sprayed water high into the sky. On the pier, the Royal Marine Band, wearing white cork helmets, played briskly.

As we stood at attention, I could see the flag that commemorated the polar trip hooked to the periscope. James Morley and John Krawczyk won the contest with the design that showed a map of the polar region and an arrow representing our route across the Pole. Ambassador Whitney, on behalf of President Eisenhower, formally presented *Nautilus* with the Presidential Unit Citation.

It was hard to tell whether the crew was most happy about the award, the joyous reception we received, or the liberty that awaited them. The basis of their joy did not matter. Soon, about eighty excited *Nautilus* sailors had piled ashore. The rest remained aboard on watch, waiting for their turn at liberty.

The welcome we received as we came into port should have been an indication of how each sailor would be treated by the general British population, but still, no one was prepared. Clarence Price and Tom Deane tell a story about visiting the historic Tower of London where they were mobbed when someone noticed their *Nautilus* shoulder patches. Many insisted on touching them and practically demanded autographs. Elsewhere, three officers and six enlisted men took in a traditional military concert and marching

Nautilus crew members James Prater and David Greenhill unfurl the flag designed to commemorate the transit through the North Pole. The flag flew from the shears as *Nautilus* sailed into Portland, England, after the trip.

event called the Searchlight Tattoo at White City Stadium. They received a spontaneous standing ovation from sixteen thousand people, and then were invited to sit in the queen's box to watch the rest of the exhibition.

Perhaps that event inspired Tom, a smart, likable fellow who had been a crew member since *Nautilus*'s pre-commissioning days, to serve in the navy for more than thirty years and retire at the rank of commander.

The notorious British tabloid

On a dreary August morning, *Nautilus* sails past the Statue of Liberty in New York harbor on the way to a rousing heroes' welcome after the North Pole transit.

newspapers had photos of *Nautilus* crew members on the front pages practically every day that we were there. One featured a spectacular picture of Quartermaster Richard Williamson. He was planting a big kiss on the girl in his arms while two of his shipmates looked on. The headline read: "Who says they are sub-men?"

There were so many celebratory events lined up for us in England that Frank Adams had to detail crew members to attend them. We did not want to insult or ignore anyone. I could not say for sure, but I would bet that few on liberty in London actually had to pay for food or drink.

The amazing reception in England—official and unofficial—and the word we were getting about how our voyage was front-page news all over the world were overwhelming. It was finally sinking in to every crew member that they had accomplished something special and that it was having a tremendous impact on nearly everyone.

Walter Harvey holds a tray with a chunk of pack ice retrieved from the deck of *Nautilus* and preserved for the entire polar transit and presented it to Admiral Hyman Rickover.

"You would think we had just gone to the moon or something," Al Charette recalled. "Hey! All we did was bore a hole in the ocean. What's the big deal?"

He was kidding, of course. It was clearly a historic event and was followed shortly by another U.S. achievement of historic proportions. Jim Calvert and *Skate* had reached the North Pole on August 12, at 9:47 p.m. EDT, just short of eight days after *Nautilus*. *Skate*, in fact, had departed New London July 30. She had surfaced in a polynya about forty miles from the Pole and reported her success via radio. I sent Jim and his crew my personal congratulations on their accomplishment—just as they had for us.

Nautilus pulled away from quayside at Portland, England, on the afternoon of Monday, August 18, as a British military band accommodatingly played "Yankee Doodle." Everyone on board was exhausted but happy. We settled down to our usual jobs, performing routine chores. Soon, four hundred feet of Atlantic Ocean was above us. Our ship, pointed toward our next port of call—New York City—was moving at a brisk twenty knots.

During our record run across the Atlantic, we slowed long enough to engage in a practice "attack" on a merchant ship that happened to be steaming near our course. I felt that we had been so occupied lately with our special mission and festivities that we needed a drill to keep us sharp. Of course, the freighter never knew we had her in our periscope. *Nautilus* may have been a ship full of explorers, but she was still a man-of-war.

As Navigator Shep Jenks guided us to the entrance of New York harbor, a tugboat carrying a very special passenger—the personal representative of President Dwight Eisenhower—approached us. I watched from the bridge as the slight figure climbed aboard and shook hands with the welcoming crew members. It was Admiral Rickover, and he was once again uncharacteristically dressed in uniform. After the controversy over the failure to invite Rickover to the press conference, President Eisenhower was trying to make amends by appointing Rickover as his personal representative in the public celebration of our voyage.

"It's a job well done," the admiral told us.

We climbed down the ladder to the wardroom where Steward Walter J. Harvey of Pascagoula, Mississippi, presented him with a chunk of Arctic ice on a silver tray.

"We were all sorry you weren't on the voyage," he told Rickover. "So as a second best, we brought a piece of ice back to you."

Rickover accepted the ice, examining it intently.

"Must I swallow it?" he asked.

The men smiled nervously, unsure of how to respond, but then everyone had a good laugh.

Rain began to fall as we followed our escort flotilla into the harbor. There were at least twenty destroyers from the U.S. Navy along with Coast Guard cutters, tankers, tugboats, and police vessels. I will never forget seeing the Statue of Liberty for the first time that day. She seemed to speak to me, saying, "Welcome home, Captain Anderson. You and your ship and

USS *Nautilus* enters New York harbor.

your fine crew can rest now." It was a very emotional time for me as the fireboats shot water high into the air in salute.

The lead vessel took us to the west of Manhattan Island and up the Hudson River. Despite the fog and rain, people stood all along the shore waving, and we could see many more greeting us from office windows in buildings that bordered the river. Parallel to 42nd Street, we swung around and headed back downriver to the Brooklyn Navy Yard. There, a marine honor guard and a navy band welcomed us back to the U.S.A.

Louise Emanuel, the nine-year-old daughter of Steward Thomas Emanuel, was one of many family members standing in the rain to welcome us. She recalled, "We went down to the Hudson River to see the ship come into New York, and when I saw the reception it got, that's when I realized how special it was [that her father had been on the polar cruise]."

Just before 10:00 a.m., we docked to a rousing welcome from those who had braved the rain. Beyond the immediate area, we could see families of crew members lined up behind a fence, patiently waiting for us, but first we had a formal welcome to conduct with the crew members lined up on the deck. Finally, as I walked off the ship, I could see the crew mingling with their families, hugging, raising kids in the air, hugging some more, all while news

New York City fireboats welcome *Nautilus* to the city after the successful transit through the North Pole. The ship set a new speed record from Portland, England, to New York City, August 25, 1958.

USS *Nautilus* makes a parade lap around Manhattan Island just after the successful Pacific-to-Atlantic transit via the North Pole, August 1958.

cameras clicked and film cameras rolled. Movietone News was there documenting the activities for theater screens all over the world. Bonny, our son Michael, Bonny's parents, and my parents were waiting dockside. My folks had flown from Tennessee as guests of the *Nashville Tennessean* newspaper and the Naval Reserve. This was their first trip on an airplane, and they made it just to greet *Nautilus* and see me. I was thrilled.

Somewhere in the swirl of activity, I managed to corral Bonny and give her a hug and kiss and greet everybody else, but not before we all were almost trampled by photographers. They insisted that Bonny and I go through the hug-and-kiss thing several times so everyone could get the shot, and we gladly obliged.

After the ceremony, the official welcome, and a brief moment with the family, Admiral Rickover and I were escorted to a waiting television camera. David Brinkley of NBC was there for an interview. Then we were off to a formal press conference, a chance for me to answer the same questions all over again. Later, we would recreate the welcome home for legendary newsman John Cameron Swayze and more film cameras.

Liberty once again awaited crew members not on watch, and each man had been given a list of area attractions, many of which were offering free or reduced admission or meals to the crew of *Nautilus* and their family members. Several television quiz and variety shows made it a point to introduce on camera the crew members that were sitting in their audiences. The sudden bright spotlight on the crew and their families had already caused some scrambling and a few moments of panic. Bonny was caught up in such a whirlwind that she hardly knew if she was coming or going. Somehow she managed to appear cool and collected given the scrutiny of many newspapers that described how she dressed or how she wore her hair.

I learned that Della Larch, a born leader like her husband, Dutch, had rallied a group of crew wives for an old-fashioned "slumber party" the night before making the trip by chartered bus to New York. Imagine the

Ceremony at city hall, New York City, after *Nautilus* returned from the North Pole. Left to right: Captain William R. Anderson, New York mayor Robert Wagner, Admiral Hyman Rickover.

excitement as they helped each other prepare to see their husbands and meet the cameras that surely would be trained on them as well.

Thankfully the rainy weather improved by Wednesday when we were guests of honor for a special welcome-home ceremony in City Hall Plaza. New York Mayor Robert Wagner presented Admiral Rickover and the

Members of the *Nautilus* crew are treated to a tickertape parade through the streets of Manhattan. Captain William R. Anderson and Admiral Hyman Rickover (in white uniforms) ride in the lead car.

Nautilus crew with the city's highest honor, the Gold Medal. I was especially appreciative that the first skipper of *Nautilus*, Captain Eugene Wilkinson, not only was present, but had obviously helped in many ways to facilitate a warm welcome for the ship and crew he once commanded.

Then we were off for the dream event—a tickertape parade along Broadway from lower Manhattan to the Waldorf-Astoria Hotel where

Sailors who made the North Pole transit aboard *Nautilus* enjoy the heroes' welcome as the tickertape rains down through the canyons of lower Manhattan, New York City. Note the official *Nautilus* insignia on the flag on the back of their vehicle.

we were to be treated to a fancy luncheon. I rode in an open convertible with Admiral Rickover and an official of New York City. Most of the crew rode in open-top jeeps behind us. Our families were stationed together and had a good view of everything. It was estimated that over a third of a million people lined our parade route. I distinctly remember the admiral's very reserved demeanor when we first started out. Soon he began to respond warmly to the cheers and waves of that wonderful crowd. That relaxed me a bit, and I started to enjoy myself, literally basking in the sun.

A number of New York's most admired celebrities paid a visit to *Nautilus*. Among them were New York Yankee shortstop Phil Rizzuto and several of his teammates. Speaking of baseball, a small group of *Nautilus* crew members arrived during a game at Yankee Stadium. Even though the famous slugger Mickey Mantle was at bat, the crowd stood and gave the submariners a standing ovation.

Our New York welcome was so wonderful that we were cheering the city as we sailed out of the harbor, past the Statue of Liberty, on our way to New London. There is nothing like home to a sailor, and everyone aboard *Nautilus* was anxious to get there.

Preparations for our arrival in New London had been under way for some time. Town officials were expecting thousands of people to line the parade route from our berth at Electric Boat.

With hardly a cloud in the sky, and the waters remarkably calm, we made our way up the Thames, its banks lined with cheering crowds who waved handkerchiefs and used pocketbook mirrors to flash the brilliant sunshine as a greeting. Many of the people on the docks at EB—including Governor Abraham Ribicoff—waved banners saying "Welcome Home PANOPOS."

After a lot of hugging and kissing and official welcoming remarks, our motorcade, made up of over one hundred vehicles, finally got started. We made our way slowly through the area, following a big circle that touched half a dozen municipalities, including Groton, New London, and Mystic.

We were especially gratified by the warm and enthusiastic welcome we received as we passed through the sub base. Sailors and officers waved and shouted, and boats along the waterfront blew their whistles. A longtime EB employee told a newspaper reporter that he had never seen any reception at the yard to rival the one thrown for *Nautilus*. "She's a great ship and we're proud of her," he said.

The New London *Evening Day* newspaper quoted an Electric Boat spokesperson as saying that despite our 1,830-mile trip beneath the polar ice pack, *Nautilus* did not have a scratch on her.

A few weeks later, in early September, Bonny and I made our way to my home state of Tennessee. Among several ceremonies and awards, we were treated to a parade through the capital city of Nashville and a luncheon at the wonderful Andrew Jackson Hotel. I will never forget the stunning replica

Nautilus and her crew are welcomed home to Groton, Connecticut, after the polar transit.

Part of the Tennessee welcome, in front of the Andrew Jackson Hotel in Nashville.

of *Nautilus* that had been carved by the catering manager from a three-hundred-pound block of ice.

We left Nashville by private aircraft heading for the town of Waverly, Tennessee, not far from my home community of Bakerville. Waverly residents rolled out the red carpet for what the *Nashville Tennessean* characterized as "the greatest celebration in the history of Humphreys County." I have no reason to doubt that. Eight bands, seven marching units, and thirteen floats, along with seven automobiles, made up the parade from the tiny Waverly airport to the high school athletic field. Schools and businesses were closed for the day. The Bakerville float featured a model of the home my parents lived in and a sign with my name and birth date. Local dignitaries paraded with U.S. senator Estes Kefauver and Frank Clement,

Captain Anderson and Bonnie with William Junior during the celebration in Tennessee after *Nautilus* made the under-ice transit.

the governor of Tennessee. A wonderful, informal reception in the school cafeteria gave me an opportunity to say hello to many friends and family I had not seen in years.

Senator Kefauver spoke, saying, "[*Nautilus*] has restored any confidence and prestige that may have been lost in the might of the United States of America."

My mother and father, especially, were touched when they learned the planned hospital in Waverly would be named *Nautilus* Hospital. For me, probably the best part of being back in my hometown was the ham dinner my mother fixed for Bonny and me that evening. Later, after changing out of my uniform, I walked around the farm with my dad and son Mike. I enjoyed a rare visit with my sister, Josephine Garner, and her family. Life was good. God had blessed me in many ways, and I was feeling particularly grateful that evening for each and every one.

Later, back in New London, newsman Edward R. Murrow broadcasted his very popular, live network news show *Person to Person* from *Nautilus*. Wearing an experimental wireless microphone, I took viewers on an unclassified guided tour of our ship. In those pre-satellite days, an elaborate system of transmitters and telephone cables relayed the television images and audio back to New York City for broadcast to the whole country.

Our crew members were honored in less-spectacular ways too. Al and Marilyn Charette told me about their apartment landlord who was normally a grumpy, miserly individual, but he was so impressed that Al was part of the *Nautilus* crew, he uncharacteristically awarded them a month's free rent. In addition, Frank Adams's hometown of Tunica, Mississippi, located just south of Memphis, proudly presented him and his wife, Novie, with a brand-new car.

One of the wonderful foreign tributes to *Nautilus*'s historic voyage was the announcement that I had been selected to receive an award known as the Medaglia de Grifone, or Christopher Columbus medal, given every year for "outstanding contributions to sea travel." Admiral Rickover had been the recipient just the year before. Bonny and I traveled to Genoa, Italy, the birthplace and boyhood home of Columbus. On October 12, 1958, Columbus Day, we attended the black-tie awards ceremony. I accepted on behalf of everyone on board *Nautilus* and emphasized that "no dramatic development in the history of modern man would be possible without the labor and genius of those who have gone before . . . and without the pioneering spirit that is our heritage . . . and will not stop with the recent accomplishment of *Nautilus*."

Italy, known for centuries as leaders in sea travel, warmly received us, and we did our best to reciprocate. I will never forget this honor or their graciousness.

There were many other honors and awards, interviews, and television appearances. It was all very wonderful but almost too much to take in. Keeping track of the appearances, speeches, and special events and answering correspondence began to wear down every sailor that called himself a PANOPO. Bonny and Mike began to show a little wear themselves. At one speaking event where they accompanied me, a reporter, noting that submariners do not get much time with their families, asked Mike if he had any questions for me about *Nautilus* and our adventures in the Arctic.

Mike did not hesitate.

Captain Anderson with Bonnie and Mike during the New York celebration after the polar transit.

"No, sir. I've read all I want to know about it in the newspapers," he answered almost bluntly.

Of course, the White House exploited our accomplishment and kept us in the public eye, which was to be expected. Our mission was, in part, a demonstration of U.S. technology and military might. *Nautilus* and *Skate* and the subsequent well-publicized missions in the Arctic Ocean by our sister nuclear submarines no doubt played a vital part in maintaining the peace during tense moments of the Cold War. Any aggressor would have to assume that we had submarines deployed beneath the Arctic ice pack, armed with nuclear weapons.

For me personally, however, an often-repeated phrase—well meaning as it might have been—began to grate on me a bit. I was often introduced as "the fellow who took that submarine to the North Pole." That did not tell the whole story. If I could have made a wish, the introduction would have been something like, "This fellow, along with 115 highly trained individuals, took that submarine from the Pacific to the Atlantic via the North Pole. They called themselves PANOPOs."

In June of the following year, my tour as skipper of *Nautilus* ended. A very fine gentleman, now-retired Vice Admiral Lando Zech, relieved me. By that time, *Nautilus* was one of several nuclear submarines in the U.S. fleet and not alone in being able to claim under-ice exploration. She remained, however, number one with her crews, the record books, and me.

I left my submarine command and sea duty with a heavy heart. I think sea captains are always sad at journey's end. It makes no difference what the future might hold. It is hard to suddenly not have that intense responsibility and closeness to the men on board. I knew I would miss it.

My next assignment was not a bad one. I went back to Washington to work again in Rickover's Naval Reactor Branch. I served as his director of personnel selection and training, part of the Navy Nuclear Propulsion Training Program. It was nice to be with old friends, but the admiral had not softened very much. He was all business and would remain so until his retirement in 1982, at age eighty-two. His sixty-three years of continuous navy service is no doubt a record. However, his innovations in ship propulsion, quality control, personnel selection, and training, as well as in the civilian nuclear energy field, are legendary and still in practical use. What a wonderful, lasting mark he made on history.

A promotion for me came in July 1960. At age thiry-nine, I became the youngest line officer in the navy with rank of captain. I remain indebted to the dedicated officers and enlisted men with whom I served, who helped me along the way. They remain my inspiration.

I left Rickover's shop to work as naval aide to Secretary of the Navy William Franke, then went on to serve two other SecNavs, John Connally and Fred Korth.

It was during that time that I made the decision to retire at my twenty-year anniversary with the navy. Thus, in June 1963, I separated from the service that I loved so much and one that had brought me so much fame and honor. I had no immediate plans, but politics was firmly on my mind. I think I got that bug while working at SecNav.

The fifty years since I took command of *Nautilus* have flown by. Good luck and health remained my fortune. Politically speaking, I enjoyed four terms in the U.S. House of Representatives, serving the Sixth Congressional District of Tennessee, an area that included Bakerville and Waverly. Bonny and I divorced. My business partner and wife for the last thirty years has been Patricia Walters of Wake Forest, North Carolina. We founded a computer services enterprise at a time when processors and disk storage were the size of refrigerators and washing machines, and cost more than a four-bedroom house. Pat understood it all; I pushed a pencil. Michael now teaches at a private university in Washington, D.C., and William Jr. is presently involved in innovative technology developing a highly fuel-efficient combustion engine. The two children with whom Pat and I were blessed, Jane Hensley and Thomas "Mac" McKelvey, are young adults and still students.

Though I did not work again with the navy or nuclear energy, *Nautilus* and the men I commanded were never far from my heart and mind. I regret I could not make it to Mare Island in 1980 for the decommissioning ceremony of *Nautilus*. I am sure it was a grand, if somewhat, sad event. Her service history remained unblemished. Records were broken with each successive skipper and crew, logging nearly half a million nautical miles. After official service, she made the record books one last time. *Nautilus* became a National Historic Landmark and the second ship in U.S. history to be designated "historic." The first was the USS *Constitution*, otherwise known as "Old Ironsides," now permanently berthed in Boston, Massachusetts.

It also gives me great satisfaction that several PANOPOs, notably Stu Nelson and his wife, Kathy, worked diligently to form the *Nautilus* Alumni Association. This very successful organization welcomes every individual who ever served on board *Nautilus* and sponsors lively, interesting reunions on even years, selecting a date as close as possible to the September 30 commissioning date of *Nautilus*.

Today, *Nautilus* lies quietly berthed on the Thames River adjacent to the New London sub base, the feature attraction of the Submarine Force Library and Museum. Thus, the extraordinary ship that transported the world into the atomic age and carried her crews through uncharted waters under the Arctic ice pack and across the North Pole remains, appropriately, the center of attention. Visitors can explore this beautiful complex year round. Each treasured relic is a tribute to U.S. submariners and submarine history and lore. I encourage everyone to visit the exhibits and then walk up the ramp and go aboard *Nautilus*. Check out the torpedo room, wardroom, officer quarters, attack center, galley, and crew's mess and quarters.

I think you will find her as grand and accommodating as ever.

Looking back, nothing fills me with more joyful emotion than my association with *Nautilus* and her Arctic explorations. I am grateful to the men and women who conceived this marvelous ship, the first true submarine, as well as those who built her strong, powerful, and safe. I have always tremendously admired her brave commissioning crew—every one a true pioneer in the safe, effective use of atomic energy. I remain in awe of the courage of the leaders who supported *Nautilus*'s explorations to parts unknown.

I am also in awe of the other submarine pioneers whose exploration to parts unknown followed on the heels of *Nautilus*. As recently as November 1997, the world-renowned Explorers Club and Rolex USA brought together and honored Vice Admirals James Calvert, John Nicholson, and George Steele, as well as Waldo Lyon and myself, at a special Lowell Thomas Awards Dinner in New York City. Rolex generously awarded each of us a beautiful, personally inscribed "Submariner" diving wristwatch.

Jim was noted for commanding several Arctic explorations in USS *Skate* as well as for being the first to surface at the North Pole in March 1959. Nick Nicholson commanded USS *Sargo* in 1960 during the first winter Arctic voyage, successfully negotiating the shallow ice-covered waters of the Beaufort, Bering, and Chukchi Seas. That same year, George Steele commanded USS *Seadragon* on the first voyage from the Atlantic to the Pacific via the Arctic Ocean, conducting a complete hydrographic survey of the Northwest Passage. In addition, our host and then president of the Explorers Club, Captain Alfred McLaren, USN (Ret.) PhD, as commander of USS *Queenfish* in 1970, measured sea ice thickness over most of the 1958 *Nautilus* track for global-warming research purposes, then completed a first-ever hydrographic survey of the Siberian continental shelf.

But I am most proud and appreciative of the men who traveled with me on *Nautilus*'s three trips beneath the ice. It was their bravery, ingenuity, sacrifice, and hard work that made our successes known around the world. They carried their commander in every way. It was always my privilege to stand with that group of men, knowing that each one of them was loyally doing what he had been trained to do. They served their country very well. I am equally appreciative of the families of those men. Their sacrifice and support should also be fully noted.

In the true spirit of the explorers who went before us, we on *Nautilus* did what we were asked to do, and we did it to the best of our abilities. The only thing we ever wanted were words like those from our commander in chief, delivered in a note on the pitching deck of our ship off the coast of Iceland:

"Congratulations on the magnificent achievement—WELL DONE."

Captain Anderson boarding a "cruise" on the Potomac River in Washington, D.C. in 1994 with son Thomas, family friend Reyna Burgoa, daughter Jane, and wife Pat.

EPILOGUE

aptain William R. Anderson embarked on what submariners call "eternal patrol" on February 25, 2007, just as he and I were completing the first draft of this book. He was buried with full military honors in Arlington National Cemetery on March 16. It is appropriate that he rests only a few steps from Eisenhower Drive and within sight of the Pentagon. Captain Anderson greatly admired President Eisenhower and appreciated his support of the *Nautilus* polar mission. And the Pentagon, where he so often visited and later worked, was the scene of his chance meeting with Pete Aurand, the event that ultimately sent him and his shipmates on the voyage of a lifetime.

I believe it was also appropriate that the weather the day of Bill's memorial service was cold and windy, with icy rain and sleet. Ice played a role, right to the end.

It had been our intention to allow the epilogue of this book to be a short look at the legacy of *Nautilus*. We would bullet-point what her voyage from the Pacific to the Atlantic through the North Pole ultimately meant, what her place in history was. I believe he would have agreed with most of my summation that follows. I also am convinced that his unassuming modesty would have deflected most any credit directed toward him to President Eisenhower; Admirals Rickover, Burke, and Bayne; and Dr. Lyon, as well as others, but especially toward the *Nautilus* crew members he loved so much.

Nautilus and her crew ventured to one of the last frontiers on our globe, collecting scientific and navigational data that enabled those who followed to operate in that region effectively and with relative safety. It is worth noting that we have not lost a submarine beneath the ice, despite the hazards that still exist there. This does not mean it is not a hostile, dangerous region. What the crew of *Nautilus* learned on each of her three daring missions north was immediately put to good use by other submarine crews in the U.S. fleet as well as those who designed and constructed them. The ice observations, sea floor mapping, navigational testing, and other knowledge gained were of great value. For the first time, U.S. submarines could operate beneath the Arctic ice pack, a short missile ride from the Soviet Union, and do so virtually undetected.

William Anderson, second captain of revolutionary first nuclear submarine USS *Nautilus*.

I will leave it to historians to decide how much the three under-ice cruises of USS *Nautilus* contributed to the eventual victory by the free world in the Cold War. My contention is that it was considerable.

There were other practical contributions that are indisputable in their value. During one of our final visits together, Bill pointed out that building a new nuclear submarine in the twenty-first century requires a staggering investment. He had been following the construction of USS *Texas* (SSN-775), commissioned only a few months before, and built at a cost of over

$2.5 billion. It is simply impractical to construct enough of these vessels to maintain full capability and a reliable deterrence in both hemispheres. However, since *Nautilus* showed the way—the much shorter route across the top of the world—it is now far more practical to redeploy submarines from one ocean to another if needed, thus requiring fewer vessels. That transit can be accomplished beneath the cover of the ice too, without the risks of the bottleneck of the Panama Canal or the delay of taking the long trip around Cape Horn or the Cape of Good Hope.

Bill was also adamant about the ocean-to-ocean voyage being the biggest accomplishment of the 1958 trip, not simply "piercing the Pole." It was true that *Nautilus* reaching the North Pole was what inevitably captured the imagination of the world, but proving that a submarine could transit from the Pacific to the Atlantic beneath the ice pack was the real victory. That was the primary reason Bill was worried about Jim Calvert and *Skate* possibly getting to the Pole first without also making a complete transpolar transit. Aside from the natural and beneficial competition between the ships, their crews, and these two great skippers, Bill was afraid that such a glamorous achievement would deflect attention from the real value of a transpolar cruise. And he was correct. *Nautilus*'s split-second crossing of that geographic location called the North Pole has always overshadowed what Bill knew to be the real triumph.

Still I believe the greatest contribution—the true legacy of *Nautilus* and her crew—will not be found in sea charts, ice graphs, or scientific notations. It does not directly pertain to a shift in naval or technological superiority or the cost savings of not having to build so many expensive new submarines.

America desperately needed heroes in 1958. The Cold War, upon the launch of *Sputnik I*, had turned dramatically in favor of the Soviet Union. The countries in the free world were questioning—openly or internally— the long-term value of their alignment with the United States. Americans suddenly realized that a technology that could launch an earth satellite could probably send far more sinister payloads our way. I remember my

Captain Anderson and his wife, Pat.

own Cold War fears, even as a ten-year-old, as I listened to the beeps of the Soviet satellite on an old shortwave receiver in my dad's ham radio workshop.

Americans had little about which to cheer in 1957. Our space program was failing spectacularly. The country was finally, painfully, confronting its own dark side—racial discrimination. The euphoria that followed the end of World War II was replaced by the unsatisfying completion of the non-war in Korea. Americans were wondering if our leaders had the ability to keep our country a superpower.

Sputnik was the spectacular flashpoint that focused attention on the potential new order in the world dominated by the Soviets. America needed something or somebody to show that we were still in the game.

Bill Anderson was plucked from the deck of *Nautilus* near Iceland and brought to Washington for that hastily called White House press conference, and there was immediate euphoria. The news of Operation Sunshine burned through the gloom.

The free world cheered for its new set of 116 heroes. Americans were out of breath with excitement and treated the new heroes appropriately. Bill talked of the many people from all over the world who wrote letters to him and the *Nautilus* crew. I was struck that so many of them came from grade-school children.

Clearly, after the *Nautilus* exploration, the United States was back in the technology race in a spectacular way and with a military component that did not go unnoticed, even if the crew of *Nautilus* and President Eisenhower chose at the time not to flaunt it.

It is my opinion—and one on which Bill might have disagreed with me—that the accomplishments of *Nautilus* and their effect on the nation's disposition would not be exceeded until the heroic feats of the astronauts who went to the moon a decade later. Oh, Bill would have been fine with his crew getting that kind of comparison, but not him alone. It was also his wish that the many other courageous and thoughtful people who took risks, from *Nautilus*'s commissioning crew to President Eisenhower, share in the accolades of this particular historic accomplishment. That was his prime impetus for doing this book.

That and to finally get the complete story told to coincide with the fiftieth anniversary of the polar crossing.

I appreciate the opportunity to assist Captain Anderson in doing both. I am honored he and his wife, Pat, allowed me to help, to get to know him and to work with him on this project. I hope that I—with Pat's help—polished it up the way he wanted. He was a man who achieved great stature in the eyes of others, but you would have never known it by his calm, polite, and modest demeanor. He was always a gentleman, and I miss working with him.

In the commemorative booklet distributed at Bill's memorial service, a crew member summed up his devotion and admiration by simply stating, "I would have followed him anywhere." So would I.

Though Bill was quite ill the last year of his life, I believe he held on until he was confident he and his "crew" had accomplished this one last mission. Only then did this sailor rest his oar.

Don Keith
Indian Springs Village, Alabama
December 2007

SAILING ROSTERS

List of those men who were aboard for each *Nautilus* under-ice mission:

1957

OFFICERS

William Anderson
Kenneth Carr
Warren Cobean
Richard Dobbins
Paul Early
Donald Fears
Frank Fogarty
John Harvey
Shepherd Jenks
William Lalor
Laurence McNamara
Thomas Tonseth
Francis Wadsworth
Steven White

ENLISTED

John Aberle
Jack Baird
Richard Bearden
Roy Beckner
Robert Bell
Philip Boyle
Donald Brady
Dennison Breese
Daniel Brigman
William Brown
Robert Burnside
Arthur Callahan
Gayle Campbell
Melvin Carson
Alfred Charette
John Cleere
Frank Clifford
Boyd Cohenour
Floyd Corbin
Thomas Deane
Joseph Degnan

James Delaney
John Draper
Edward Dunn
Wallace Durkin
John Dyer
Ronald Eisenman
James Ellsworth
Thomas Emanuel
George Fields
Leeland Fischer
Dale Fisher
Charles Fletcher
William Furnholm
William Gaines
Richard Hadley
Marc Haglund
John Hargraves
Harry Hedin
Albert Herrera
Stonewall Hilton
Carl Hoffman
Ernest Holland
Walter Hyde
James Irvin
Richard Jackman
Howard James
James Johnson
Charles Kates
Raymond Kazebee
Ronald Kloch
James Knotts
John Krawczyk
Raymond Kropp
John Kurrus
Lynus Larch
Thomas La Susa
Allan Lewis

Paul Lovejoy
Raymond McCoole
John McGovern
Marvin Megason
John Michaud
John Monk
James Morley
Richard Murphy
Hercules Nicholas
William O'Neill
James Owens
Charles Parshall
Charles Payne
John Pendleton
James Phelps
Imon Pilcher
James Prater
Clarence Price
Terrence Provost
Raymond Raczek
Lyle Rayl
Thomas Reece
Robert Ringer
Edward Riordan
Robert Scott
George Shabenas
Charles Shaffer
Robert Simonini
James Sims
John Smarz
Malcom Snelgrove
James Sordelet
Gilbert Spurr
Richard Szramiak
Norman Vitale
Curtis Wagner
Ronald Waldron

William Williams
Donald Wilson
Richard Wood
Jimmy Youngblood
John Yuill

CIVILIANS
Waldo Lyon
John Ropek
Archie Walker

1958 (FIRST CRUISE)

OFFICERS
Frank Adams
William Anderson
Dave Boyd
Kenneth Carr
William Cole
Richard Dobbins
Paul Early
Donald Fears
John Harvey
Shepherd Jenks
Robert Kelsey
Jack Kinsey
William Lalor
Thomas Tonseth
Steven White

ENLISTED
John Aberle
Bruce Aquizap
Jack Baird
Ralph Barnhart
Richard Bearden
Robert Bell

Nils Bergquist
Charles Black
Freddie Boswell
Philip Boyle
Dennison Breese
Daniel Brigman
James Brown
William Brown
Arthur Callahan
Roland Cave
Alfred Charette
Boyd Cohenour
Thomas Deane
Earl Diamond
John Draper
Edward Dunn
Wallace Durkin
Thomas Emanuel
Leslie Evans
Bobby Faircloth
William Furnholm
William Gaines
David Greenhill
William Hansen
Dowell Harrell
Walter Harvey
Harry Hedin
Albert Herrera
Joseph Higgins
Stonewall Hilton
Ernest Holland
James Irvin
Richard Jackman
Howard James
Robert Jarvis
Ronald Jett
James Johnson

Raymond Kazebee
Ronald Kloch
James Knotts
John Krawczyk
Raymond Kropp
John Kurrus
Lynus Larch
Barry Lerich
Allan Lewis
David Long
Joseph Marchand
Raymond McCoole
William McNally
Marvin Megason
John Michaud
Roger Miller
James Morley
Richard Murphy
Stuart Nelson
Hercules Nicholas
James Norris
William O'Neill
Charles Parshall
Gary Patterson
Charles Payne
John Pendleton
Robert Pfeiffer
James Phelps
Imon Pilcher
James Prater
Clarence Price
Terrence Provost
Lyle Rayl
Robert Rockefeller
Robert Scott
George Shabenas
Robert Simonini

Frank Skewes
Malcom Snelgrove
James Sordelet
Gilbert Spurr
Robert Stroud
Kirby Talley
Harry Thomas
Norman Vitale
Curtis Wagner
Richard Williamson
Richard Wood
John Yuill
John Zaretki

CIVILIANS
George Bristow
Thomas Curtis
Waldo Lyon
Rexford Rowray

1958 (SECOND CRUISE)

OFFICERS
Frank Adams
William Anderson
Kenneth Carr
William Cole
Richard Dobbins
Paul Early
Donald Hall
John Harvey
Shepherd Jenks
Robert Kassel
Robert Kelsey
Jack Kinsey
William Lalor
Steven White

ENLISTED

John Aberle
Bruce Aquizap
Jack Baird
Ralph Barnhart
Richard Bearden
Robert Bell
Nils Bergquist
Charles Black
Freddie Boswell
Philip Boyle
Donald Brady
Dennison Breese
Daniel Brigman
James Brown
William Brown
Arthur Callahan
Roland Cave
Alfred Charette
Boyd Cohenour
Thomas Deane
Joseph Degnan
Earl Diamond
John Draper
Edward Dunn
Wallace Durkin
Thomas Emanuel
Leslie Evans
Bobby Faircloth
Billy Fowlkes
William Furnholm
William Gaines
David Greenhill
Roger Hall
William Hansen
Dowell Harrell
Walter Harvey

Harry Hedin
Albert Herrera
Joseph Higgins
Stonewall Hilton
Ernest Holland
James Irvin
Richard Jackman
Robert Jarvis
Ronald Jett
James Johnson
Raymond Kazebee
Richard King
Ronald Kloch
James Knotts
John Krawczyk
Raymond Kropp
John Kurrus
Lynus Larch
Barry Lerich
Allan Lewis
David Long
Joseph Marchand
John McGovern
William McNally
Marvin Megason
John Michaud
Roger Miller
James Morley
Richard Murphy
Stuart Nelson
Hercules Nicholas
James Norris
William O'Neill
Clemente Ortega
Charles Parshall
Gary Patterson
Charles Payne

John Pendleton
Robert Pfeiffer
James Phelps
Imon Pilcher
James Prater
Clarence Price
Terrence Provost
Lyle Rayl
Robert Rockefeller
Robert Scott
George Shabenas
Robert Simonini
Frank Skewes
Malcom Snelgrove
James Sordelet
Gilbert Spurr

Robert Stroud
Kirby Talley
Harry Thomas
Norman Vitale
Curtis Wagner
Richard Williamson
Richard Wood
John Yuill
John Zaretki

CIVILIANS
George Bristow
Thomas Curtis
Waldo Lyon
Archie Walker

INDEX

A

Aberle, John (Chief Hospitalman), 209, 276, 285, 339, 341, 343
Adams, Frank, 159, 190, 194, 200–1, 212, 220, 247, 257–58, 271, 280, 287, 298, 313, 326, 341, 342
Adams, Novie, 271, 326
Adams, Sherman (Presidential Counsel), 158
Air Force, 63
Air Force H-19 helicopter, 298
Alabama, 172, 338
Alaska, 60, 64, 175, 191–92, 201, 212–13, 217, 238, 240–41, 268–69, 274
Aleutian Chain, 205, 256
Aleutian Islands, 201, 232, 252–53
Allendorfer, Harry (Commander), 167–68
Allies (U.S.), 67, 119, 136, 139, 148
Alpha-Mendeleev, 275
American Civil War, xvii
American Vanguard rocket payload, 145, 172

Anderson, Bonny, 7, 14, 18, 24–25, 27, 72, 89, 158, 176, 178, 194, 238, 241, 245, 247, 302–3, 306–7, 318, 323, 325, 327, 329
Anderson, Jack, 146
Anderson, Michael, 14, 18, 302, 308, 318, 327, 329
Anderson, Pat(ricia) (Walters, xi, 329, 332, 336–37
Anderson, William (Captain), xii, 5, 24, 29, 55, 68, 85, 131, 155, 171, 195, 200, 215, 220, 239, 267, 302, 304–7, 310, 315, 319–20, 327, 332–37, 341, 342
Anderson, William, Jr., 238, 241, 302, 308, 325, 329
Annapolis, MD, 3, 5, 7, 24, 30, 41
Antarctica, 61–62
antisubmarine forces, 11, 37, 47, 69
Arco, ID, 33–34, 245
Arctic Basin, 129, 171, 176, 186, 202, 218, 241, 269, 274
Arctic charts, 71, 147, 245
Arctic Circle, 60, 101, 219

Arctic Ocean, x, xix, 43, 57–59, 62, 92, 147, 152, 156, 166, 175, 186, 213, 219, 225, 227–28, 240, 256, 270, 276–77, 284, 301, 328, 331
Arctic Ocean charts (also Arctic charts), 71, 147, 245
Arkansas Democrat, 146
Arkansas Gazette, 146
Arkansas National Guardsmen, 164
Arlington National Cemetery, 239, 333
Armed Forces of the United States, 295, 305
Army Air Force, 61
Arnold, H. H. "Hap" (General), 61
Atlantic Fleet, 16–17, 47, 166, 298
Atlantic Fleet Headquarters, 47
Atlantic Fleet vessel, 166
Atlantic Ocean, ix, 60, 90, 173, 264, 289, 292, 315
Atomic Energy Commission (A.E.C.), 12, 30, 32–33
Atomic Energy Commission's desert test center, 33
Atomic Energy Commission's Oak Ridge plant, 30
atomic-powered submarine, 31, 42
Atomic Submarine and Admiral Rickover, The (Blair), 20
Attack Center, 95–96, 124, 224, 280, 283, 330
Aurand, Pete (Captain), 154–58, 162, 164–65, 168–69, 171, 228, 265, 290, 297, 301–2, 304, 333

B
Baird, Jack ("Mother") (Chef), 213, 275, 286, 339, 341, 343
Baldwin, Hanson, 309

ballast tanks (also "trim" tanks), 51, 97, 112
Barrow Sea Valley, 265, 269–70
bathythermograph, 93, 204
Bayne, Marmaduke G. "Duke" (Commander), 163, 165, 167–70, 176, 238, 265, 301, 333
Beach, Edward L. (Commander), 12, 162
Bearden, Richard, 118, 122–24, 184, 206, 339, 341, 343, 359
Benedict, William (Lieutenant), 61
Bering Sea, 157, 205–6, 208, 210–11, 218, 232, 252, 254, 256–57, 304
Bering Strait, 60, 167–68, 171, 191–92, 200, 203, 210, 212, 214, 216–18, 220, 229, 232, 242, 253, 255–57, 304
Big Diomede, 217
Blair, Clay, ix, 20
Block Island Sound, 90, 92, 148–49, 177
blocks and brash (also "B & B"), 108, 267
Boston, MA, 330
Bowman, Frank Lee (Admiral), 256
BPS-1 radar well, 114
Braddon, Fred, 174, 247
Brigman, Daniel (Helmsman), 264, 289, 339, 341, 343
Brinkley, David, 318
Bristow, George, 174, 237, 253, 278, 342, 344
Bronze Star, 17
Brooklyn Navy Yard, 316
Brooks, Dan, 41
Brown, Nelson, xviii
Brown, William, 53, 264, 339, 341, 343

Bureau of Ships (BUSHIPS), 30, 32, 194

Burke, Arleigh (also "31 Knot" Burke, Chief of Naval Operations) (Admiral), 65, 162–63, 165, 167–69, 171, 176, 186, 196, 225, 227, 229, 231, 265, 293, 301, 333

BUSHIPS Nuclear Power Division, 32

Butte County, 33

Byrd, Richard E. (Admiral), 61–62, 282

C

Cairns, Ernie, 192–93

Callahan, Arthur "Gunner," 124, 183, 339, 341, 343

Calvert, James (Vice Admiral), 331

Calvert, Jim (Commander), 40, 44, 244–46, 255, 265, 288, 298, 314, 335

Cape Canaveral, FL, 164, 172

Cape Prince of Wales, AK, 192

Captain Nemo, 37, 43, 74, 100

Carr, Ken (Lieutenant), 267, 270, 292, 339, 341, 342

Cave, Roland, 70, 213, 341, 343

Central High School (Little Rock, AR), 146, 164

Charette, Alfred (Al) (Sonarman), 109, 222–26, 256, 308, 314, 326, 339, 341, 343

Charette, Marilyn, 308, 326

Chicago, IL, 30, 189–90

Chukchi Sea, 191–92, 206, 216, 218, 223, 238, 240–41, 259, 264, 331

CinCPacFlt, 241

City Hall Plaza (New York), 320

Clement, Frank (Governor), 324

Coast Guard cutters, 315

Cobean, Warren R. "Bus" (Lieutenant Commander), 68, 90, 93, 96, 136, 159, 339

Cold War, x–xi, 40, 47, 60, 84, 160, 202, 247, 328, 334–36

Cole, William (Bill) (Lieutenant), 53, 220, 223, 267, 341, 342

Columbia Military Academy, 18, 24

Columbia University, 30

Columbia, TN, 18

Combs, Thomas S. (Vice Admiral), 237–38

Communist Party, 151

Confederate South, xvii

Congress, 55, 65

Connecticut General Assembly, xviii

Constitution Avenue, 22

Cook, Frederick (also Captain Cook), 61, 273, 289

cormorant, 213

Cramer, Shannon, 41

Crary, Albert P., 61

Curtis, Tom, 174, 237, 249, 253, 257, 278, 280, 283, 293, 342, 344

D

Daily Telegraph, 310

Daspit, Dan (Rear Admiral), 170–71, 187, 196, 237–38

Deane, Tom (Commissaryman Second Class), 312, 339, 341, 343

Defense Department, 55

Degnan, Joseph (Joe) (Electrician's Mate), 190, 237, 339, 343

Denmark Strait, 294

Destroyer Squadron 23, 163

Diamond Head, 232, 234

Dick, Ray, 30

diesel submarines, xvii, 10–11, 36, 101

Diomede Islands, 217, 259

dive klaxon, 139, 200

diving officer, 203, 225

diving planes, 258

Dobbins, Richard (Dick) (Commander), 52, 124, 209, 339, 341, 342

dolphin insignia, 41, 76

Dunford, Jim (Captain), 29–30, 39

DuPont, 30

E

Early, Paul (Chief Engineer), 80, 118, 120–22, 129, 159, 180, 182–83, 187–88, 190–91, 194, 197, 214, 230, 247, 339, 341, 342, 359

East Siberian Sea, 291

EB pier, 13

Eielson Air Force Base, 240

Eisenhower, Dwight "Ike" (President), xi, 12, 35–36, 143, 146, 148–51, 154–55, 160–63, 165–66, 168–69, 171–72, 175, 186, 192, 228, 246, 265, 285, 290, 294, 297, 299–305, 308–9, 312, 315, 333, 337

Eisenhower, Mamie (Mrs.) (First Lady), 12–13, 35–36, 173, 285, 300–1

Electric Boat (Company) (EB), xvi–xvii, 11–13, 34, 89, 90, 92, 174–75, 194, 322–23

emergency breathing apparatus, 184

equator, 79, 233–34

escort flotilla, 315

escort vessel, 6

Etzel, Gastao, 190

Etzel, Yvonne "Bonny," 7

Europe, 4, 57, 251, 258, 276, 309

Evening Day, 323

Everett,WA, 186, 190

F

Fairway Rock, 217, 259

Falls Church, VA, 28

Fathometer, 63–64, 71, 77–78, 93, 107, 109–12, 115, 117, 127, 205, 231, 263, 269–70, 273–75

Fears, Don (Lieutenant), 185, 187, 236, 339, 341

First Lady, 12, 35–36, 173, 285. *See also* Eisenhower, Mamie

Fleet Ballistic Missile (FBM) program, 195

Fletcher, Joseph (Lieutenant), 61

Fowlkes, Billy (Seaman), 237, 343

G

Gaines, Bill (William) (Sonarman Second Class), 256, 340, 341, 343

Gates, Thomas (Secretary of the Navy), 303

General Dynamics Corporation, xvi, xviii, 12

Gorshkov, Sergei, 34

Greenhill, David, 35, 270, 312, 341, 343

Greenland, 60, 73, 76, 91, 135, 167, 174–75, 210, 223, 346, 287, 289–91

Greenland Sea, 135, 290–92, 301

Greenland-Svalbard portal, 287

Grenfell, E.W. (Rear Admiral), 235, 241, 246–47, 255

Groton, CT, x, xi, xv, 323

Gulf of Siam, 9

Gunfight at the O.K. Corral, 202

gyrocompass(es), 63, 78–79, 92, 104, 129–31, 133, 209, 213–14, 242, 246–47, 278, 289
gyroscope, 78, 174

H
Hagerty, James (Jim) (Press Secretary), 158, 162, 228, 302–3
Hall, Donald (Lieutenant), 237, 342
Hall, Roger (Seaman), 49, 237, 343
Harvey, John (Lieutenant), 257, 267, 342
Harvey, Walter, (Steward), 314–15, 341, 343
Harvey, Wes (Lieutenant), 214
Hawaii, 235, 242–43, 251, 264, 270
Hawaiian Village, 232
Hedin, Clara, 253
Hedin, Harry (Engineman First Class), 253, 340, 341, 343
"Henderson, Charles A.," 191, 193
Henry, Tom (Captain), 70, 72–73
Herbert Islands, 254
Herter, Christian (Undersecretary of State), 148
Himalayas, 275
Hitler, Adolf, 60
Holland, Frank (Crewman), 277
Holland, Ernest, 182–83, 340, 341, 343
Holland, John, xvi, 118
Honolulu, 293
Hopwood, H. G. (Admiral), 235, 237, 241
Hudson River, 316
Huey, Enders P. (Commander), 20, 22
Huey, Jane, 20
Humphreys County, 324
Hunley, xvii
Huntsville, AL, 172

Hydrographic Office (Navy), 71, 98, 176, 231

I
Iceland, 91, 176, 290, 297–99, 301, 332, 336
In the Course of Duty, xi
Indian Ocean, 57
inertial navigator (N6A), 173, 276, 278, 289, 293
intercontinental ballistic missile (ICBM), 146, 151
interlocks, 268
International Boundary Line, 211
International Geophysical Year, 61

J
Jackman, Richard (Torpedoman First Class), 275, 340, 341, 343
Jackson, Henry M. "Scoop" (Senator), 65, 309
James, Howard (Chief Yeoman), 236–37, 340, 341
Japan, 293
Japanese Current, 204
Jarvis, Robert (Hospitalman First Class), 209, 271, 341, 343
Jenks's Deep, 231
Jenks, Barbara, 239
Jenks, Shepherd (Shep), 159, 174, 176, 201, 206, 212, 231, 239–41, 246, 252, 258–59, 264–65, 270, 275–76, 281–82, 293, 315, 339, 341, 342
July "stopover," 174

K
Kansas City, 7, 9
Kassel, Robert (Bob) (Lieutenant), 237, 266, 270, 342

Kauai Channel, 252
Kefauver, Estes (Senator), 324–25
Kelly, Les (Chief Engineer), 13, 72,
    76, 81, 95, 102–3, 111, 114,
    126–28, 134–36, 140–41, 350
Kelsey, Robert (Bob) (Lieutenant /
    Diving Officer), 198, 204, 257,
    341, 342
Khrushchev, Nikita, 151
King Island, 216
King, Richard (Fireman), 237, 343, 359
Kinsey, Jack (Captain), 195–96, 237,
    267, 341, 342
Kloch, Ronald (Quartermaster), 281,
    340, 342, 343
Kodiak, AK, 240
Korean conflict, 245
Korean War, 18, 40
Kotzebue, BC, 192
Krawcyzk, John. J. "Mr. Nautilus"
    (Chief Fire Control Technician),
    xii, 118–22, 138–39, 199, 213,
    312, 340, 342, 343
Krenitzin Islands, 295
Kropp, Raymond (*also* Ray), 53, 118,
    121, 122, 124, 138–39, 223, 340,
    342, 343
Kurrus, John, 118, 122–24, 184, 189,
    202, 233, 277, 340, 342, 343

L
Lagarto (SS-371), 9
Laika, 152
Lalor, Bill (Lieutenant), 76, 147, 159,
    181–82, 216, 221–23, 226, 230,
    257, 259, 262, 267, 339, 341, 342
Larch, Lynus "Dutch" (Chief of
    Boat), 103, 118, 124, 138–39,
    183, 233, 235, 319, 340, 342, 343

Larch, Della, 319
Larson, G. Edward, 148–49
Latta, Frank, 8–9
Lawson, Dunbar, 4, 7
Legion of Merit, 304–5
Lerich, Barry (Electronics
    Technician), 253, 342, 343
Life magazine, 20, 309
Lincoln Memorial, 155
Lincoln Sea, 223
Little Diomede, 217
Little Rock, AR, 146, 149, 164
Lockwood, Vice Admiral Charles A.,
    6–7, 9, 17
London, England, 310–13
Long Beach, CA, 69, 186
Long Island Sound, xvi
LORAN (Long Range Navigation),
    92, 98, 213, 270
LORATT (long-range sonar
    communications system), 92, 101
Lyon, Waldo, 62–64, 71–72, 75–77,
    90, 95–96, 107–11, 115, 134, 137,
    150, 171, 174, 186, 191–92,
    199–201, 203, 206, 209, 212, 237,
    253, 267, 272–73, 281, 331, 333,
    341, 342, 344

M
Magellan, 138, 273
magnetic compass(es), 63, 78–79, 92,
    130, 136, 209
magnetic North Pole, 63
magnetic pole, 78–79, 209
Mandil, Harry, 29
Manhattan, 320–21
Manhattan Island, 316–18
Manhattan Project, 4, 9
Mantle, Mickey, 322

Mare Island, CA, 48, 185–88, 330
Mare Island Naval Shipyard, 186
Marine honor guard, 316
Mark 19 (Sperry) (compass), 79, 92, 104, 129, 131, 242, 247
Marrowstone Point, 199
McCoole, Ray, 213–14, 236, 340, 342
McGovern, John P. (Auxiliaryman / Engineman First Class), 51, 118, 120, 122, 268, 340, 343
McKechnie, A.W. (Rear Admiral), 240–41
McNally, William J. (*also* Bill) (Engineman), 182–83, 233, 258, 277, 286, 342, 343
McNamara, Laurence (Ensign), 118, 121, 339
McWethy, Robert (Commander), 47, 62–66, 75–75
Mediterranean Sea, 57
Michaud, John H. (Sonarman Chief), 256, 294, 340, 342, 343
Momenta Sera, 309
Monterey, CA, 63
Morley, James (Electrician's Mate), 204, 312, 340, 342, 343
Morse key, 293
Moscow, Russia, 151–52
Movietone News, 318
Murmansk, 152
Murphy, Richard, 204, 340, 342, 343
Murrow, Edward R., 326
Mystic, 16, 18, 27, 46, 176–77, 194, 239, 247, 308, 322

N
N Building, 22
N6A (inertial navigator), 173, 280, 289–90

N6A navigation system, 253, 278
Narwhal, 8
Nashville, TN, 323–24
National Geographic, 20
National Historic Landmark, 330
National Security Council, 148
NATO. *See* North Atlantic Treaty Organization
NATO exercise, 67, 71, 91, 95, 113, 115, 141, 153–54, 311
Nautilus 90 North (book), ix
"Nautilus 90 North," 289, 293
Navaho missile, 173
Naval Reactors Branch (NRB), 27–30, 32–34, 38, 40–41, 43–46, 62, 65, 194, 245, 256
Naval Reserve, 318
NROTC (naval reserve officers training corps program), 245
Naval Submarine Force Museum, x
Navy Annex,22
Navy Bureau of Personnel, 40, 64
Navy Department, 45, 150
Navy Hydrographic Office, 71, 98, 176, 231
navy pier, xiii, xv
Navy radio station, 293
Navy's Bureau of Personnel, 40, 64
NBC, 318
Nelson, Stuart (*also* Stu) (Chief Petty Officer), 180–81,191, 194, 221, 270, 330, 342, 343
New London, CT, xvi, 5, 9, 14–16, 24, 30, 54, 69–75, 77, 79, 81–83, 85, 94, 96, 102–3, 105, 147, 153–54, 167, 177, 180, 191, 194, 236–40, 242–43, 255, 314, 322–23, 326, 330

New York City, NY, 315, 317, 319, 321–22, 326, 331
New York harbor, 313, 315–16
New York Times, ix, 145, 307, 309
Newport, Rhode Island, 236
Nimitz, Chester (Admiral), 32
Norris, James (Jim) (Chief Sonarman), 208, 256, 342, 343
Norris, John, 309
North American Aviation, 173
North American inertial navigator, 278
North Atlantic, 69–70
North Atlantic Treaty Organization (NATO), 69, 71, 91, 95, 113–15, 118, 152–54
North Korea, 11
North Pole, ix–xi, xix, 43–44, 56–61, 63, 71, 73, 77–79, 81, 92, 97, 102, 104–5, 116, 125, 127, 129, 131–32, 136, 140, 143, 146–47, 154, 156–57, 161–63, 166–67, 171–73, 193, 198–99, 204, 219, 227, 232–33, 236, 238–39, 244–47, 251, 253, 257–58, 262, 265, 269, 271, 273–74, 277–89, 291, 298, 302–4, 308–10, 312–14, 317–19, 321, 328, 330–31, 333, 335
Northwest Passage, 44, 147, 157, 279, 305, 309, 331
Nuclear Power School, 41, 54, 236
nuclear reactor, 1, 3, 10, 21, 30–31, 33, 52
nuclear submarine, ix–xi, xiii, xvii–xviii, 14, 19, 28–30, 39, 41, 44–45, 47–48, 56, 65, 67, 69, 91, 136, 147, 152, 156, 159, 185, 187, 204, 236, 243, 247, 256, 277, 285, 305–6, 309, 328, 334

O

Oahu, Hawaii, 234, 242, 252
Oak Ridge, TN, 9–10, 30
omni-directional hydrophones, 92
OP-33, 240
Operation Strikeback, 69–70, 81, 101–2, 146, 309
Operation Sunshine, 143, 163, 173, 186–97, 225, 228, 232, 244, 260, 264, 278, 294, 298, 337
Operation Sunshine I, Part III, ch. 20
Operation Sunshine II, 243, 249, Part IV,
Order of Bluenoses, 219
Ortega, Clemente (Yeoman Second Class), 237, 298, 343
Oval Office, 165–66, 168
Owens, James, 96, 340
Oxygen, 4, 36, 51, 167, 202, 275, 307

P

P2V, 240
Pacific Coast, 166
Pacific Fleet, 1, 32, 67, 235
Pacific (Ocean), 244, 246–47, 251, 254, 279, 286, 304, 306, 318, 328, 331, 333, 335
Pacific submarine commander, 6
Pacific submarine fleet, 9
Pacific theater, 41
Pali, HI, 232
Panama, 71–72, 79, 167, 175, 179–81, 198, 233–42, 251, 257
Panama–Arctic–Pearl Shuttle Boat News, The, 253
Panama-Arctic Shuffle, The, 214
Panama Canal, 147, 166, 180, 198, 335
Panoff, Bob, 29, 306–7
PANOPOS, 286, 322, 328, 330

Papanin, Ivan, 284
Pearl Harbor, HI, 6, 8, 14–15, 151,
  227–29, 232–36, 241–42, 247,
  251, 255, 259–60, 281
Peary, Robert (Admiral), 60–61, 271,
  273, 282, 284, 289
Pentagon, 47, 62, 66, 69, 83–84,
  150–55, 159, 161, 163, 165–67,
  169–70, 186–87, 194, 227–29,
  238, 265, 293, 297, 301, 333
periscope(s), xiv–xv, 6, 36, 67, 81,
  92–93, 96–102, 110–15, 117–28,
  133–34, 137, 141, 184, 202–10,
  213–19, 229–30, 234, 237,
  254–55, 258–59, 261–62, 266–67,
  270, 275, 277–78, 291–92, 298,
  312, 315
Philippine guerillas, 8
Pilcher, Imon, 183, 204, 340, 342, 344
Plaisted, Ralph, 61
Plummer, Jake, 8
Point Barrow, AL, 193, 268, 272, 274
polar crossing, 157, 159, 304, 337
polar cruise, 316
polar expedition, 72
polar ice, 6, 43–44, 47, 51, 59, 76,
  91–92, 95–96, 104, 117, 150, 171,
  200, 215, 220, 273, 276, 309, 323
polar submarine operations, 62
Polaris missile submarine program,
  167
Polaris-missile-toting nuclear submarines, 306
Pole of Inaccessibility, 272, 277
polynyas, 43, 58, 63, 108, 237, 277
Portland, England, 91, 176, 198–99,
  290, 300, 311–12, 314, 317
Portsmouth Naval Shipyard, 11
Portsmouth, VA, 85

Potomac River, 62, 154, 332
practice depth charge, 127–28
Prater, James H. (Torpedoman First
  Class), 275, 312, 340, 342, 344
Presidential Unit Citation, 295, 303,
  312
Presley, Elvis, 149
Pribiloff Islands, 256
Price, Clarence, 223, 264, 312, 340,
  342, 344
Professor Arronax, 37
Pro-Submarine Section, 163
Provost, Terrence (Radioman), 293,
  340, 342, 344
Puget Sound,WA, xiii, xv, 55, 69, 186,
  188–89, 198, 205

R
radar, 6, 81, 99, 114, 139–41, 217,
  254, 265–66, 269
radiation monitoring program, 52
radio, 61, 64, 80–81, 98–99, 140–41,
  150, 202–4, 208, 229, 252–53,
  255, 264–65, 288, 292–94, 297,
  301, 306, 314, 336
Radio Londonderry, 293
radioactive exposure, 52
Rayl, Lyle "Doggie" (Chief
  Quartermaster), 130, 220, 270,
  276, 281, 340, 342, 344
reactor, 1, 3, 9–10, 13, 21, 27, 30–33,
  39, 49, 52–53, 89, 179, 181, 185,
  187, 206, 245, 252
Red Star, 34
Redstone Arsenal, 172
Reece, Thomas (Crew member), 118,
  125, 340
Reykjavik, Iceland, 297–98, 301
Ribicoff, Abraham (Governor), 322

Rickover, Hyman G. (Admiral), 10, 12–14, 19–33, 35, 38–40, 42–43, 45, 49, 52, 62, 83–84, 100, 104, 116, 132, 139, 154, 162, 194–95, 245, 254, 302, 306–7, 314–15, 318–20, 322, 326, 328–29, 333

Rizzuto, Phil, 322

Rockefeller, Robert (Electronics Technician), 253, 342, 344

Rockwell, Ted, 29, 306

Roddis, Lou, 30

Ropek, John, 90, 341

Ross, Sir John, 273

Rowray, Rexford (also Rex), 203, 222–23, 226, 237, 342

Royal Marine Band, 312

Russell, Jane, 221

Russia, 47, 60–62, 64, 168, 211, 291, 309

Russian chart, 176

Russian Empire, 30

Russian fishing fleet, 99

Russian land ice, 212

S

S-48 (SS-159), 30

S-9 (SS-114), 30

San Diego, CA, 62, 69, 71, 75, 167, 186, 191, 237

San Francisco Bay, 48, 104, 188

San Francisco, CA, 46, 48, 69, 167, 176, 185, 188

San Juan, Puerto Rico, 14

SCAR, 98, 100. *See also* Sperry Celestial Altitude Recorder

Schlech, Wally (Captain), 16

Scotland, 115, 141

Scott, Robert (Seaman), 118, 120–22, 223, 340, 342, 344

sea floor contours, 92

sea ice, 58, 96, 110, 174, 206, 218, 223–24, 238, 273, 331

sea route, 59, 152

sea trials, ix, xviii–xix, 13–14, 67

sea walls, 235

seagoing operations, xvi

seagoing vessel(s), 3

Searchlight Tattoo, 312

Seattle, WA, xiii, xv, xix, 46, 49, 55, 67–68, 94, 167, 186, 191–92, 198, 202–3, 234, 251–52

Secretary of Defense, 36

Secretary(ies) of the Navy, 55, 303, 329

Sedov (Russian icebreaker), 136

Sextant, 92

Shamble (lightship), 311

Siberia, 60, 152, 210, 258

Siberian coast, 209–12, 217, 230

Skewes, Frank (Chief Engineman), 53, 223, 268, 342, 344

Smith, A. C. (Captain), 174, 243–44

"Smith" (Lieutenant), 243–44

smoke, 80, 164, 181–85

snorkel, 114, 182, 202, 219, 215

sonar, xv, 92, 99–101, 107, 110–12, 133–94, 139, 141, 159, 166, 174, 201, 208, 213, 219–24, 226, 229–30, 259, 262–63, 266, 270–71, 274, 274, 282, 298

Sordelet, James R. (Electrician's Mate First Class), 285, 340, 342, 344

Sounding(s), 65, 71, 92, 129, 147, 176, 206, 210, 257, 269, 274, 284, 290–91

South Pacific, 51, 234

South Pole, 43, 61

Southern California, 70, 186

Soviet(s), x, 34, 52, 60, 84, 119, 129, 139, 145–46, 148–49, 168, 208, 211, 215, 218, 247, 310–11, 336

Soviet Union, x, 61, 119, 139, 145–46, 151, 232, 258, 310, 334–35

Space Age, 145

space flights, 205

Sperry Celestial Altitude Recorder, 98. *See also* SCAR

Sperry Corporation, 79, 247

Sperry gyro-syn, 278

Spitsbergen, 73, 107, 140–41, 152, 289–90

Sputnik, x, 145–46, 148, 150–51, 155, 160, 162, 164, 309–10, 335–36

Sputnik II, 151

SQS-4 scanning sonar, 111

St. Lawrence Island, 201, 209–14, 218, 252, 256, 258

St. Matthew Island, 256

Stalin, Joseph, 60

starboard whip radio antenna, 292

Stassen, Harold, 148

Statue of Liberty, 313, 315

steam condenser, 179

steam generator, 180, 191

steam plant, 10, 125

steam propulsion equipment, 182

steam system, 179–81

steam turbine, 31

steam-turbine system, 31

Strait of Juan de Fuca, xiii, 200

sub base (*also* submarine base), xvi–xvii, 14–15, 89, 149, 194, 235, 237, 242, 323, 330

sub base repair shop, 242

sub school, 5, 16–17, 22, 30, 237, 244

Submarine and Arctic Division of the U.S. Naval Electronics Laboratory, 62

submarine commander, 6, 41

Submarine Force Library and Museum, xi, 226, 330

Submarine Force Museum. *See* Naval Submarine Force Museum

Submarine School, New London, 15

Submarine Tactics Department, 15

submarine tender, 13, 121, 255

submarine training facility, xvi

Submarine Warfare Branch, 170

Super-Constellation radar-warning plane, 75

Swayze, John Cameron, 318

Swiftsure Lightship, 200

Szarzynski, Theodore "Ski" (Torpedoman), 189–90, 237

T

tactic(s), 6, 15, 17, 22, 30, 41, 111

Tarpon, 6–7

Task Group Alpha, xvii

Tass, 311

Tatsuta Maru, 7

Tennessean (Nashville), 318, 324

test depth, 101, 204

Thach, John S., (Rear Admiral), xvii

Thames channel, 13

Thames River, xvi, 12–13, 34, 82, 89–90, 104, 148, 322, 330

The Constellation

The Greatest Adventures of All Time

The Nashville Tennessean

The Tennessean

Thomas, Harry (Radioman), 229, 293, 342, 344

Thule Air Force Base, Greenland, 76

tickertape parade, 320–21
Time magazine, 35, 164, 305, 309
Titanic, 66
Tonseth, Tom (Lieutenant), 236–37, 339, 341
top secret drills, 40
top secret mission, 196
torpedo, 202, 219, 275, 285
torpedo room, 275, 330
Tower of London, 312
transmitting key, 229
troop ship, 7
Truman, President Harry S., xviii, 11, 35
20,000 Leagues Under the Sea (Verne), 1, 10, 43, 74
Type VIII periscope, 92, 97–98

U

U.S. Air Force, 61
U.S. antisubmarine forces, 11
U.S. Atlantic Fleet, 17
U.S. Naval Academy, 3, 5, 18, 30, 57
U.S. Naval Academy (Annapolis), 3, 5, 18, 30
U.S. Naval Submarine School, 15
U.S. Navy, xii, xvo, 3, 10, 19, 38, 68, 75, 104, 139, 282, 293, 311, 315
U.S. Navy Radio, Japan, 293
U.S. nuclear submarines, xi
U.S. submarines, 44, 115, 298, 334
Unimak Pass, 205
Union Station, 24, 154, 157
United Statesxvi, 12, 30, 32, 54, 67, 99, 145–46, 148, 150–51, 160, 162, 168, 186, 211, 228, 285, 285, 290, 294, 295, 308, 325, 335, 337
University of Delaware, 7
University of Idaho, 245

USS *Arizona* (BB-39), 281
USS *Batfish* (SS-310), xi
USS *Boarfish* (SS-327),63
USS *Burton Island, 64*
USS *Constitution* ("Old Ironsides"), 330
USS *Flying Fish* (SS-229), 17
USS *Fulton* (AS-11), 13, 141, 255
USS *Halfbeak* (SS-352), 166–67, 175, 244
USS *Jack* (SSN-605), 281
USS *Lapon* (SSN 661), 223
USS *Long Beach* (CGN-9), 14
USS *Nautilus* (SSN-571), ix–xix, 6, 11–14, 19–21, 28, 31, 33–37, 39, 42, 56, 58–60, 63, 65–79, 81–82, 24–85, 90–112, 115–16, 119–20, 123, 126, 132, 134–41, 146, 148–51, 153–56, 165–69, 171–95, 195–205, 209, 214–15, 219–53, 256–60, 264–344
USS *Redfish* (SS-395), 64
USS *Seawolf* (SSN-575), 19, 40
USS *Skate* (SSN-578) (also *Skate*), 19, 40–41, 44, 166–67, 175, 227, 237, 243–47, 255, 265, 278, 288–89, 298, 314, 328, 331,335
USS *Tang* (SS-563), 11, 20, 271
USS *Thresher* (SSN-593), 214,
USS *Tiru* (SS-16), 159
USS *Triton* (SSRN-586), 162, 236
USS *Trutta* (SS-421) (*Trutta*), 9, 114, 245
USS *Wahoo* (SS-565), 11, 14, 18

V

Vanguard rocket, 145, 172
Vanguard TV-3, 164
Verne, Jules, 1, 10, 19, 31, 37, 43

Vietnam Veterans' Memorial, 22
Vitale, Engineman Norman A., 206, 340, 342, 344
von Braun, Werner, 172

W

Wagner, Robert (Mayor), 319–20
Waikiki, HI, 232
Waldorf-Astoria Hotel, 321
Walker, Archie, 90, 108, 237, 253, 341, 344
Walker, Frank (Captain), 163, 170
Warder, Frederick "Fearless Freddy" (*also* F. B. (Rear Admiral), 174–75, 237, 240, 302
Washington, D.C., 20, 26–27, 237, 285, 302, 329, 332
Washington Post (also *Post*), 35–36, 309
Watkins, Frank (Admiral), 16–18
Waverly, TN, 324, 326, 329
West Coast SOSUS (Sound Surveillance System), 166–67
Westinghouse Corporation, 10
Whidbey Island, xiii
whip antenna, 98, 133–34, 137
White City Stadium, 312
White House, 148, 150, 155–59, 161, 164, 168, 171–72, 187, 194, 227–28, 237, 265, 290, 297, 300–2, 304, 306–9, 311, 328, 336
White, Steve (Lieutenant), 105, 133, 137, 181, 232, 257, 339, 341
Whitney, John Hay (U.S. Ambassador), 311–12
Widmark, Richard, 203
Wilde, Cornel, 221
Wilkins, C. W. (Rear Admiral), 75, 85, 87

Wilkins, Hubert, 43–44, 51, 63–64, 109, 311
Wilkinson, Eugene "Dennis" (Admiral), xi, xiv–xv, xviii–xix, 11, 13–14, 19, 34, 40, 42, 44, 46, 48, 67–68, 236, 321
Williamson, Richard (Quartermaster), 281, 313, 342, 344
Wilson, Charles, 36
Wilson, Donald, 96, 341
Wisconsin, 9
Wogan, Tom (Captain), 6–7
Wood, Richard, 341, 342, 344
Woodall, Reuben, 7
World War I, xvi
World War II (also Second World War), xi, 4, 6, 9, 16–18, 30, 32, 36, 40–41, 44, 50, 60–62, 64, 69, 103, 161, 170, 174, 190, 193, 219, 245, 336

Y

Yankee Stadium, 322
Youngblood, Jimmy (crew member), 118, 125, 341
Yuill, John (Seaman/ Quartermaster Striker), 283, 341, 342, 344
Yukon River, 215
Yunaska Islands, 254, 358
Yunaska Pass, 252

Z

Zech, Commander Lando, 328

ACKNOWLEDGMENTS

Captain Anderson's family and I want to thank the many *Nautilus* officers and crew, along with their families and friends, who provided remembrances and carefully considered responses to our inquiries. Especially helpful throughout this project were Ken Carr, Shepherd Jenks, Joe Degnan, Richard Williamson, John Yuill, and the late John Krawczyk. We are most grateful for the hours of taped and personal interviews provided by Paul Early, Richard Bearden, Jack Kurrus, the late Tom Deane, the late Richard King, and the late Admiral Duke Bayne. Thanks also to Marilyn Charette, Jean Cobean, Anna Deane, and Della Larch for their support and great stories.

Al Charette cheerfully and graciously reviewed manuscripts, confirmed facts, supplied descriptions, and compiled crew lists. We could not have done it without him.

We appreciate the time Dr. Alfred McLaren took to clarify several points. We praise the creative talents of Gary Zambrana and his painstaking work on many old, damaged photographs. We thank Colleen Gustavson for her many hours of direct support to Captain Anderson during the early days. We recognize Brian Summerfield and Allen Browning for their special talents. Thanks go to the staff of the Eisenhower Library in Abilene, Kansas, for their research assistance and private tour during Captain Anderson's weeklong visit.

We salute our publisher, Thomas Nelson, for their special interest and enthusiasm for this project. Their editors and staff have been most patient and accommodating.

Last, but not least, we cherish the good relationship and hard work of our ever-watchful and talented agent, Robbie Robison, a former submariner who just happens to have his office on Nautilus Drive! Captain Anderson considered that an especially good omen.